Garfield life in the fat lane

BY: JIM DAVIS

Ballantine Books • New York

Published in the United States by Ballantine Books, a division of Random House, Inc., New York, and simultaneously in Canada by Random House of Canada Limited, Toronto.

Library of Congress Catalog Card Number: 95-94532

ISBN: 0-345-39776-2

Manufactured in the United States of America

First Edition: October 1995

10 9 8 7 6 5 4 3 2 1

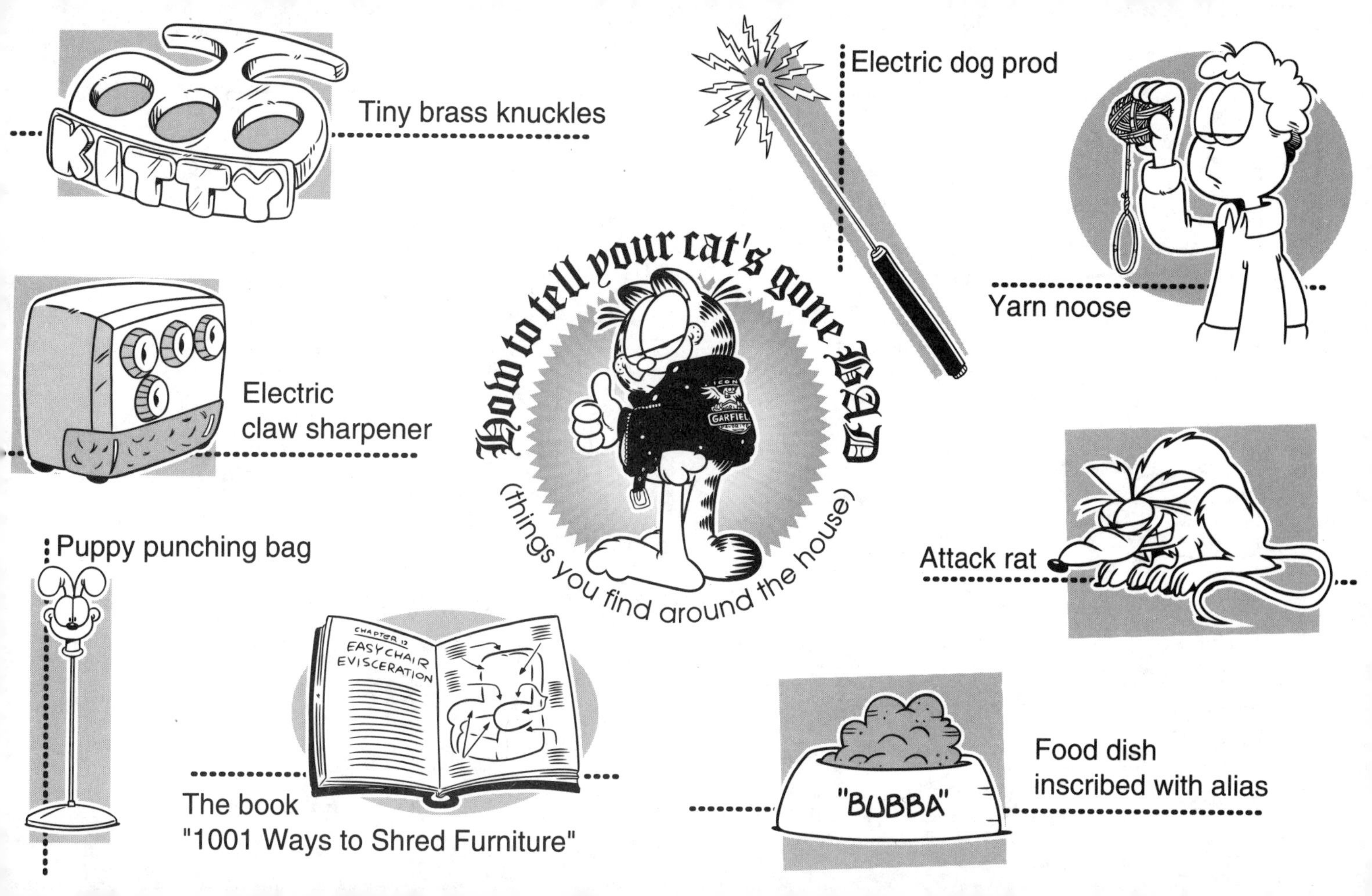
How to tell your cat's gone BAD
(things you find around the house)
KITTY
Tiny brass knuckles
Electric dog prod
Yarn noose
Electric
claw sharpener
Attack rat
Puppy punching bag
CHAPTER 12
EASY CHAIR
EVISCERATION
The book
"1001 Ways to Shred Furniture"
"BUBBA"
Food dish
inscribed with alias

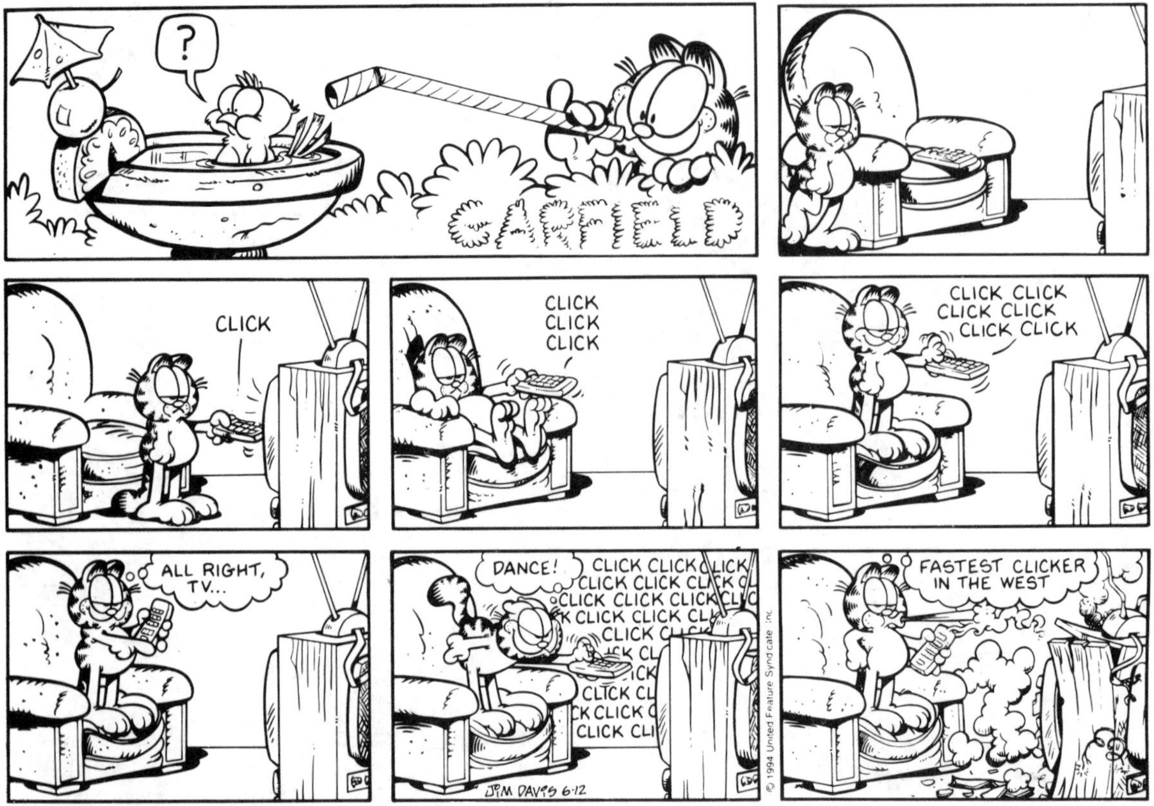
?
GARFIELD
CLICK
CLICK
CLICK
CLICK
CLICK CLICK
CLICK CLICK
CLICK CLICK
ALL RIGHT, TV...
DANCE!
CLICK CLICK CLICK
JIM DAVIS 6-12
© 1994 United Feature Syndicate, Inc.
FASTEST CLICKER IN THE WEST

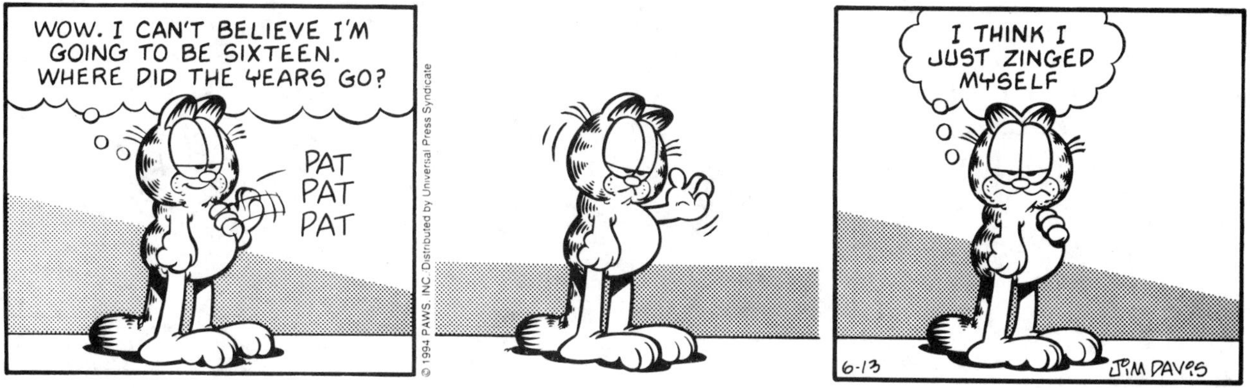
WOW. I CAN'T BELIEVE I'M GOING TO BE SIXTEEN. WHERE DID THE YEARS GO?
PAT
PAT
PAT
I THINK I JUST ZINGED MYSELF
6-13
JIM DAVIS

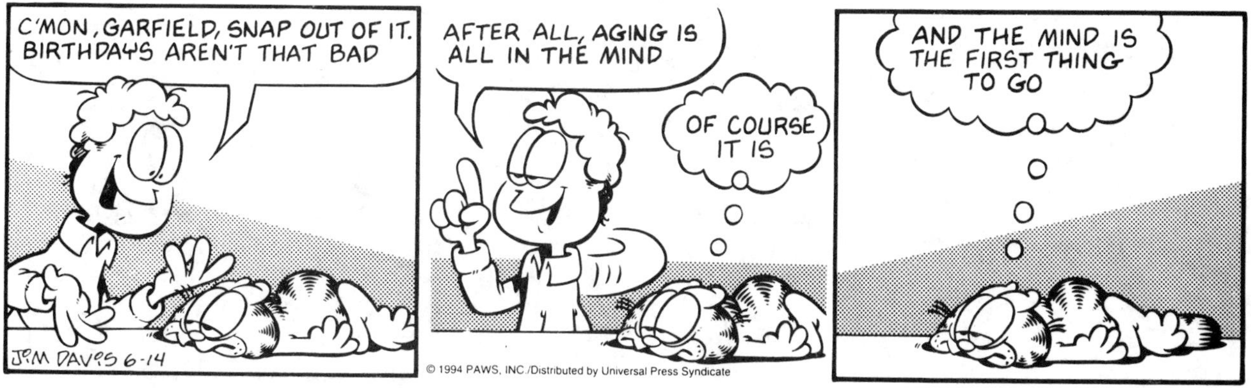
C'MON, GARFIELD, SNAP OUT OF IT. BIRTHDAYS AREN'T THAT BAD
JIM DAVIS 6-14
AFTER ALL, AGING IS ALL IN THE MIND
OF COURSE IT IS
AND THE MIND IS THE FIRST THING TO GO

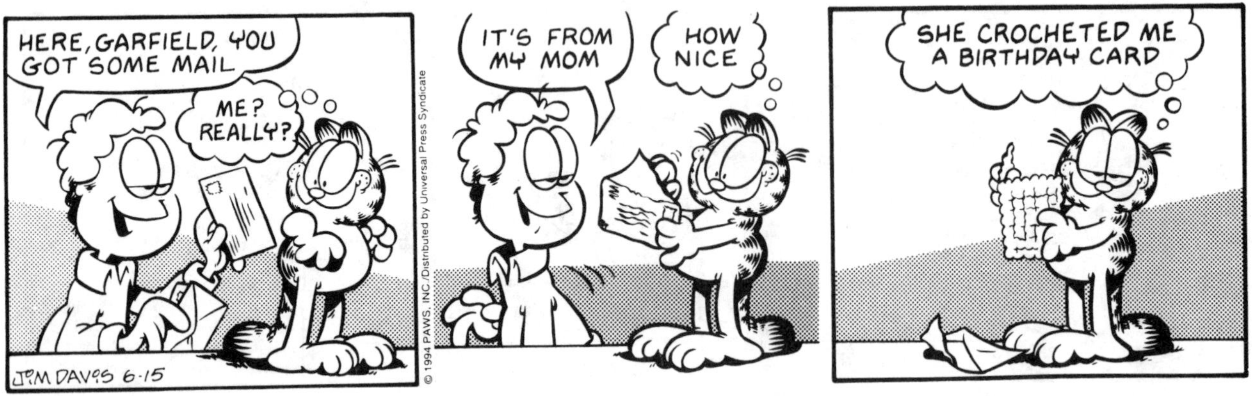
HERE, GARFIELD, YOU GOT SOME MAIL
ME? REALLY?
JIM DAVIS 6-15
IT'S FROM MY MOM
HOW NICE
SHE CROCHETED ME A BIRTHDAY CARD

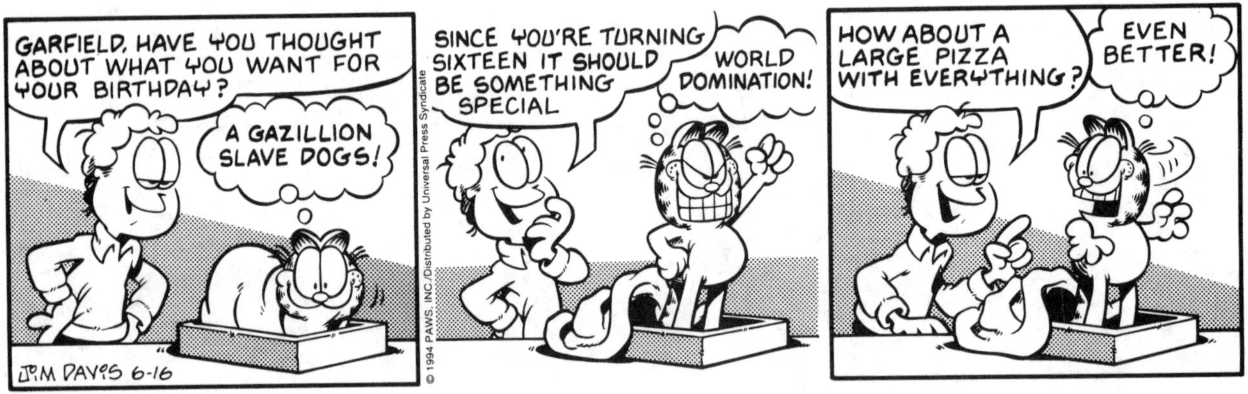
GARFIELD, HAVE YOU THOUGHT ABOUT WHAT YOU WANT FOR YOUR BIRTHDAY?
A GAZILLION SLAVE DOGS!
JIM DAVIS 6-16
SINCE YOU'RE TURNING SIXTEEN IT SHOULD BE SOMETHING SPECIAL
WORLD DOMINATION!
HOW ABOUT A LARGE PIZZA WITH EVERYTHING?
EVEN BETTER!

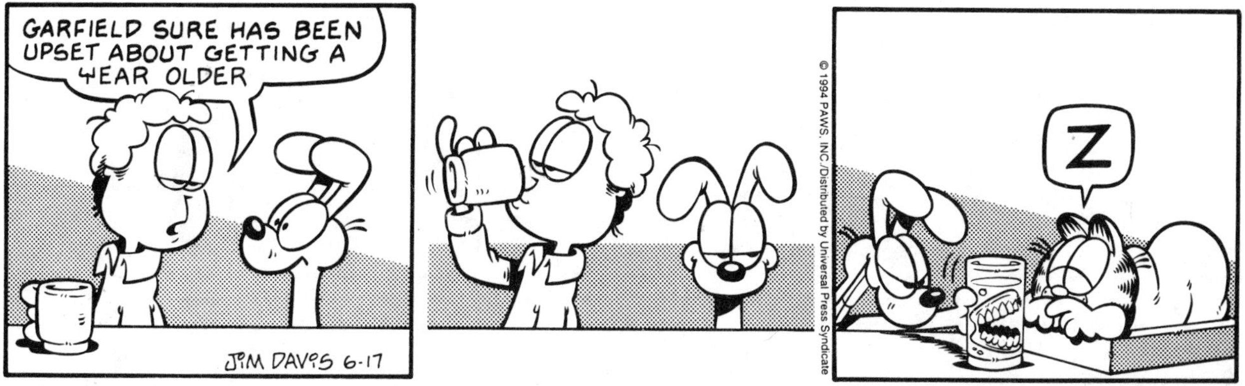
GARFIELD SURE HAS BEEN UPSET ABOUT GETTING A YEAR OLDER
JIM DAVIS 6-17
© 1994 PAWS, INC./Distributed by Universal Press Syndicate
Z

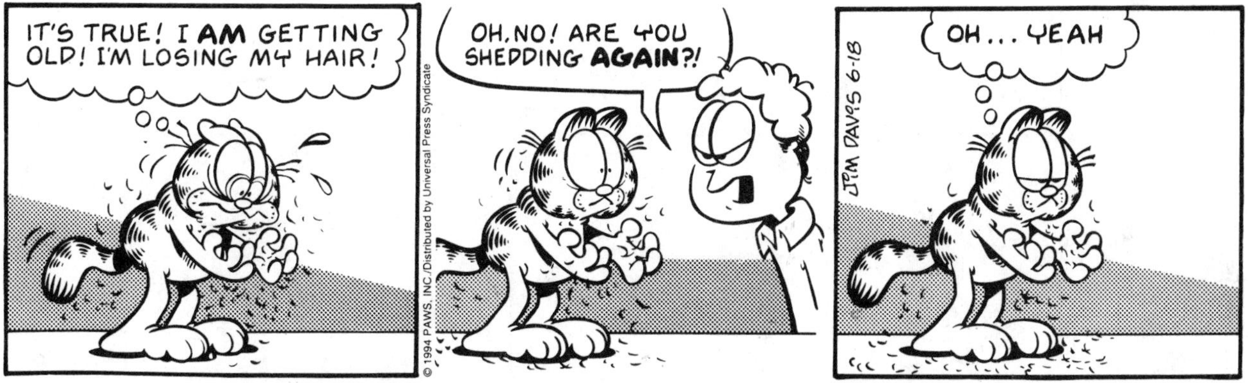
IT'S TRUE! I **AM** GETTING OLD! I'M LOSING MY HAIR!
© 1994 PAWS, INC./Distributed by Universal Press Syndicate
OH, NO! ARE YOU SHEDDING **AGAIN**?!
JIM DAVIS 6-18
OH... YEAH

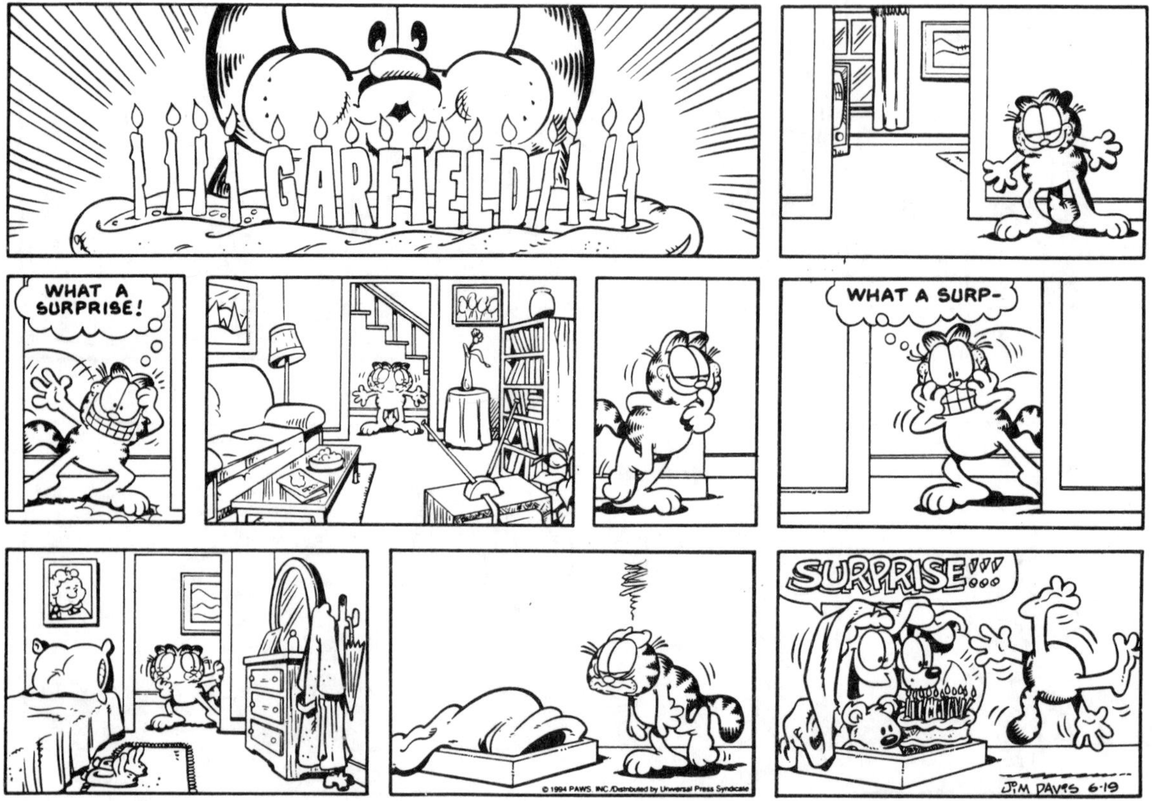
GARFIELD
WHAT A SURPRISE!
WHAT A SURP-
SURPRISE!!!
© 1994 PAWS, INC./Distributed by Universal Press Syndicate
JIM DAVIS 6-19

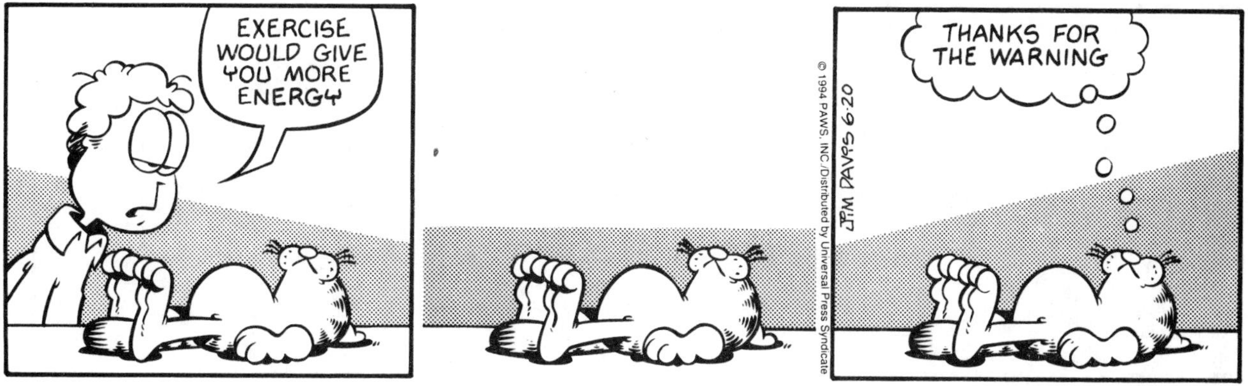
EXERCISE WOULD GIVE YOU MORE ENERGY
THANKS FOR THE WARNING
© 1994 PAWS, INC./Distributed by Universal Press Syndicate
JIM DAVIS 6-20

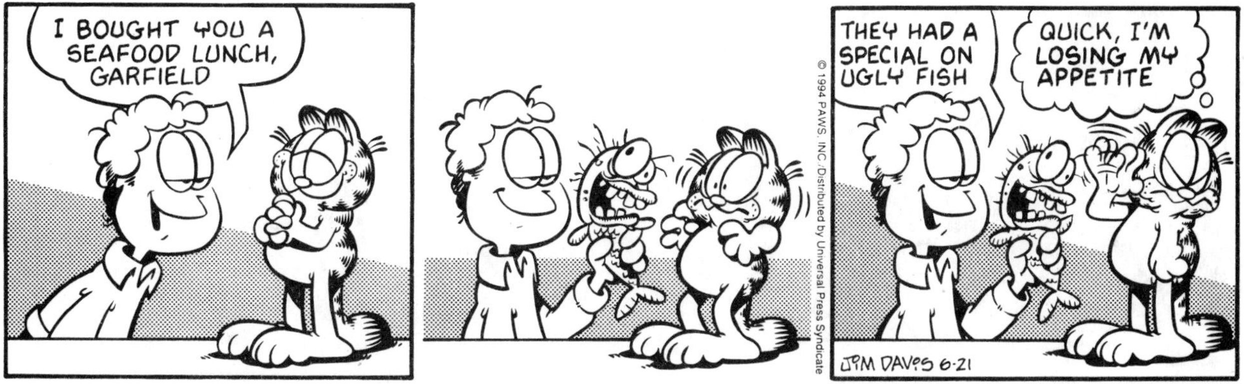
I BOUGHT YOU A SEAFOOD LUNCH, GARFIELD
THEY HAD A SPECIAL ON UGLY FISH
QUICK, I'M LOSING MY APPETITE
© 1994 PAWS, INC./Distributed by Universal Press Syndicate
JIM DAVIS 6-21

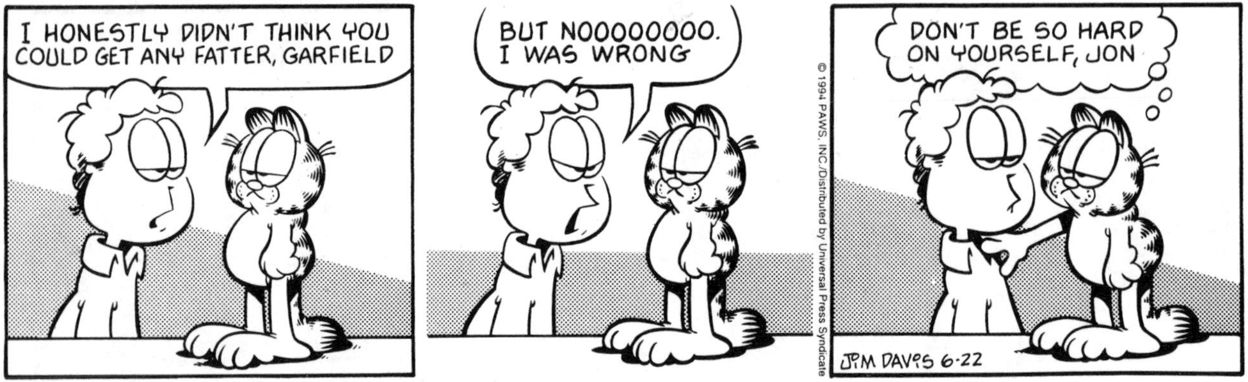
I HONESTLY DIDN'T THINK YOU COULD GET ANY FATTER, GARFIELD
BUT NOOOOOOOO. I WAS WRONG
DON'T BE SO HARD ON YOURSELF, JON
JIM DAVIS 6-22
© 1994 PAWS, INC./Distributed by Universal Press Syndicate

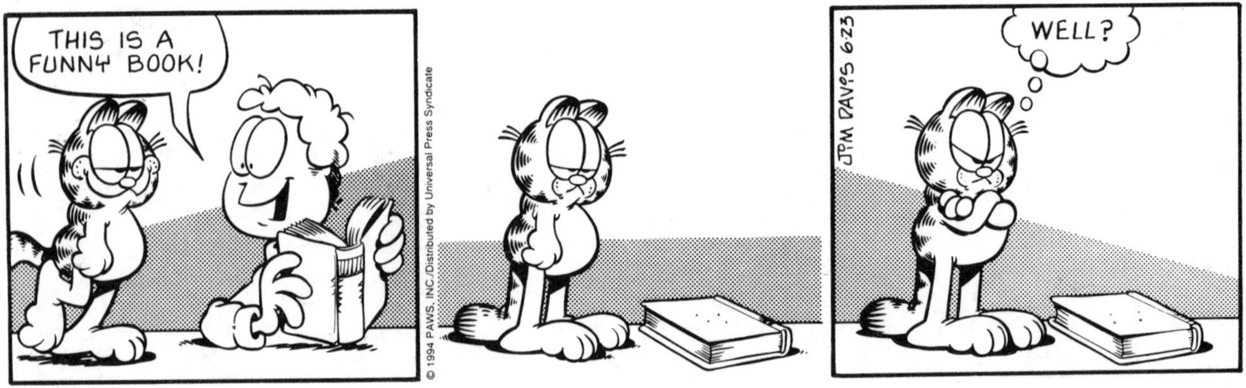
THIS IS A FUNNY BOOK!
WELL?
JIM DAVIS 6-23
© 1994 PAWS, INC./Distributed by Universal Press Syndicate

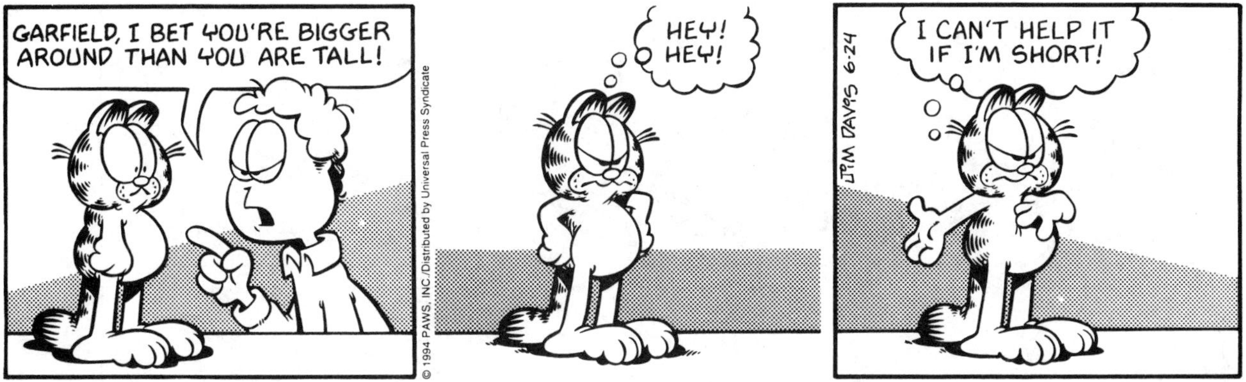
GARFIELD, I BET YOU'RE BIGGER AROUND THAN YOU ARE TALL!
HEY! HEY!
JIM DAVIS 6-24
I CAN'T HELP IT IF I'M SHORT!

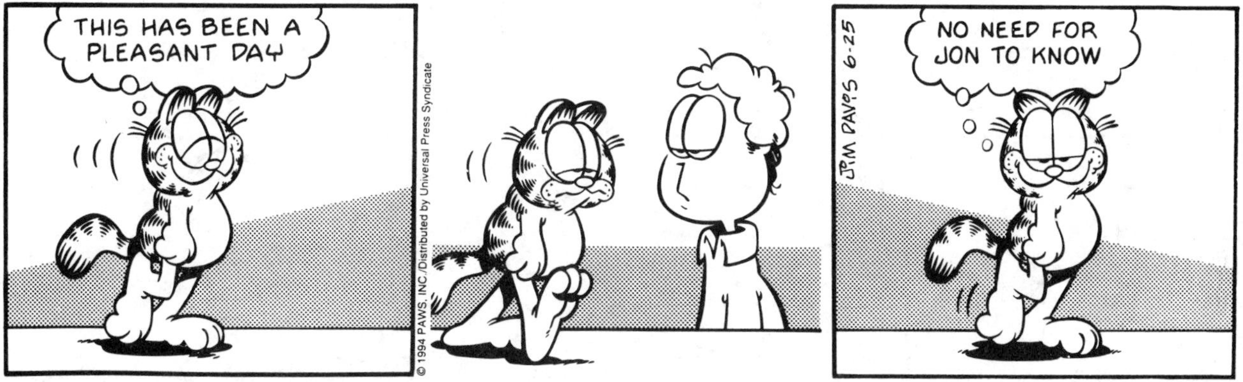
THIS HAS BEEN A PLEASANT DAY
JIM DAVIS 6-25
NO NEED FOR JON TO KNOW

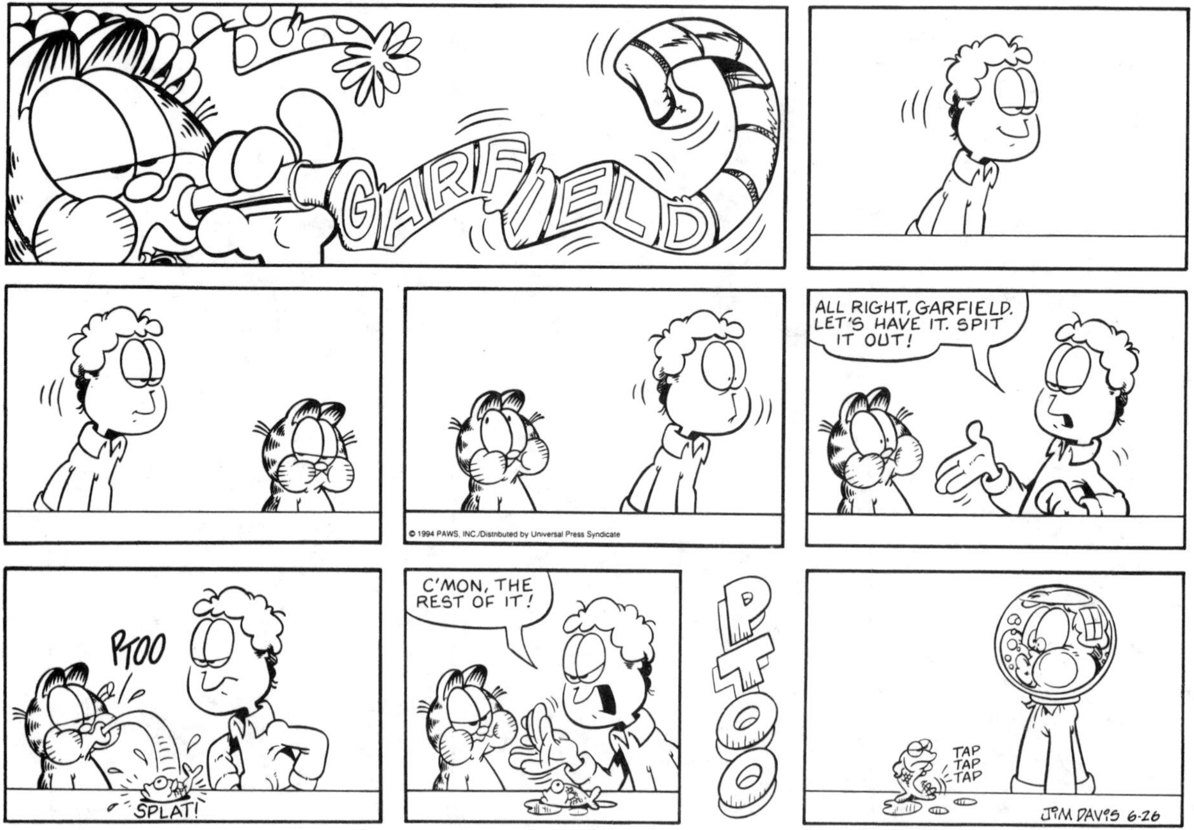
GARFIELD
© 1994 PAWS, INC./Distributed by Universal Press Syndicate
ALL RIGHT, GARFIELD. LET'S HAVE IT. SPIT IT OUT!
PTOO
SPLAT!
C'MON, THE REST OF IT!
PTOO
TAP TAP TAP
JIM DAVIS 6-26

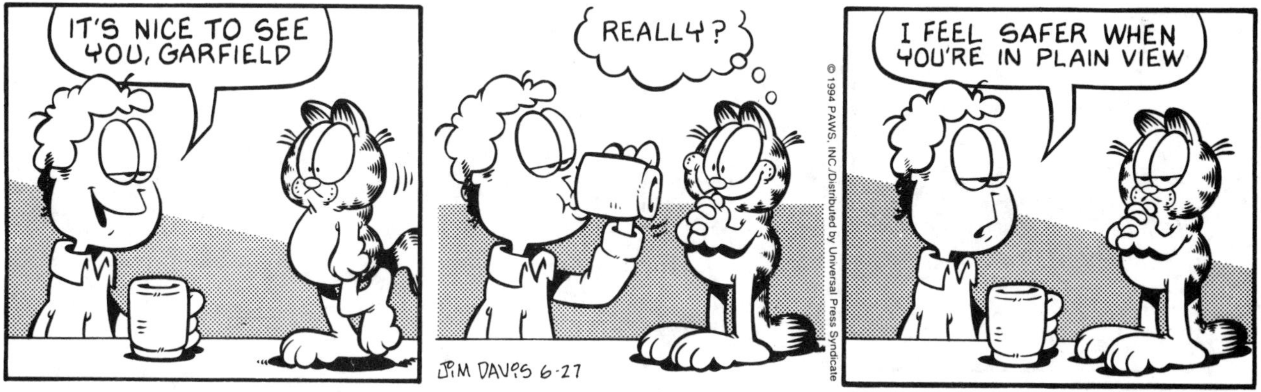
IT'S NICE TO SEE YOU, GARFIELD
REALLY?
I FEEL SAFER WHEN YOU'RE IN PLAIN VIEW
JIM DAVIS 6-27

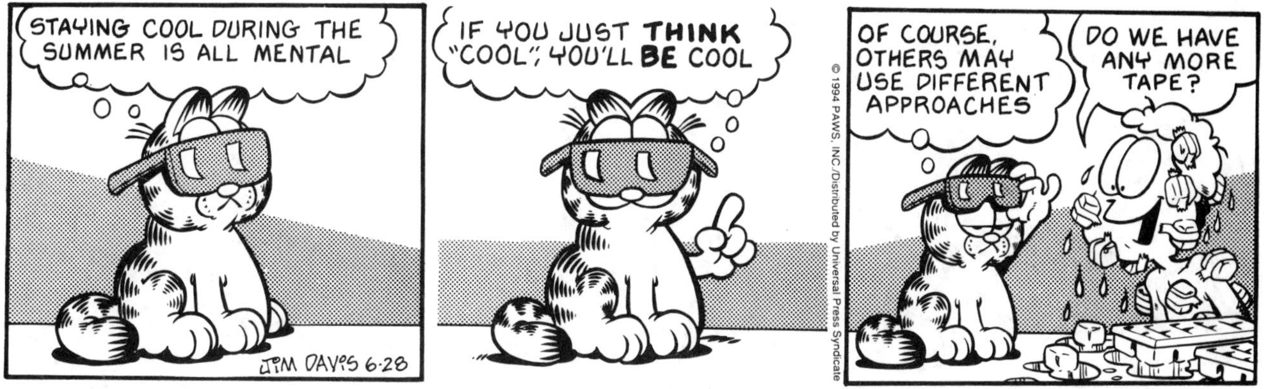
STAYING COOL DURING THE SUMMER IS ALL MENTAL
IF YOU JUST **THINK** "COOL", YOU'LL **BE** COOL
OF COURSE, OTHERS MAY USE DIFFERENT APPROACHES
DO WE HAVE ANY MORE TAPE?
JIM DAVIS 6-28

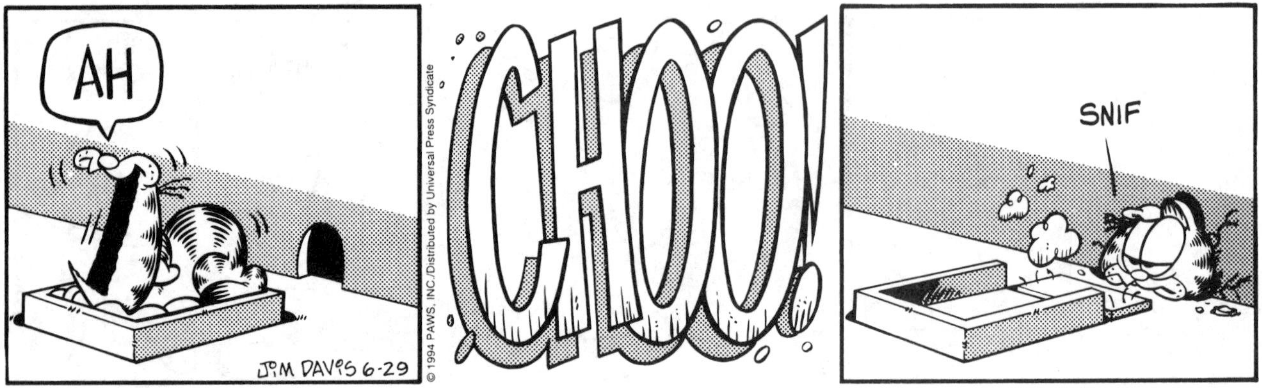
AH
JIM DAVIS 6-29
© 1994 PAWS, INC./Distributed by Universal Press Syndicate
CHOO!
SNIF

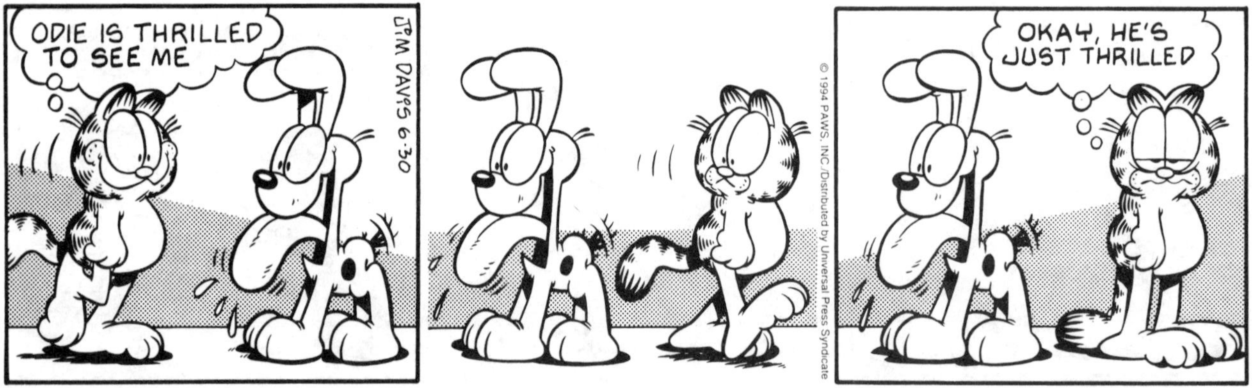
ODIE IS THRILLED TO SEE ME
JIM DAVIS 6-30
© 1994 PAWS, INC./Distributed by Universal Press Syndicate
OKAY, HE'S JUST THRILLED

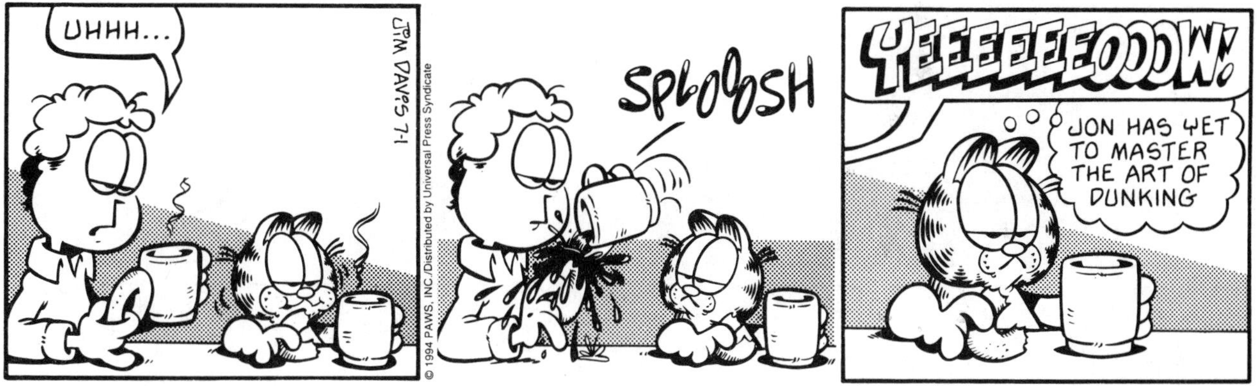
UHHH...
JIM DAVIS 7-1
SPLOOOSH
YEEEEEEOOOOW!
JON HAS YET TO MASTER THE ART OF DUNKING

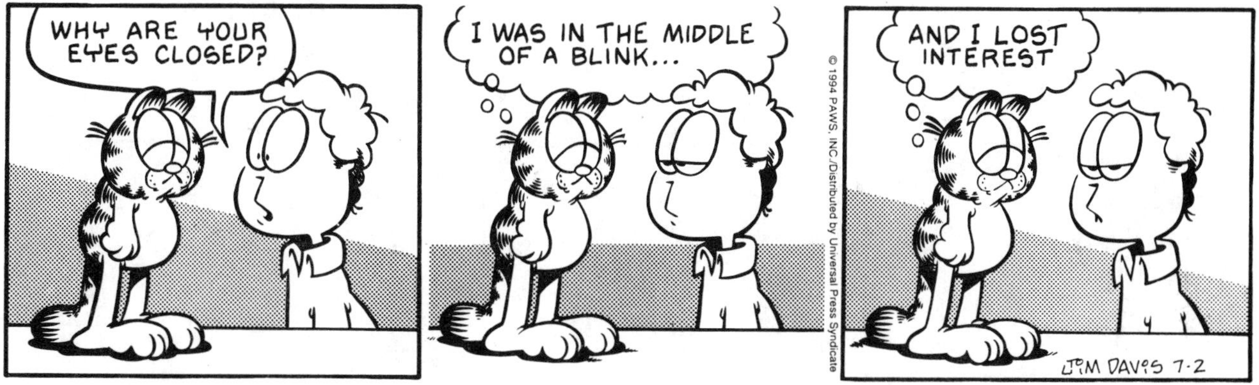
WHY ARE YOUR EYES CLOSED?
I WAS IN THE MIDDLE OF A BLINK...
AND I LOST INTEREST
JIM DAVIS 7-2

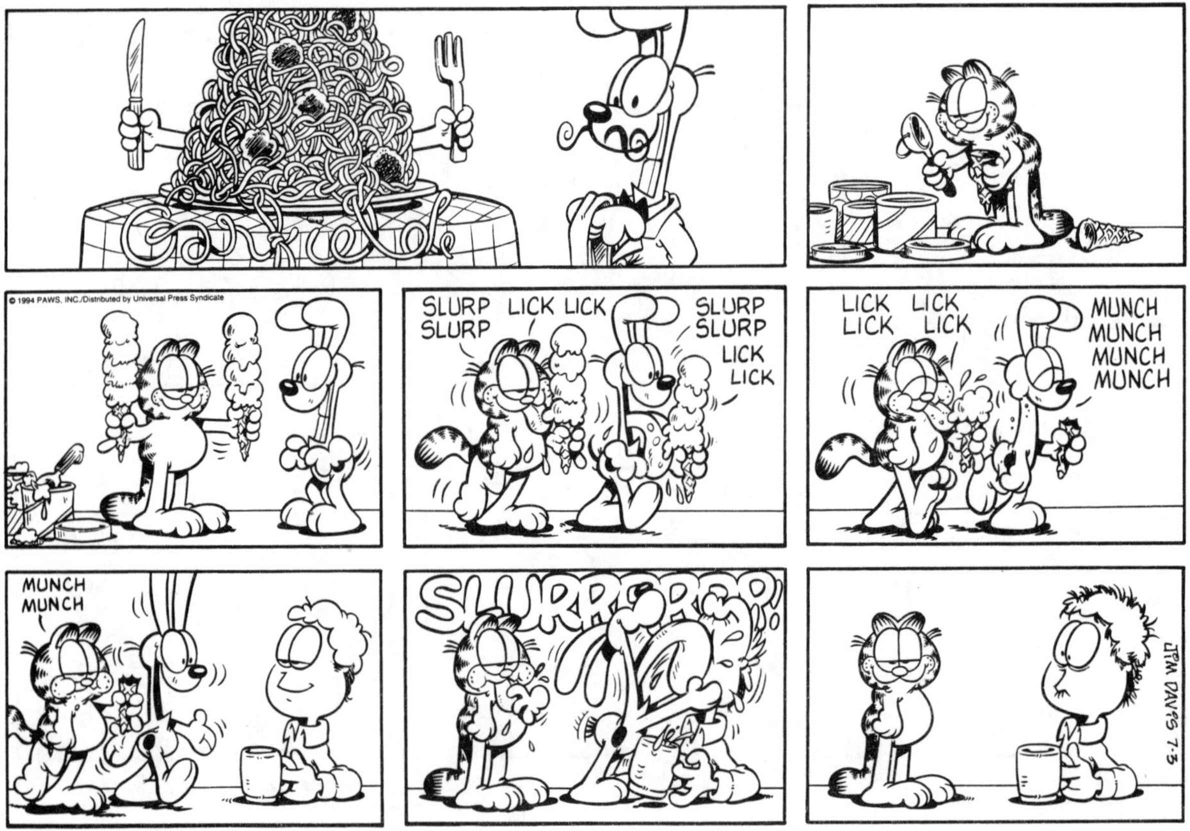
© 1994 PAWS, INC./Distributed by Universal Press Syndicate
SLURP SLURP
LICK LICK
SLURP SLURP
LICK LICK
LICK LICK
LICK LICK
MUNCH MUNCH MUNCH MUNCH
MUNCH MUNCH
SLURRRRRP!
JPM DAVIS 7-3

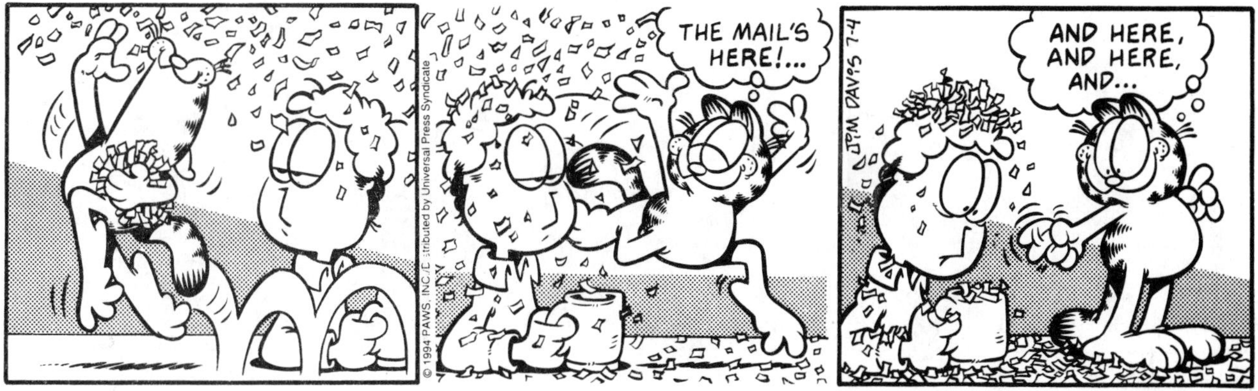
THE MAIL'S HERE!...
AND HERE, AND HERE, AND...
JIM DAVIS 7-4
© 1994 PAWS, INC./Distributed by Universal Press Syndicate

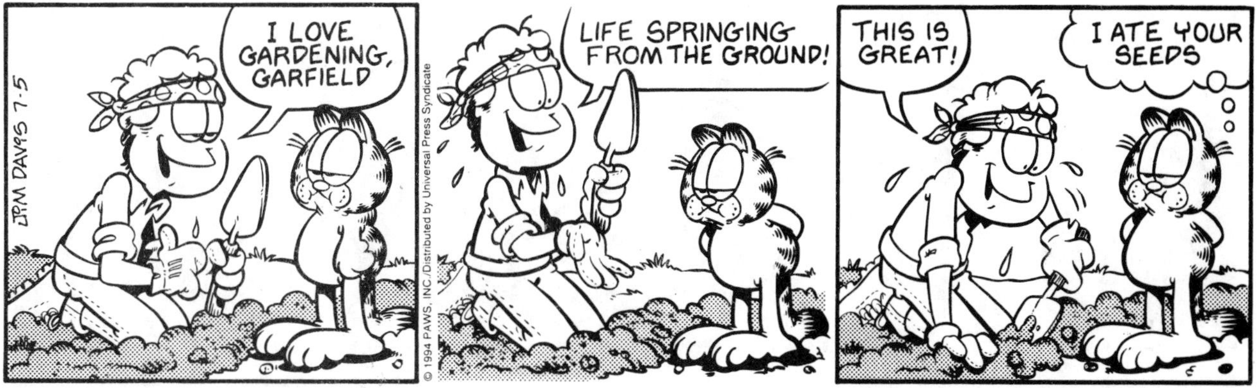
I LOVE GARDENING, GARFIELD
LIFE SPRINGING FROM THE GROUND!
THIS IS GREAT!
I ATE YOUR SEEDS
JIM DAVIS 7-5
© 1994 PAWS, INC./Distributed by Universal Press Syndicate

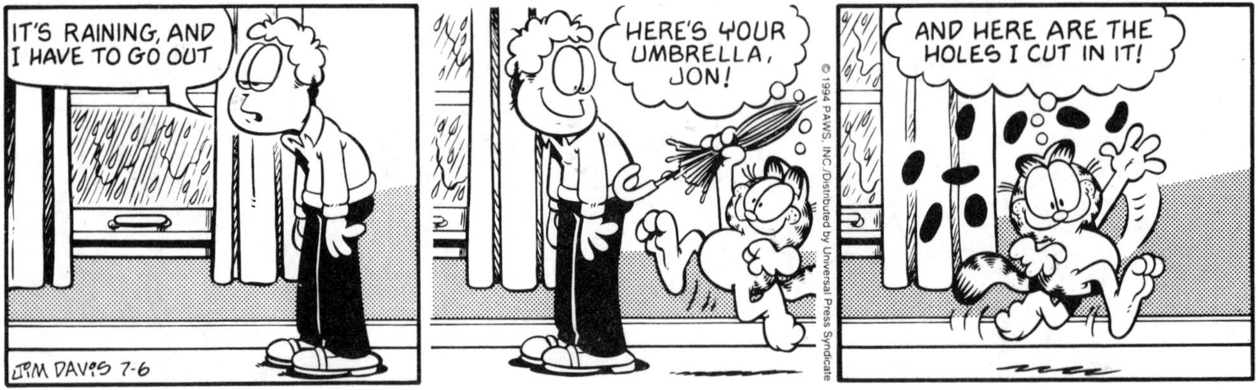
IT'S RAINING, AND I HAVE TO GO OUT
JIM DAVIS 7-6
HERE'S YOUR UMBRELLA, JON!
AND HERE ARE THE HOLES I CUT IN IT!
© 1994 PAWS, INC./Distributed by Universal Press Syndicate

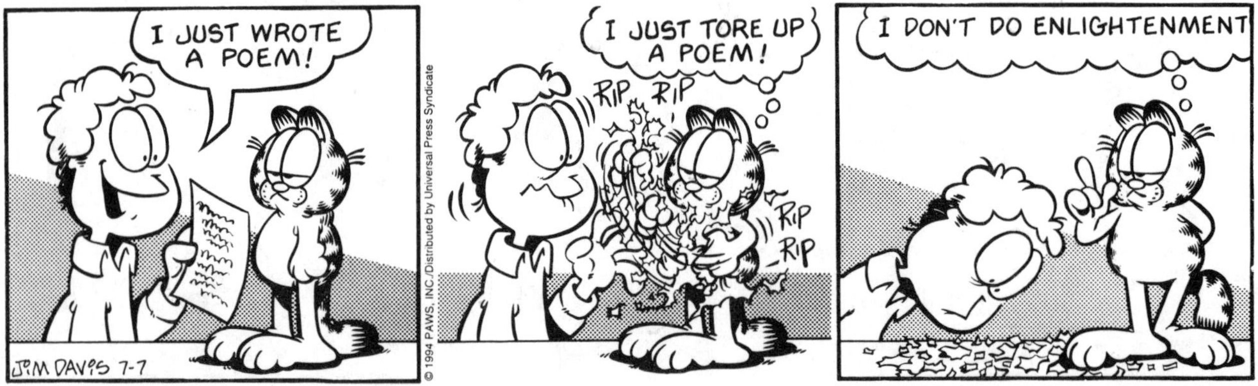
I JUST WROTE A POEM!
JIM DAVIS 7-7
© 1994 PAWS, INC./Distributed by Universal Press Syndicate
I JUST TORE UP A POEM!
RIP RIP
RIP
RIP
I DON'T DO ENLIGHTENMENT

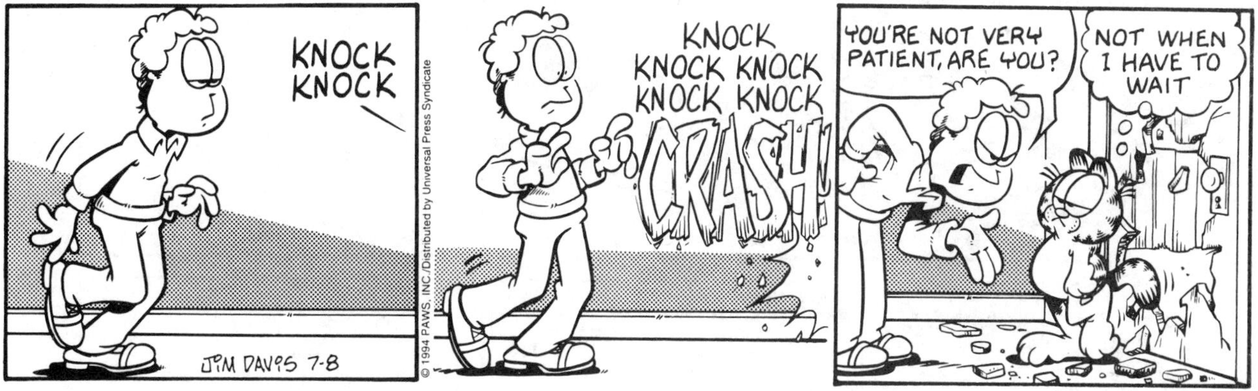
KNOCK KNOCK
JIM DAVIS 7-8
KNOCK KNOCK KNOCK KNOCK KNOCK
CRASH!
YOU'RE NOT VERY PATIENT, ARE YOU?
NOT WHEN I HAVE TO WAIT

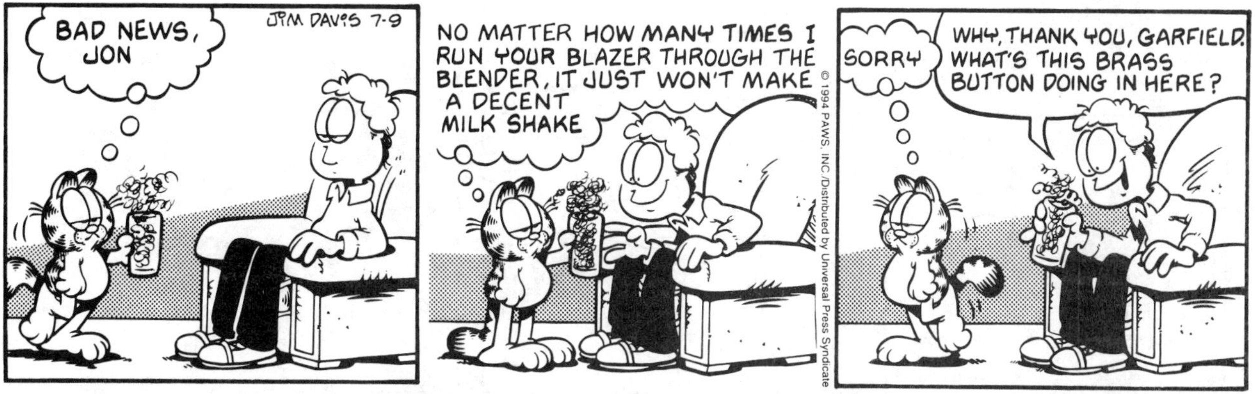
BAD NEWS, JON
JIM DAVIS 7-9
NO MATTER HOW MANY TIMES I RUN YOUR BLAZER THROUGH THE BLENDER, IT JUST WON'T MAKE A DECENT MILK SHAKE
SORRY
WHY, THANK YOU, GARFIELD. WHAT'S THIS BRASS BUTTON DOING IN HERE?

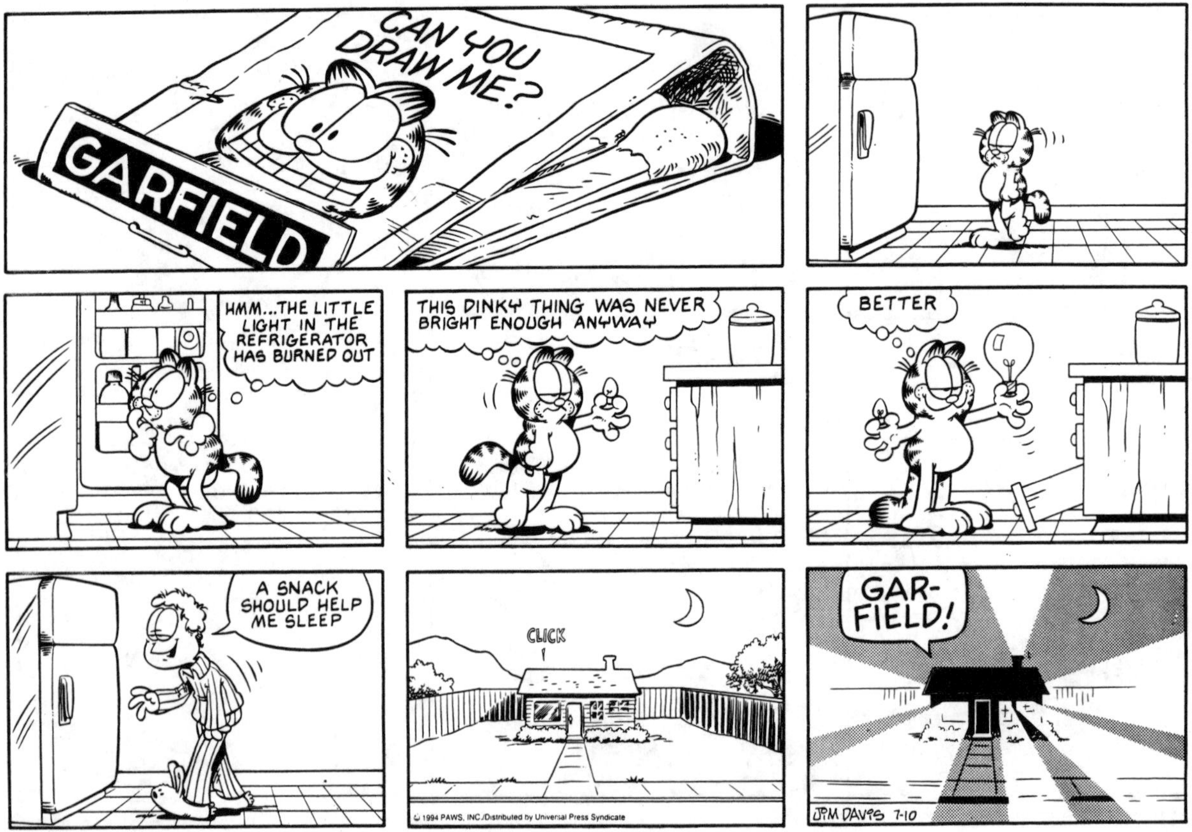
CAN YOU DRAW ME?
GARFIELD
HMM...THE LITTLE LIGHT IN THE REFRIGERATOR HAS BURNED OUT
THIS DINKY THING WAS NEVER BRIGHT ENOUGH ANYWAY
BETTER
A SNACK SHOULD HELP ME SLEEP
CLICK
GAR-FIELD!
© 1994 PAWS, INC./Distributed by Universal Press Syndicate
JIM DAVIS 7-10

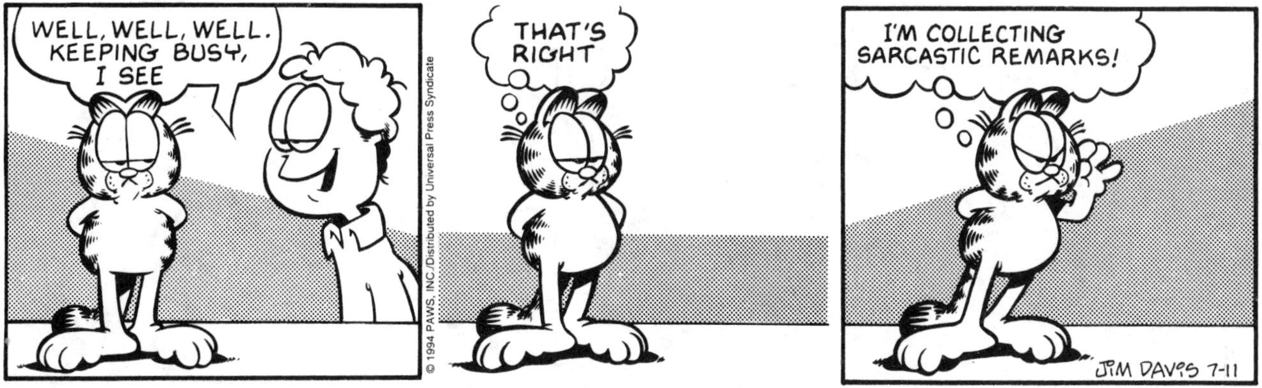
WELL, WELL, WELL. KEEPING BUSY, I SEE
THAT'S RIGHT
I'M COLLECTING SARCASTIC REMARKS!
© 1994 PAWS, INC./Distributed by Universal Press Syndicate
JIM DAVIS 7-11

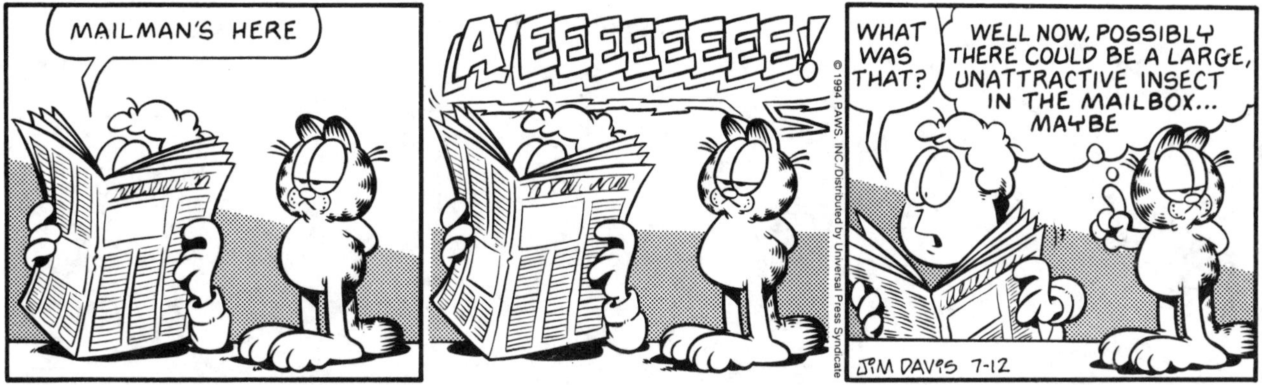
MAILMAN'S HERE
AIEEEEEEEEE!
WHAT WAS THAT?
WELL NOW, POSSIBLY THERE COULD BE A LARGE, UNATTRACTIVE INSECT IN THE MAILBOX... MAYBE
© 1994 PAWS, INC./Distributed by Universal Press Syndicate
JIM DAVIS 7-12

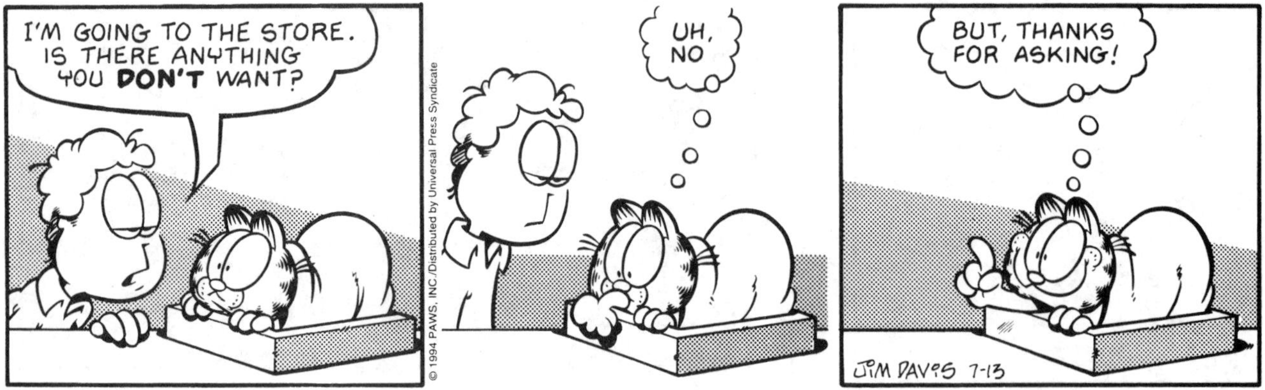
I'M GOING TO THE STORE. IS THERE ANYTHING YOU DON'T WANT?
© 1994 PAWS, INC./Distributed by Universal Press Syndicate
UH, NO
BUT, THANKS FOR ASKING!
JIM DAVIS 7-13

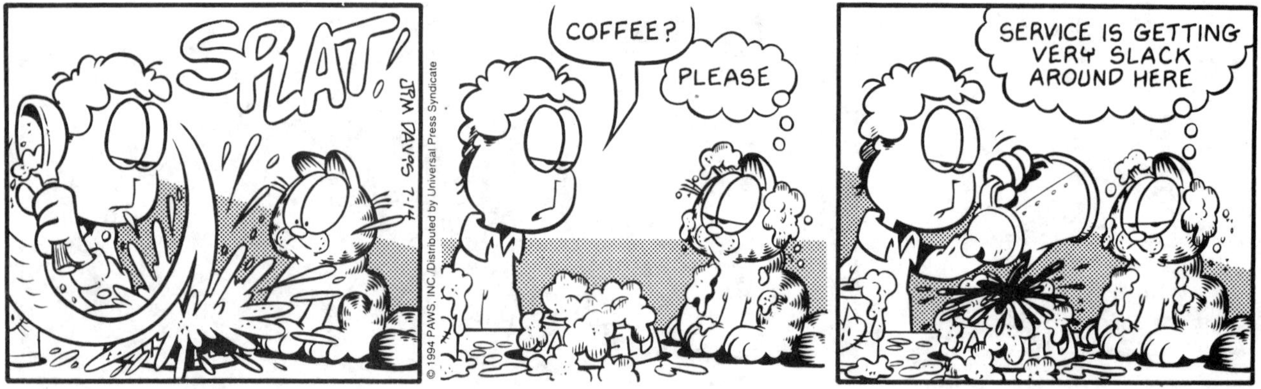
SPLAT!
JIM DAVIS 7-14
© 1994 PAWS, INC./Distributed by Universal Press Syndicate
COFFEE?
PLEASE
SERVICE IS GETTING VERY SLACK AROUND HERE

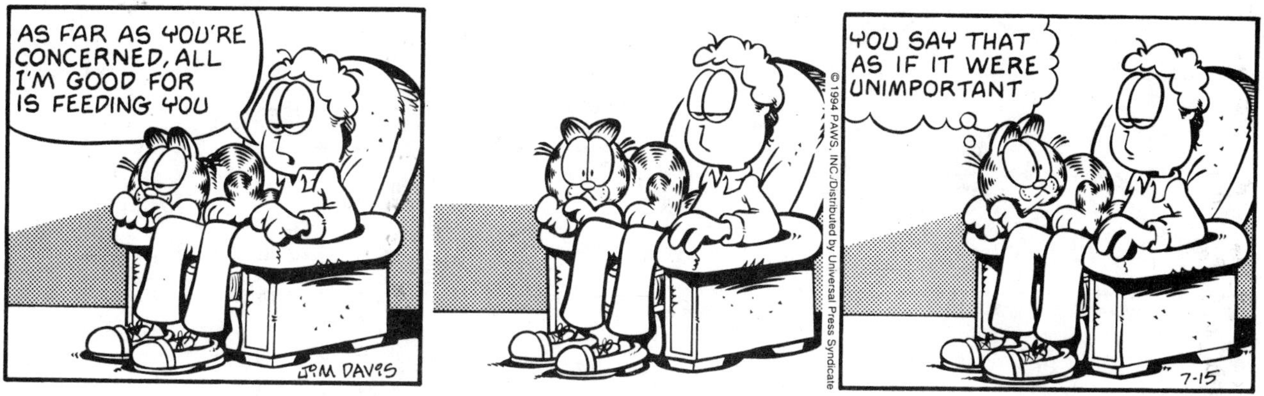
AS FAR AS YOU'RE CONCERNED, ALL I'M GOOD FOR IS FEEDING YOU
JIM DAVIS
© 1994 PAWS, INC./Distributed by Universal Press Syndicate
YOU SAY THAT AS IF IT WERE UNIMPORTANT
7-15

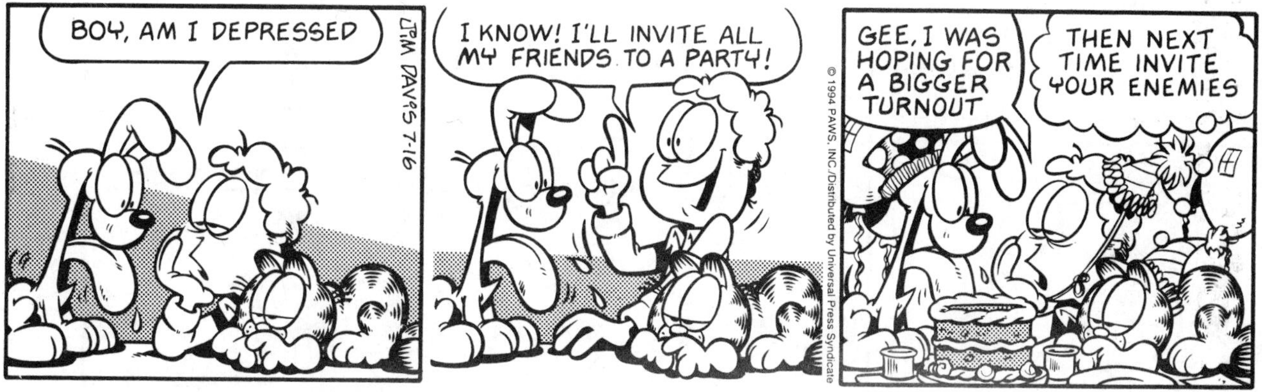
BOY, AM I DEPRESSED
JIM DAVIS 7-16
I KNOW! I'LL INVITE ALL MY FRIENDS TO A PARTY!
© 1994 PAWS, INC./Distributed by Universal Press Syndicate
GEE, I WAS HOPING FOR A BIGGER TURNOUT
THEN NEXT TIME INVITE YOUR ENEMIES

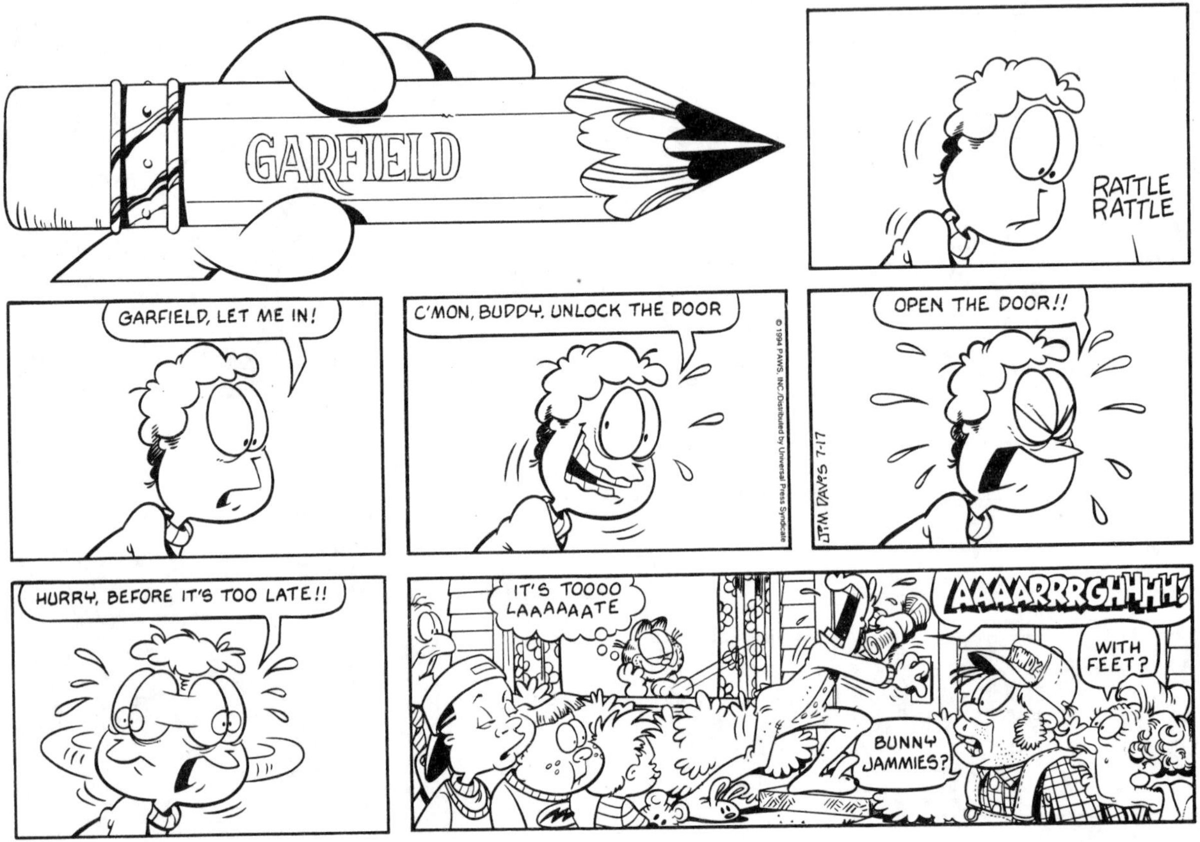
GARFIELD
RATTLE RATTLE
GARFIELD, LET ME IN!
C'MON, BUDDY. UNLOCK THE DOOR
© 1994 PAWS, INC./Distributed by Universal Press Syndicate
OPEN THE DOOR!!
JIM DAVIS 7-17
HURRY, BEFORE IT'S TOO LATE!!
IT'S TOOOO LAAAAAATE
AAAARRRGHHHH!
WITH FEET?
BUNNY JAMMIES?

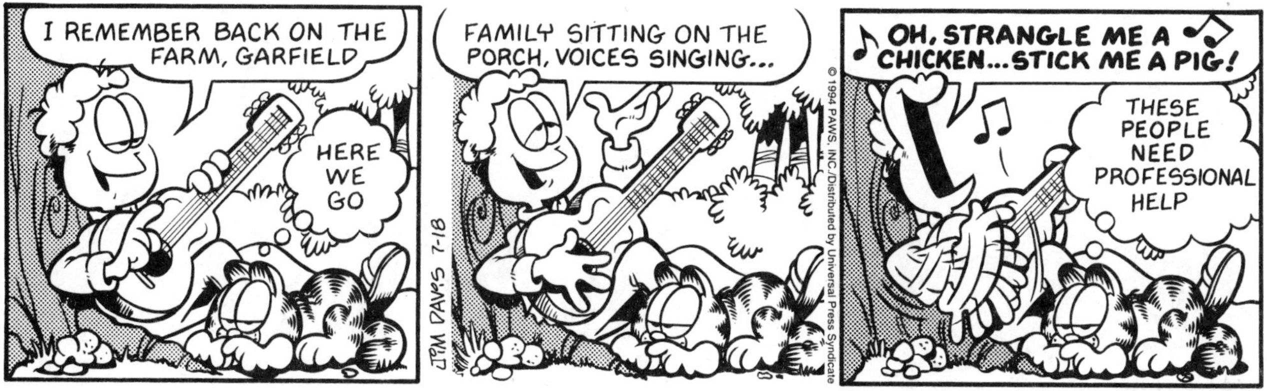
I REMEMBER BACK ON THE FARM, GARFIELD
HERE WE GO
JPM DAVPS 7-18
FAMILY SITTING ON THE PORCH, VOICES SINGING...
© 1994 PAWS, INC./Distributed by Universal Press Syndicate
OH, STRANGLE ME A CHICKEN... STICK ME A PIG!
THESE PEOPLE NEED PROFESSIONAL HELP

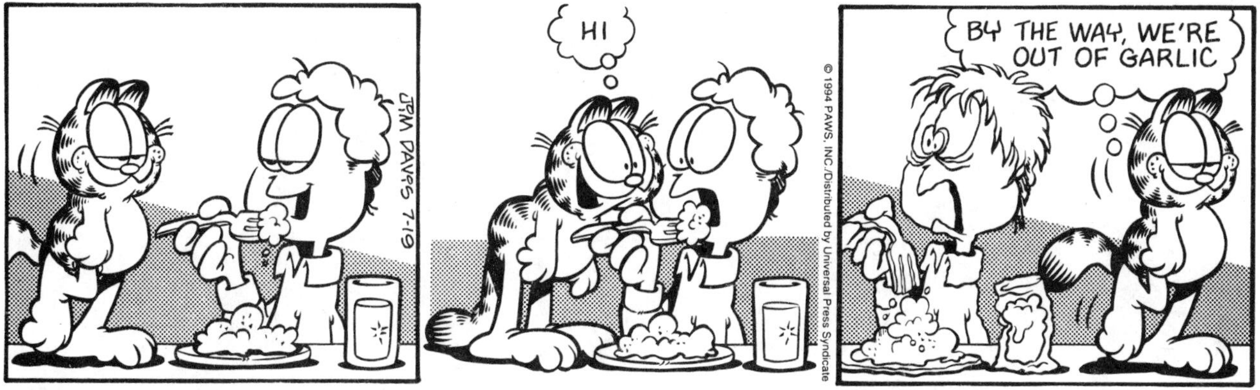
JPM DAVPS 7-19
HI
© 1994 PAWS, INC./Distributed by Universal Press Syndicate
BY THE WAY, WE'RE OUT OF GARLIC

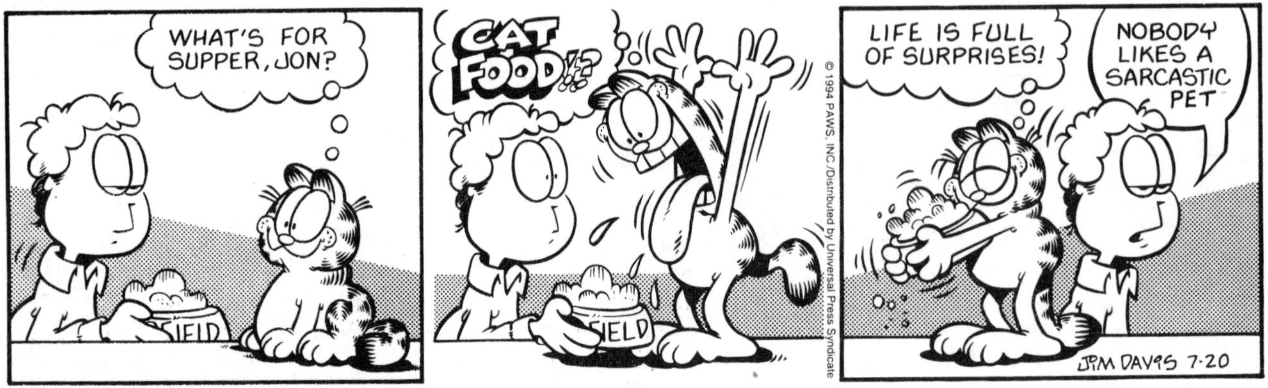
WHAT'S FOR SUPPER, JON?
CAT FOOD!?
LIFE IS FULL OF SURPRISES!
NOBODY LIKES A SARCASTIC PET
© 1994 PAWS, INC./Distributed by Universal Press Syndicate
JIM DAVIS 7-20

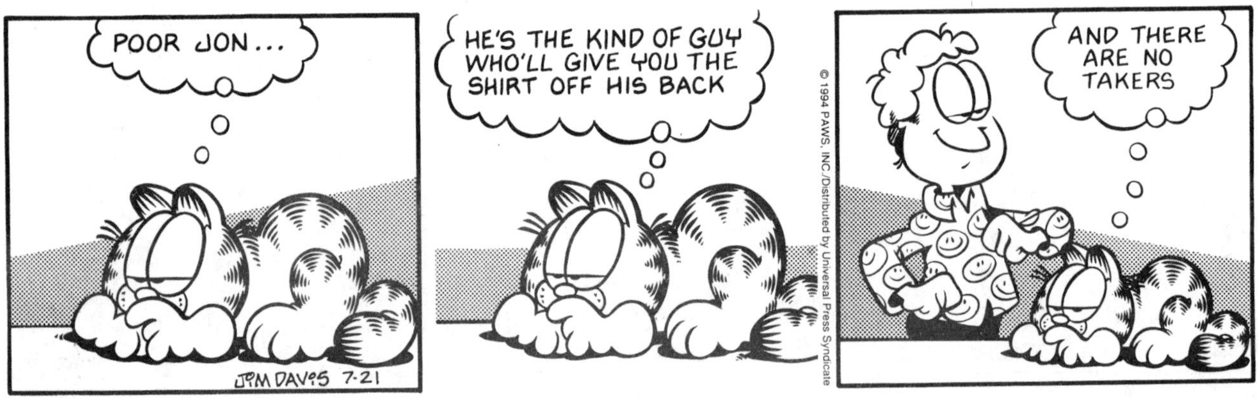
POOR JON...
HE'S THE KIND OF GUY WHO'LL GIVE YOU THE SHIRT OFF HIS BACK
AND THERE ARE NO TAKERS
© 1994 PAWS, INC./Distributed by Universal Press Syndicate
JIM DAVIS 7-21

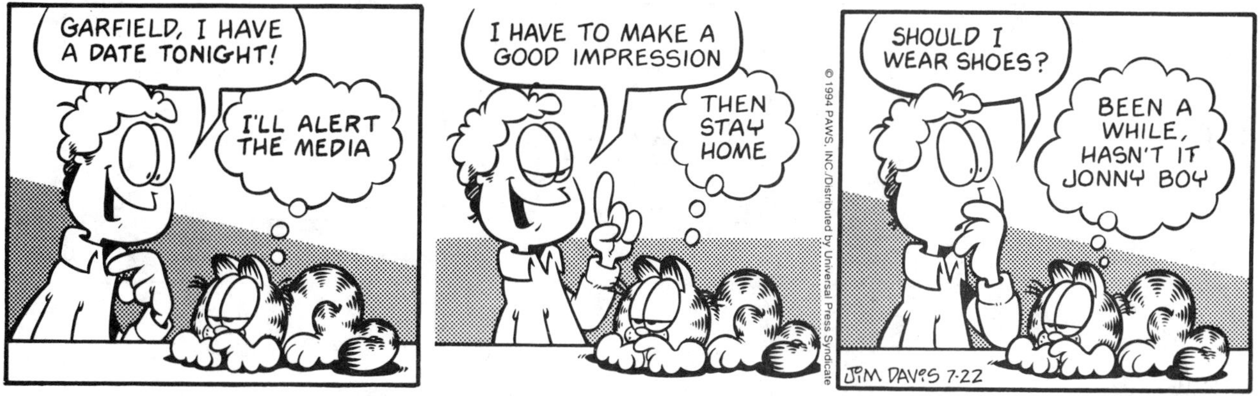
GARFIELD, I HAVE A DATE TONIGHT!
I'LL ALERT THE MEDIA
I HAVE TO MAKE A GOOD IMPRESSION
THEN STAY HOME
© 1994 PAWS, INC./Distributed by Universal Press Syndicate
SHOULD I WEAR SHOES?
BEEN A WHILE, HASN'T IT JONNY BOY
JIM DAVIS 7-22

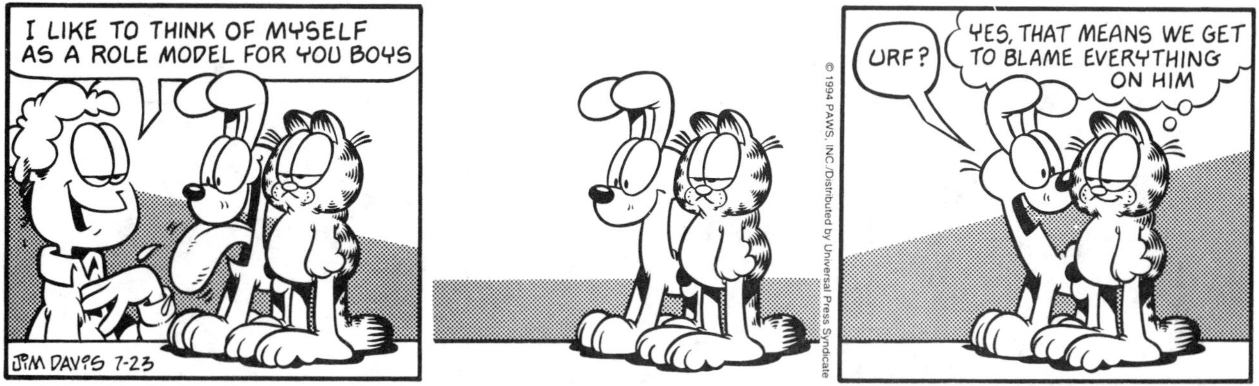
I LIKE TO THINK OF MYSELF AS A ROLE MODEL FOR YOU BOYS
JIM DAVIS 7-23
© 1994 PAWS, INC./Distributed by Universal Press Syndicate
URF?
YES, THAT MEANS WE GET TO BLAME EVERYTHING ON HIM

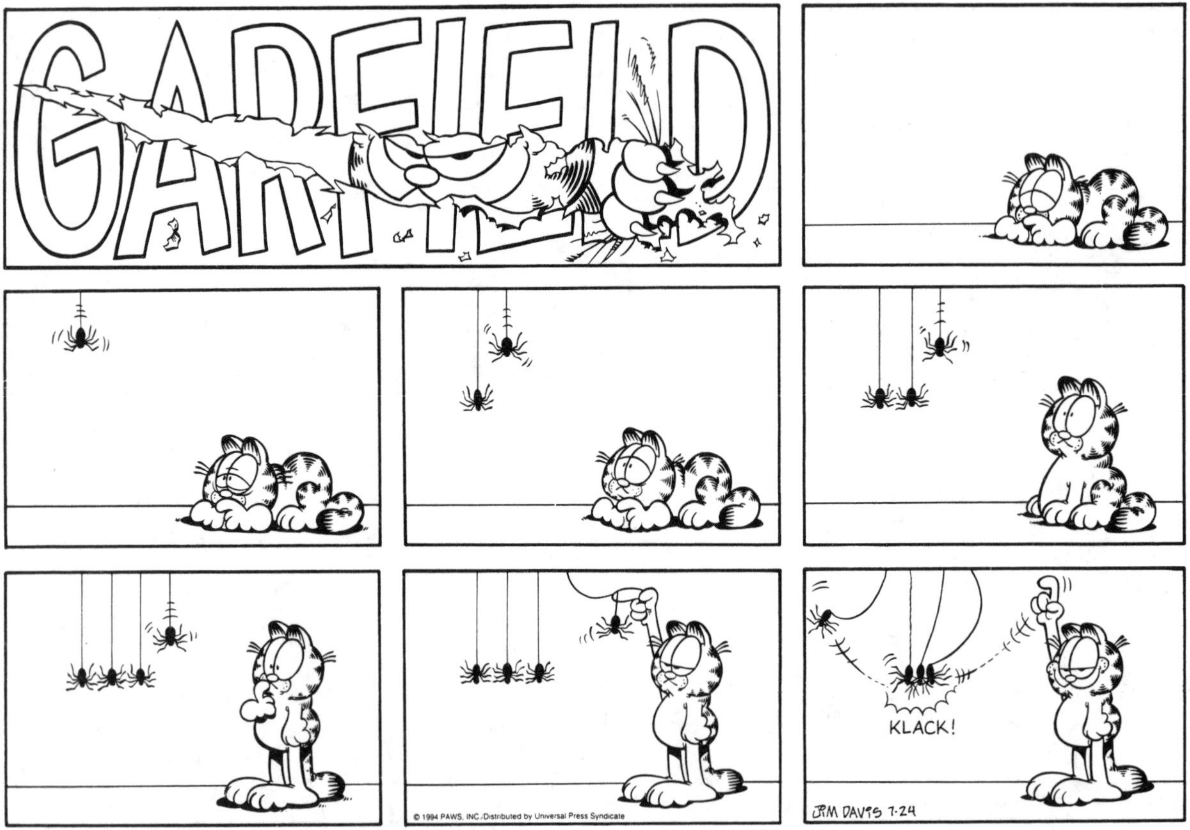
GARFIELD
KLACK!
JIM DAVIS 7-24

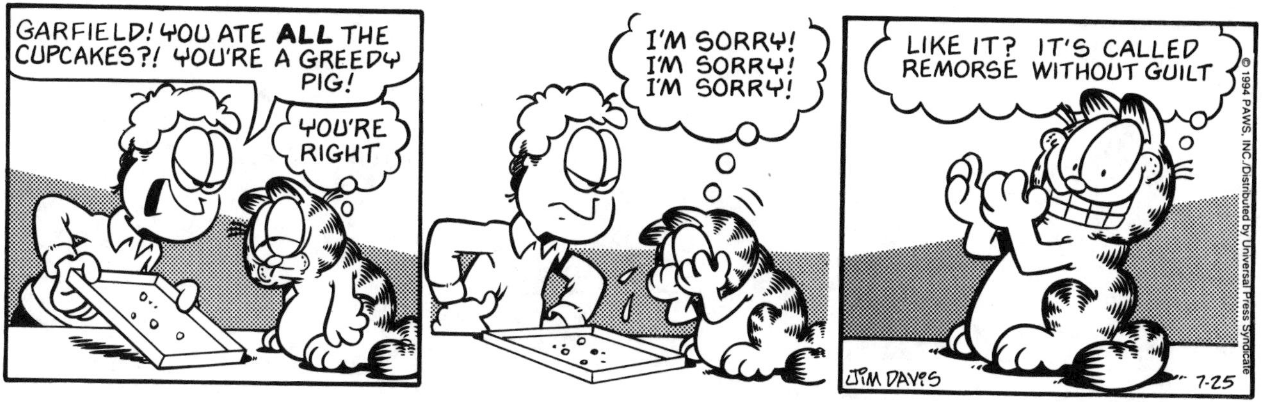
GARFIELD! YOU ATE **ALL** THE CUPCAKES?! YOU'RE A GREEDY PIG!
YOU'RE RIGHT
I'M SORRY! I'M SORRY! I'M SORRY!
LIKE IT? IT'S CALLED REMORSE WITHOUT GUILT
© 1994 PAWS, INC./Distributed by Universal Press Syndicate
JIM DAVIS 7-25

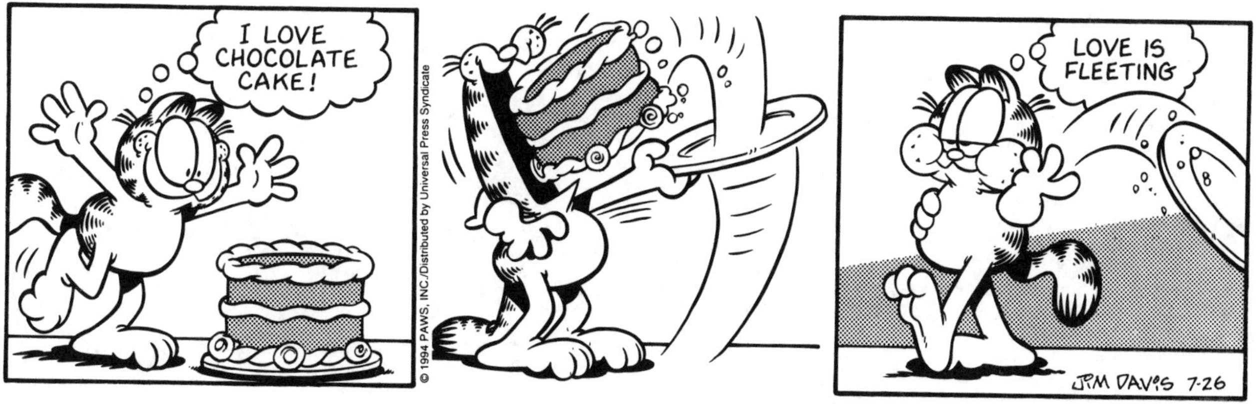
I LOVE CHOCOLATE CAKE!
© 1994 PAWS, INC./Distributed by Universal Press Syndicate
LOVE IS FLEETING
JIM DAVIS 7-26

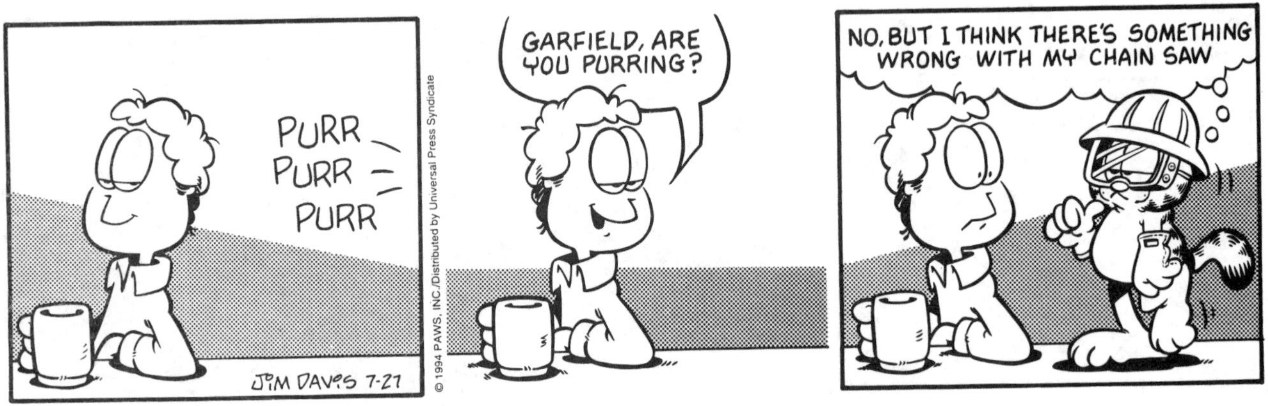
PURR PURR PURR
JIM DAVIS 7-21
© 1994 PAWS, INC./Distributed by Universal Press Syndicate
GARFIELD, ARE YOU PURRING?
NO, BUT I THINK THERE'S SOMETHING WRONG WITH MY CHAIN SAW

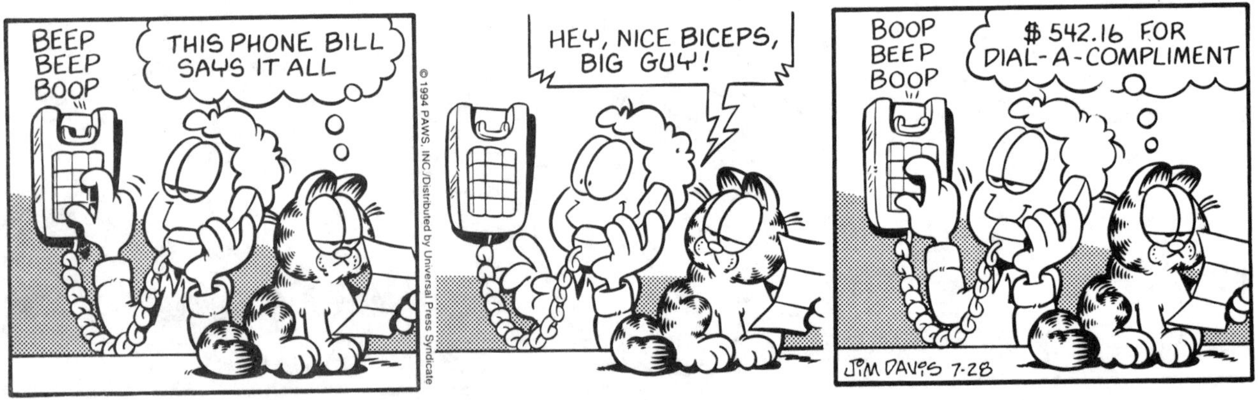
BEEP BEEP BOOP
THIS PHONE BILL SAYS IT ALL
© 1994 PAWS, INC./Distributed by Universal Press Syndicate
HEY, NICE BICEPS, BIG GUY!
BOOP BEEP BOOP
$ 542.16 FOR DIAL-A-COMPLIMENT
JIM DAVIS 7-28

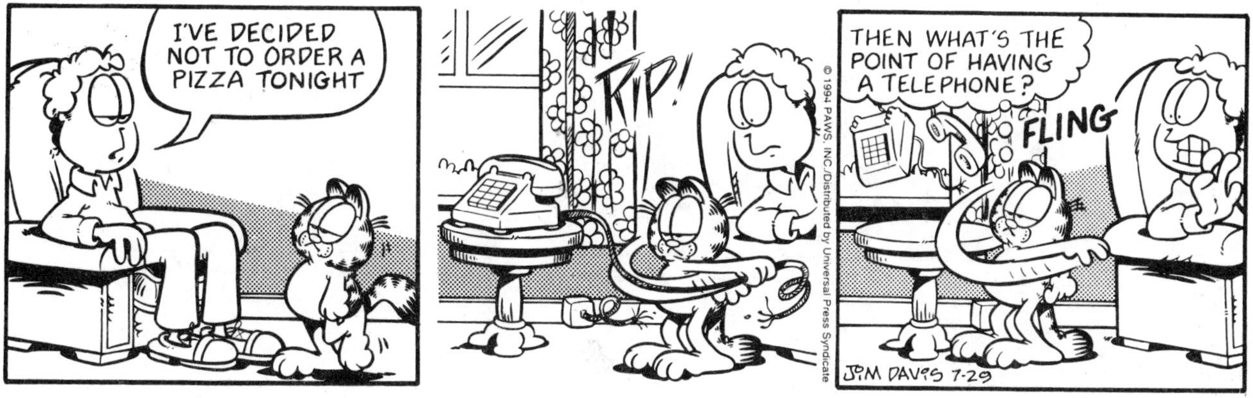
I'VE DECIDED NOT TO ORDER A PIZZA TONIGHT
RIP!
© 1994 PAWS, INC./Distributed by Universal Press Syndicate
THEN WHAT'S THE POINT OF HAVING A TELEPHONE?
FLING
JIM DAVIS 7-29

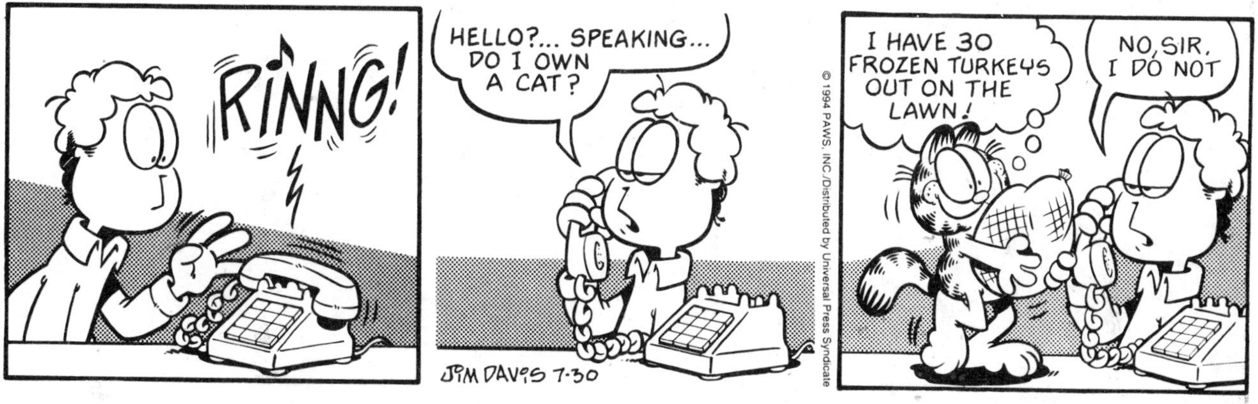
RINNG!
HELLO?... SPEAKING... DO I OWN A CAT?
JIM DAVIS 7-30
© 1994 PAWS, INC./Distributed by Universal Press Syndicate
I HAVE 30 FROZEN TURKEYS OUT ON THE LAWN!
NO, SIR, I DO NOT

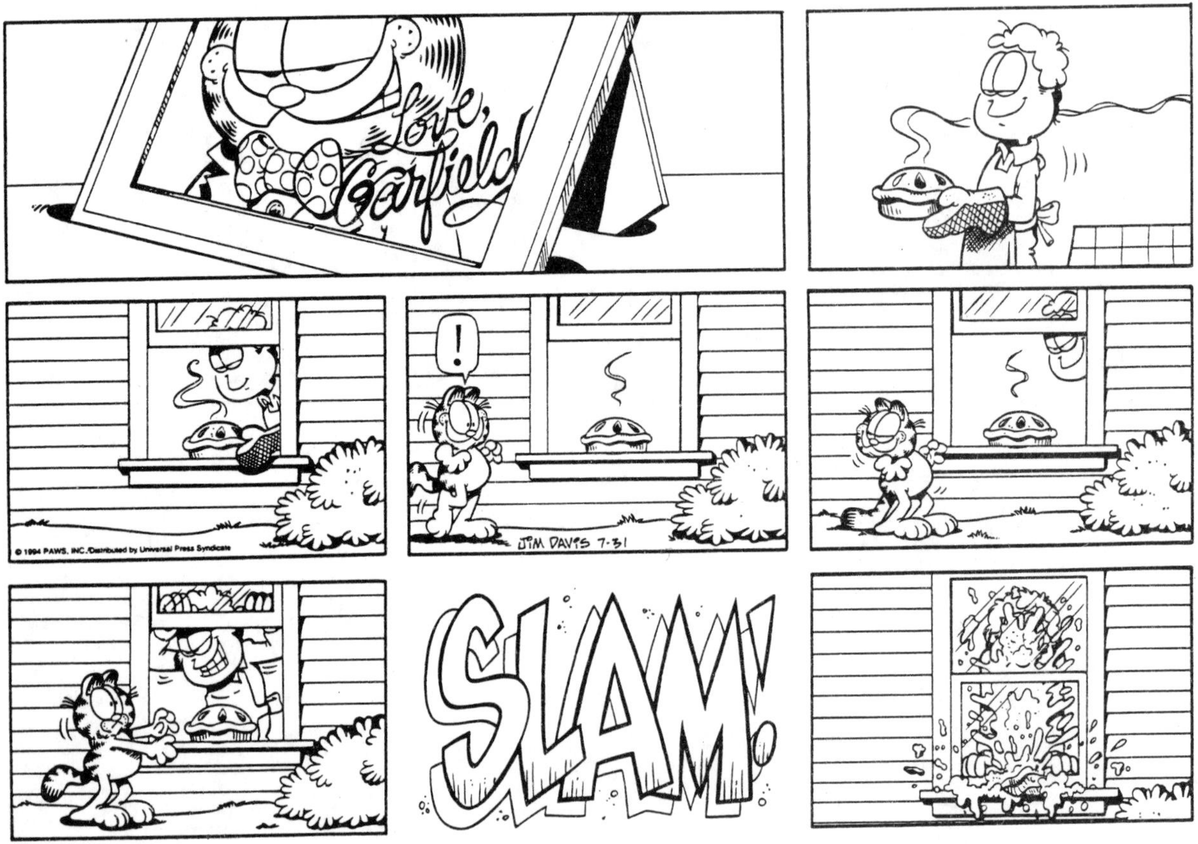
Love, Garfield
© 1994 PAWS, INC./Distributed by Universal Press Syndicate
!
JIM DAVIS 7-31
SLAM!

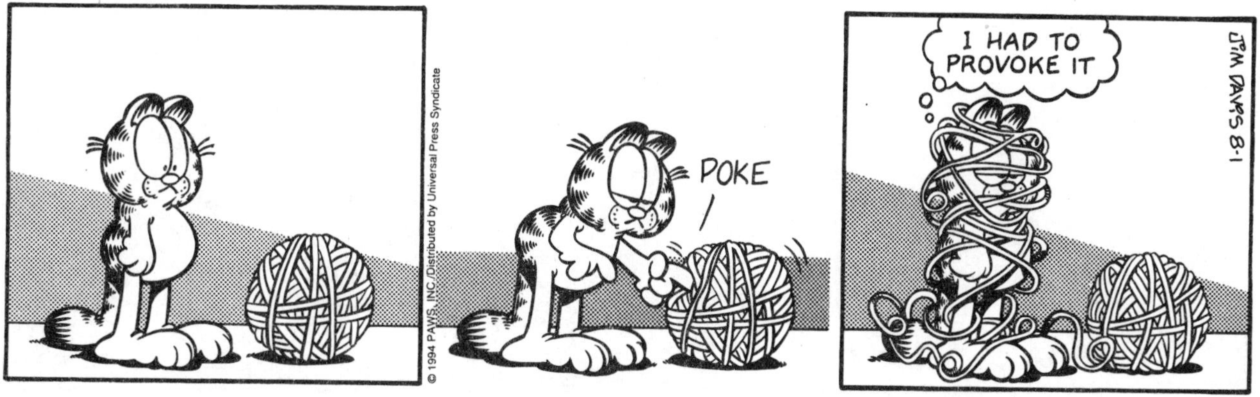
POKE
I HAD TO PROVOKE IT
JIM DAVIS 8-1
© 1994 PAWS, INC./Distributed by Universal Press Syndicate

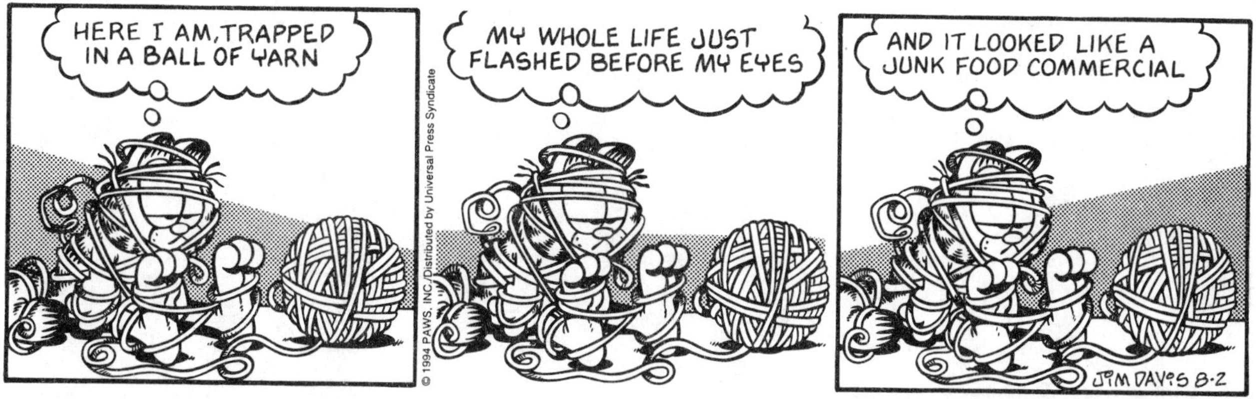
HERE I AM, TRAPPED IN A BALL OF YARN
MY WHOLE LIFE JUST FLASHED BEFORE MY EYES
AND IT LOOKED LIKE A JUNK FOOD COMMERCIAL
JIM DAVIS 8-2
© 1994 PAWS, INC./Distributed by Universal Press Syndicate

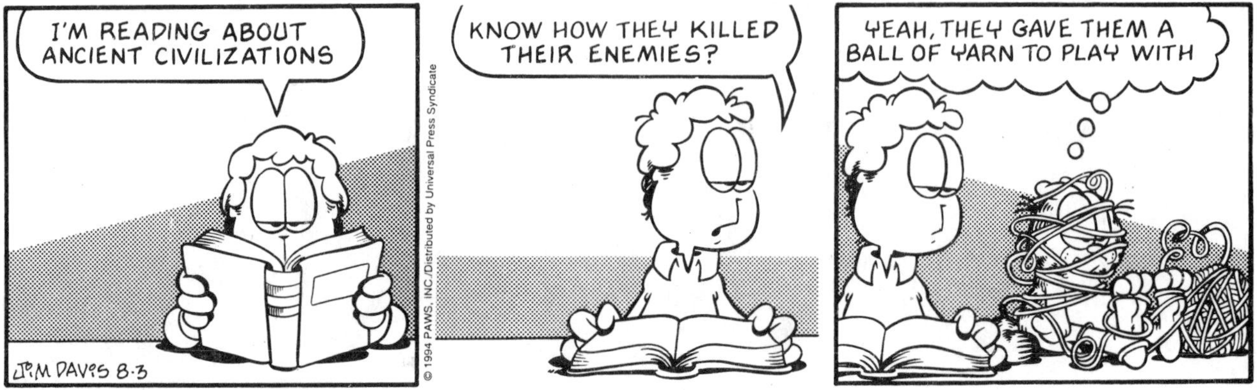
I'M READING ABOUT ANCIENT CIVILIZATIONS
KNOW HOW THEY KILLED THEIR ENEMIES?
YEAH, THEY GAVE THEM A BALL OF YARN TO PLAY WITH
JIM DAVIS 8-3

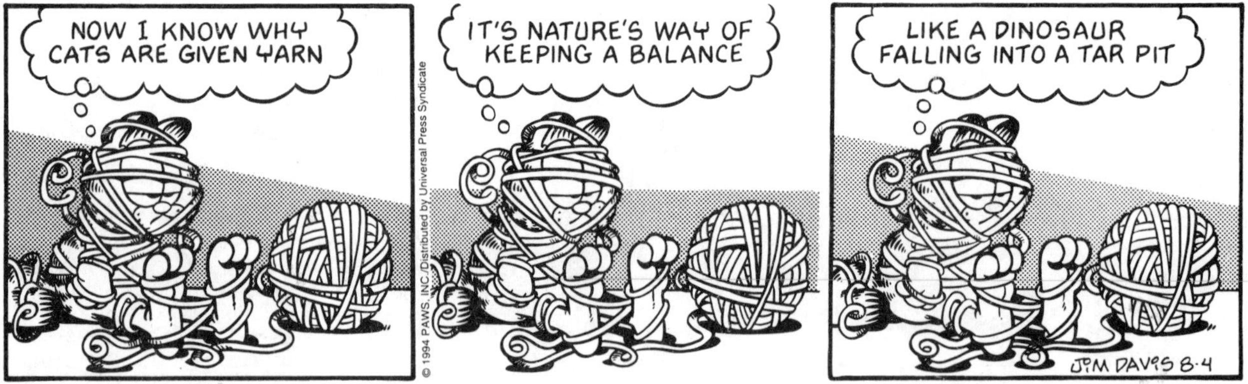
NOW I KNOW WHY CATS ARE GIVEN YARN
IT'S NATURE'S WAY OF KEEPING A BALANCE
LIKE A DINOSAUR FALLING INTO A TAR PIT
JIM DAVIS 8-4

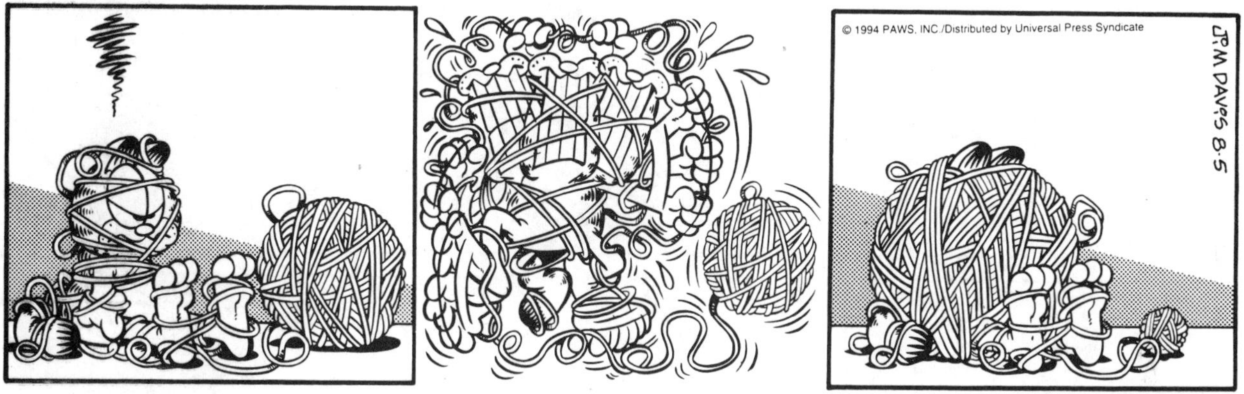
© 1994 PAWS, INC./Distributed by Universal Press Syndicate
JIM DAVIS 8-5

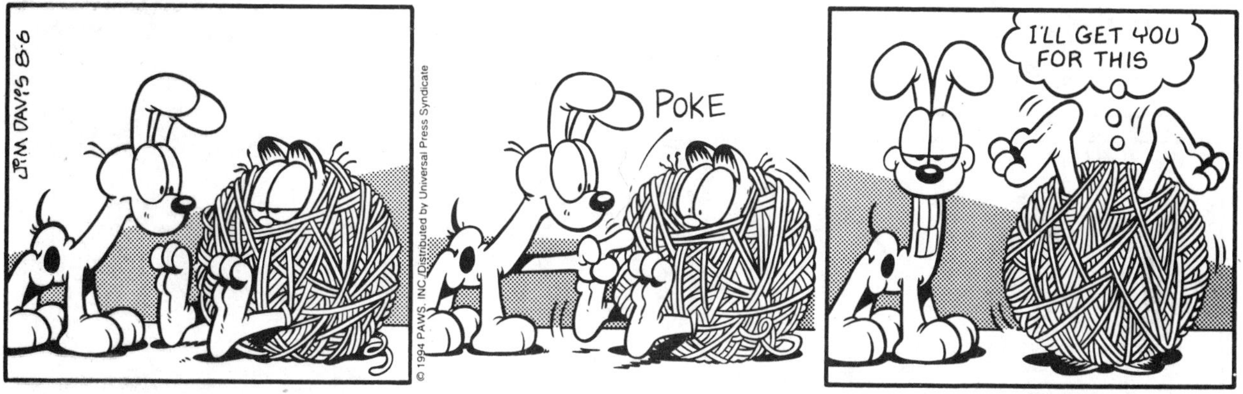
JIM DAVIS 8-6
© 1994 PAWS, INC./Distributed by Universal Press Syndicate
POKE
I'LL GET YOU FOR THIS

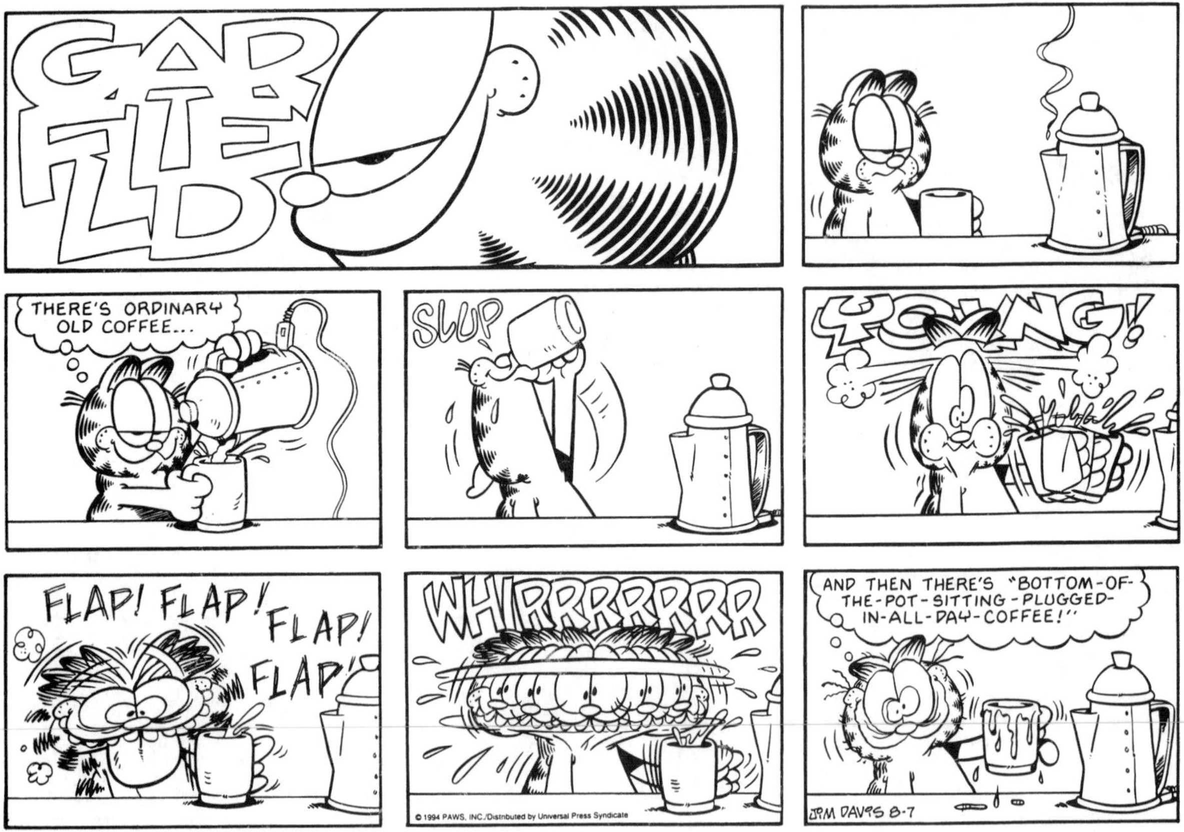
GARFIELD
THERE'S ORDINARY OLD COFFEE...
SLUP
YOING!
FLAP! FLAP! FLAP! FLAP!
WHIRRRRRRR
AND THEN THERE'S "BOTTOM-OF-THE-POT-SITTING-PLUGGED-IN-ALL-DAY-COFFEE!"
© 1994 PAWS, INC./Distributed by Universal Press Syndicate
JIM DAVIS 8-7

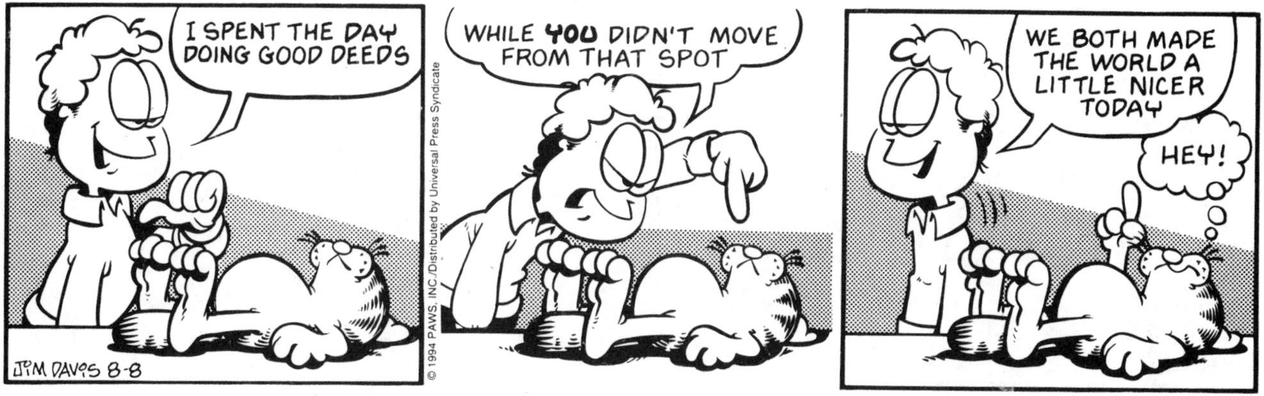
I SPENT THE DAY DOING GOOD DEEDS
WHILE YOU DIDN'T MOVE FROM THAT SPOT
WE BOTH MADE THE WORLD A LITTLE NICER TODAY
HEY!
JIM DAVIS 8-8

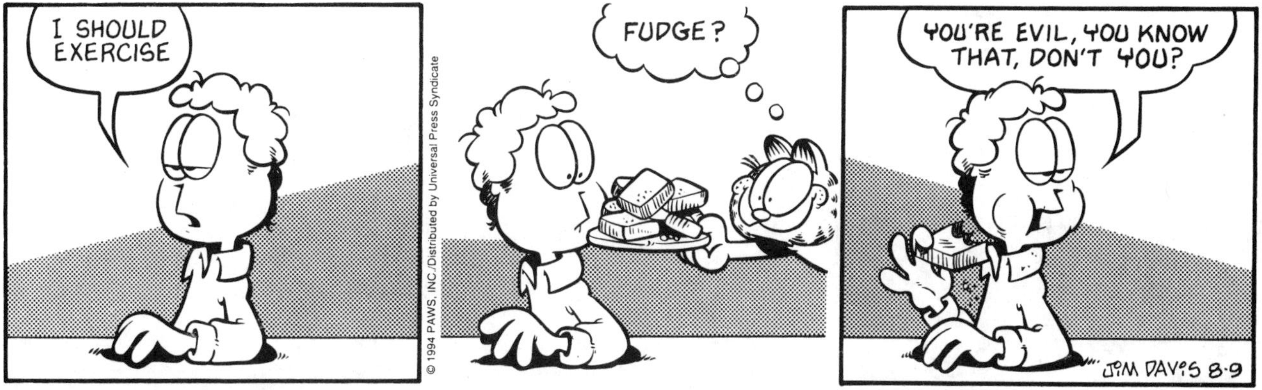
I SHOULD EXERCISE
FUDGE?
YOU'RE EVIL, YOU KNOW THAT, DON'T YOU?
JIM DAVIS 8-9

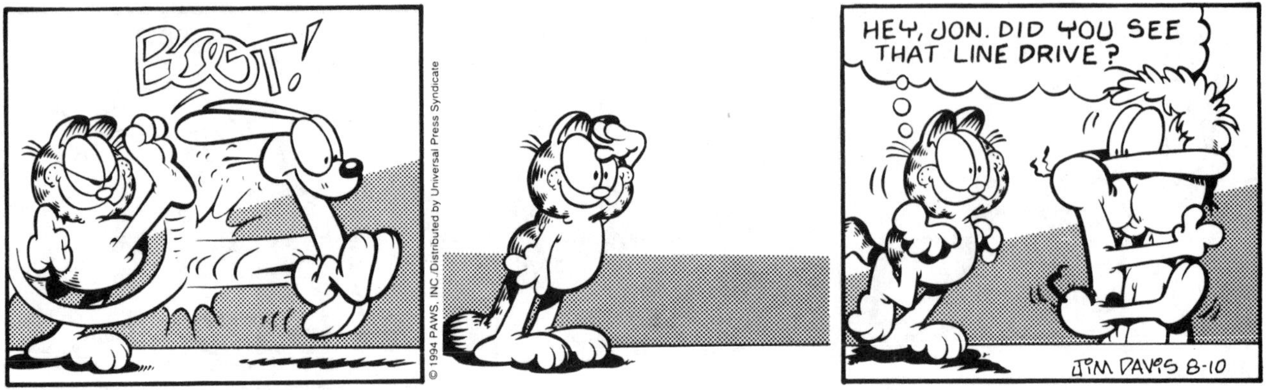
BOOT!
© 1994 PAWS, INC./Distributed by Universal Press Syndicate
HEY, JON. DID YOU SEE THAT LINE DRIVE?
JIM DAVIS 8-10

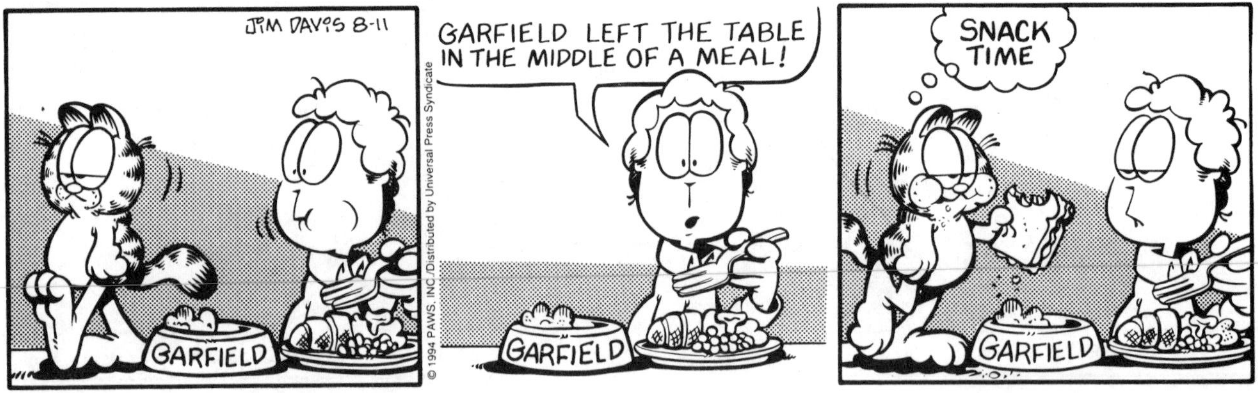
JIM DAVIS 8-11
GARFIELD
© 1994 PAWS, INC./Distributed by Universal Press Syndicate
GARFIELD LEFT THE TABLE IN THE MIDDLE OF A MEAL!
GARFIELD
SNACK TIME
GARFIELD

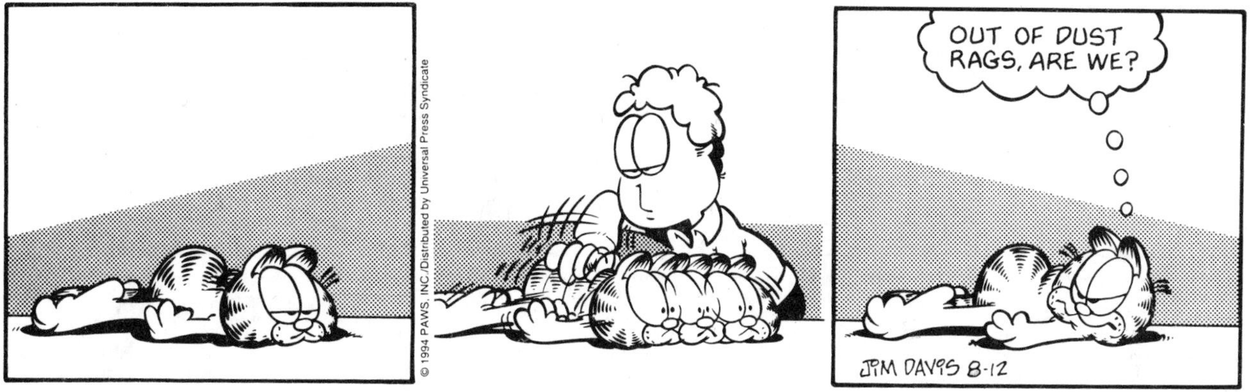
OUT OF DUST RAGS, ARE WE?
JIM DAVIS 8-12

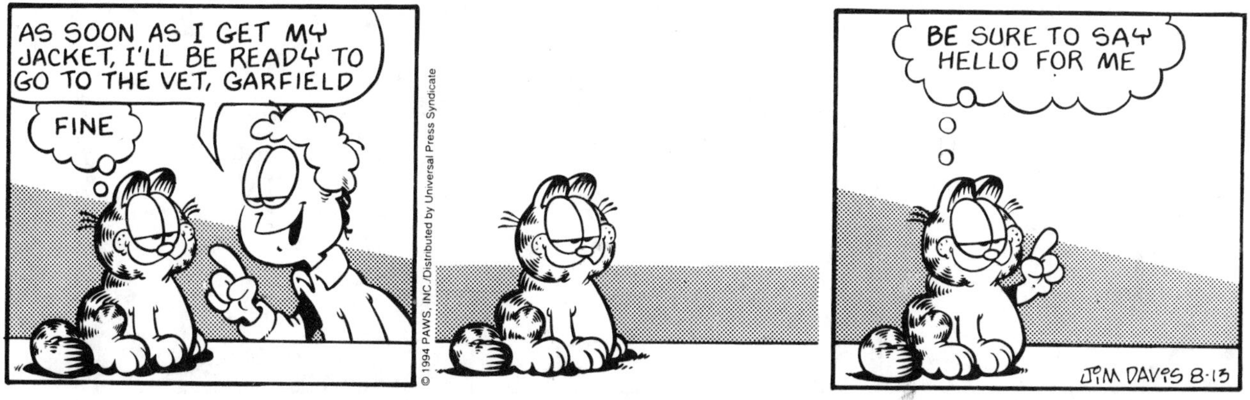
AS SOON AS I GET MY JACKET, I'LL BE READY TO GO TO THE VET, GARFIELD
FINE
BE SURE TO SAY HELLO FOR ME
JIM DAVIS 8-13

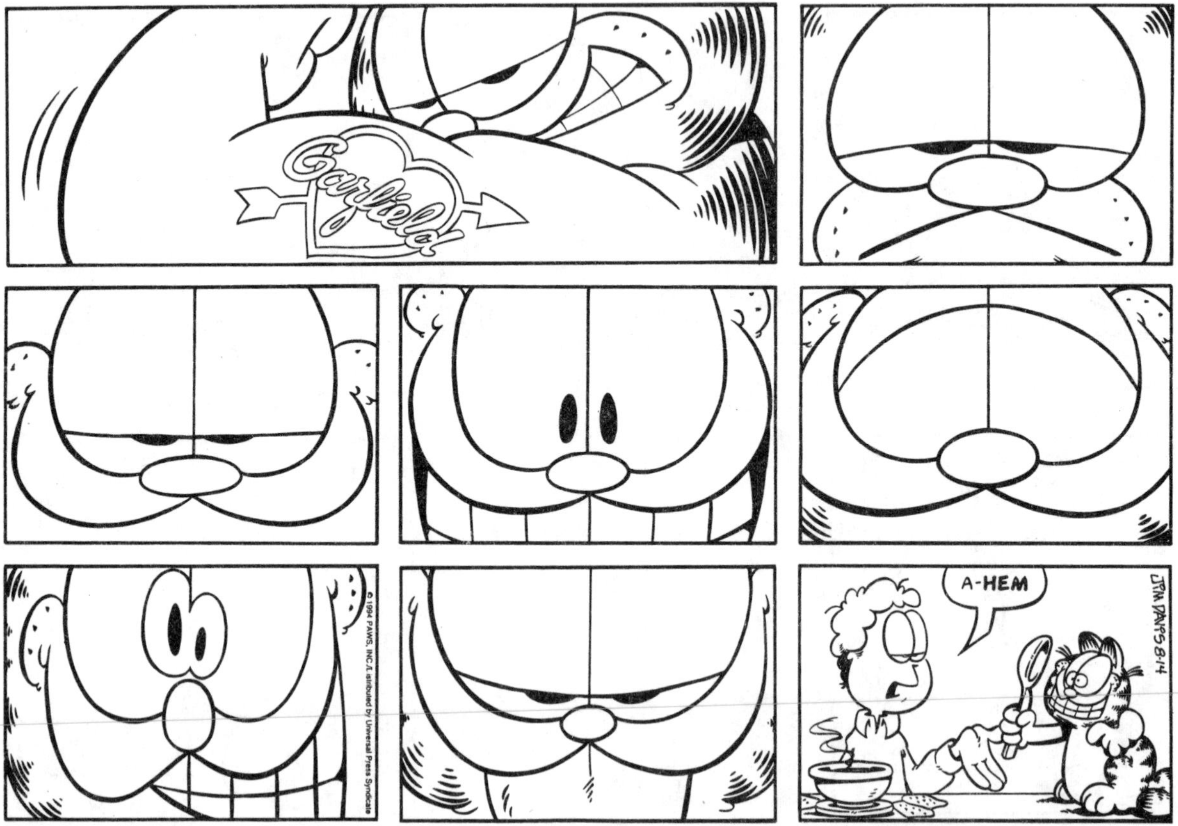
Garfield
A-HEM
JIM DAVIS 8-14
© 1994 PAWS, INC./Distributed by Universal Press Syndicate

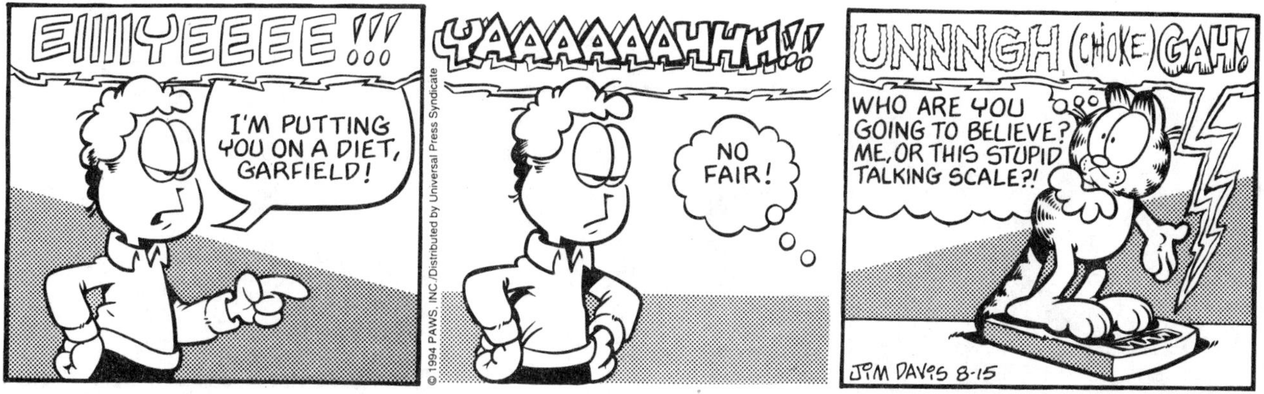
EIIIIYEEEEE!!!
I'M PUTTING YOU ON A DIET, GARFIELD!
© 1994 PAWS, INC./Distributed by Universal Press Syndicate
YAAAAAAAHHH!!
NO FAIR!
UNNNGH (CHOKE) GAH!
WHO ARE YOU GOING TO BELIEVE? ME, OR THIS STUPID TALKING SCALE?!
JIM DAVIS 8-15

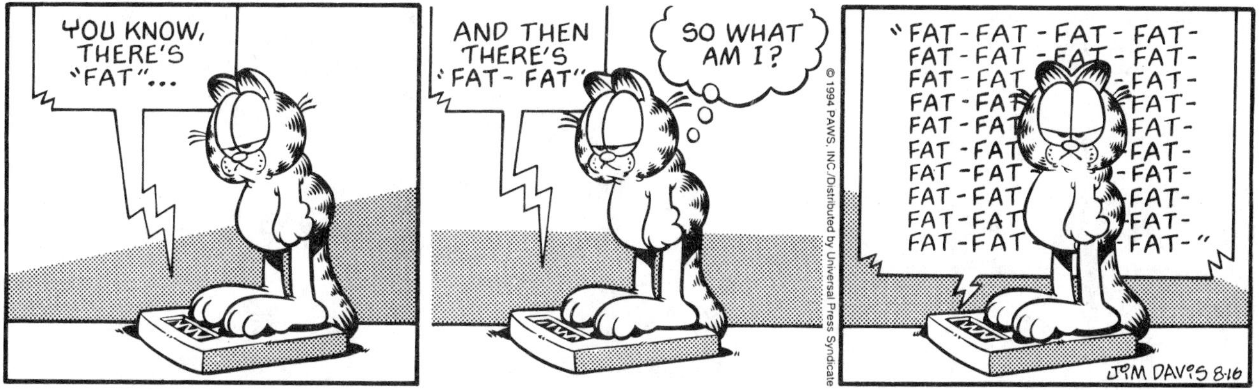
YOU KNOW, THERE'S "FAT"...
AND THEN THERE'S "FAT-FAT"
SO WHAT AM I?
© 1994 PAWS, INC./Distributed by Universal Press Syndicate
"FAT-FAT-FAT-FAT-
FAT-FAT-FAT-FAT-
FAT-FAT
-FAT-
FAT-FAT
FAT-
FAT-FAT
FAT-
FAT-FAT
-FAT-
FAT-FAT
-FAT-
FAT-FAT
-FAT-
FAT-FAT
-FAT-
FAT-FAT
-FAT-"
JIM DAVIS 8-16

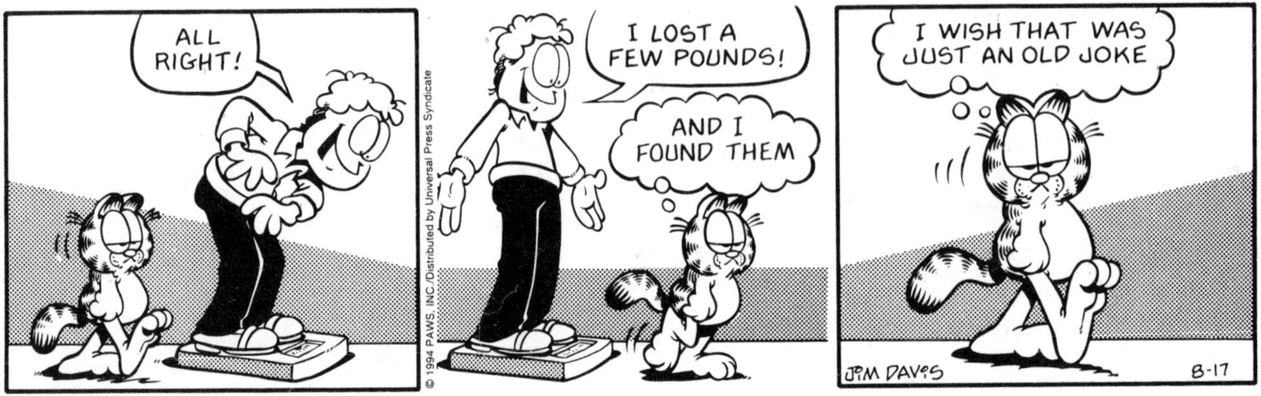
ALL RIGHT!
© 1994 PAWS, INC./Distributed by Universal Press Syndicate
I LOST A FEW POUNDS!
AND I FOUND THEM
I WISH THAT WAS JUST AN OLD JOKE
JIM DAVIS 8-17

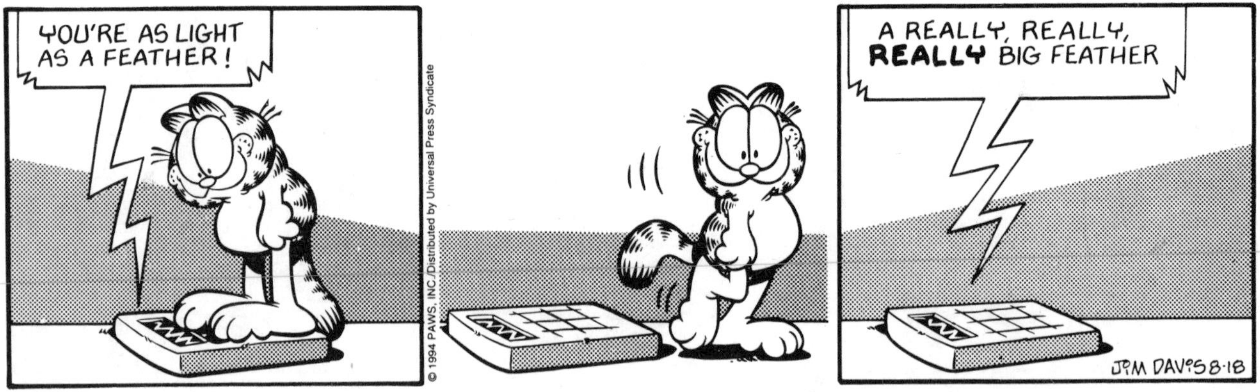
YOU'RE AS LIGHT AS A FEATHER!
© 1994 PAWS, INC./Distributed by Universal Press Syndicate
A REALLY, REALLY, **REALLY** BIG FEATHER
JIM DAVIS 8-18

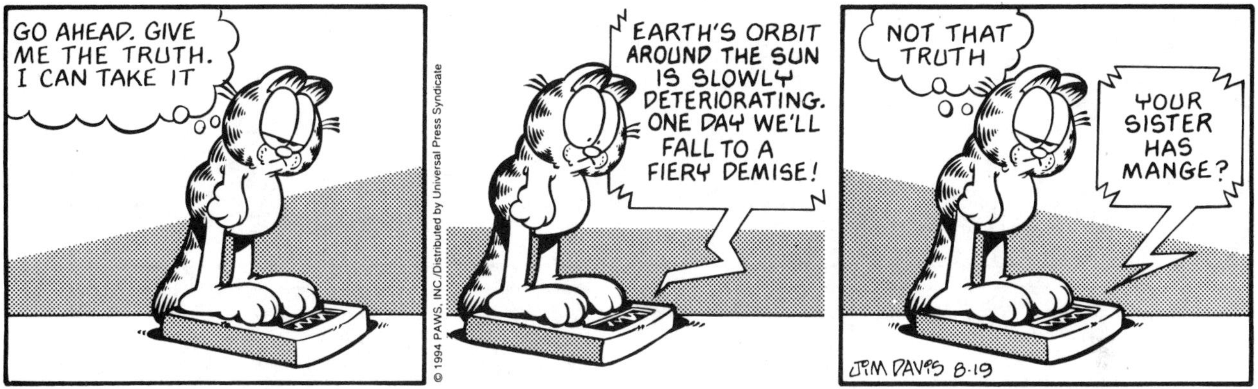
GO AHEAD. GIVE ME THE TRUTH. I CAN TAKE IT
EARTH'S ORBIT AROUND THE SUN IS SLOWLY DETERIORATING. ONE DAY WE'LL FALL TO A FIERY DEMISE!
NOT THAT TRUTH
YOUR SISTER HAS MANGE?
© 1994 PAWS, INC./Distributed by Universal Press Syndicate
JIM DAVIS 8-19

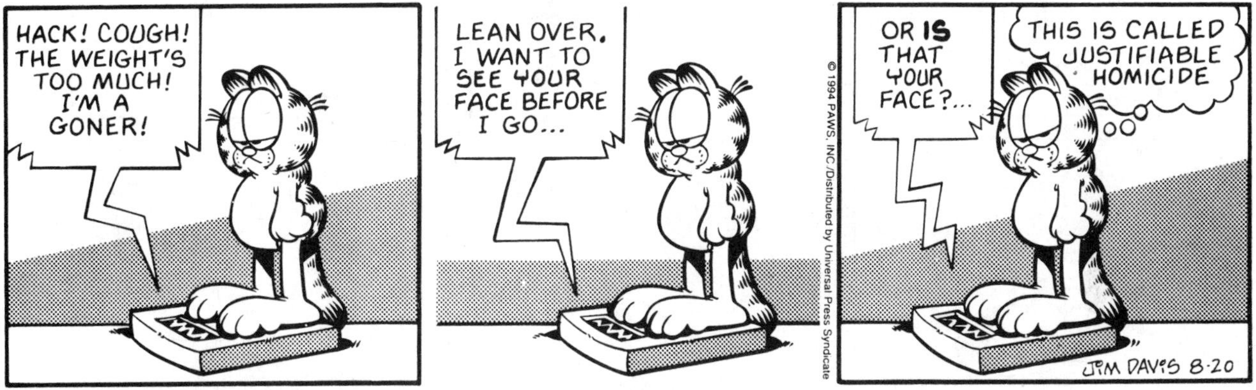
HACK! COUGH! THE WEIGHT'S TOO MUCH! I'M A GONER!
LEAN OVER. I WANT TO SEE YOUR FACE BEFORE I GO...
OR **IS** THAT YOUR FACE?...
THIS IS CALLED JUSTIFIABLE HOMICIDE
© 1994 PAWS, INC./Distributed by Universal Press Syndicate
JIM DAVIS 8-20

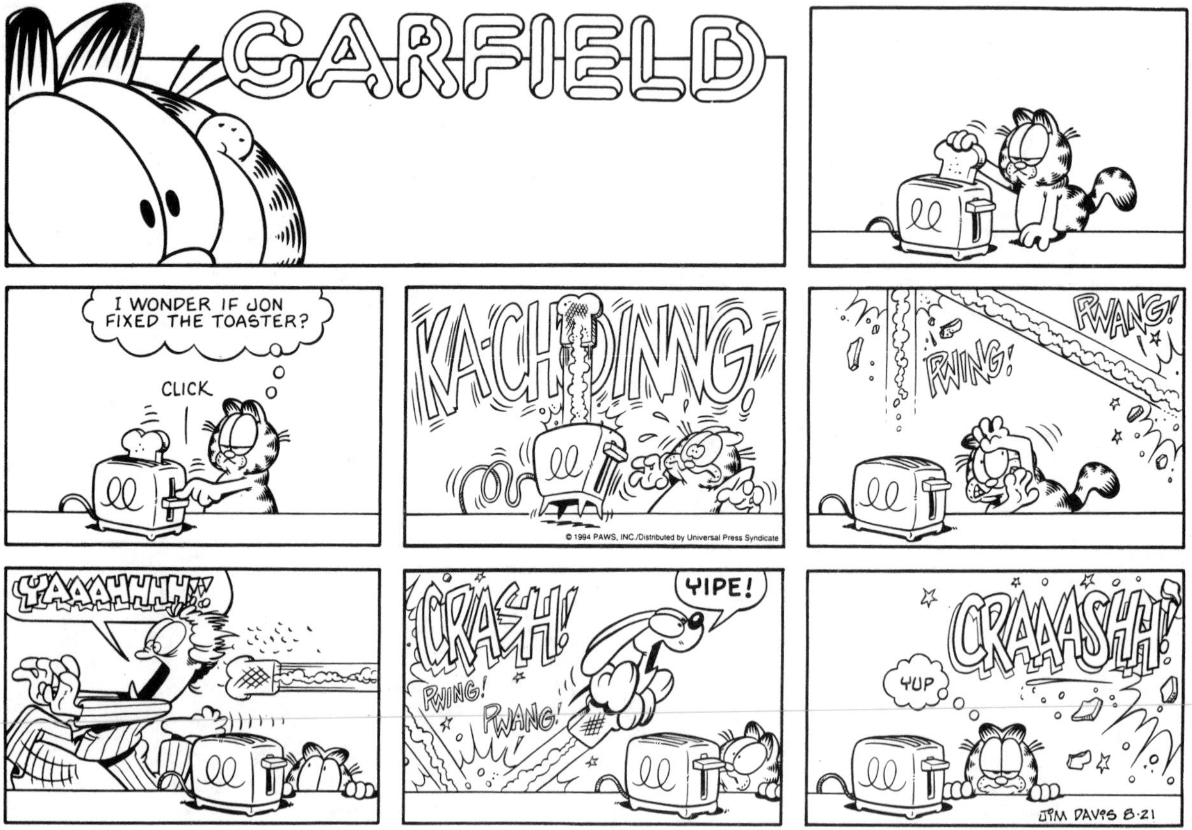
GARFIELD
I WONDER IF JON FIXED THE TOASTER?
CLICK
KA-CHOINNG!
PWANG!
PWING!
YAAAHHHH!!
CRASH!
YIPE!
PWING!
PWANG!
YUP
CRAAASHH!
JIM DAVIS 8-21

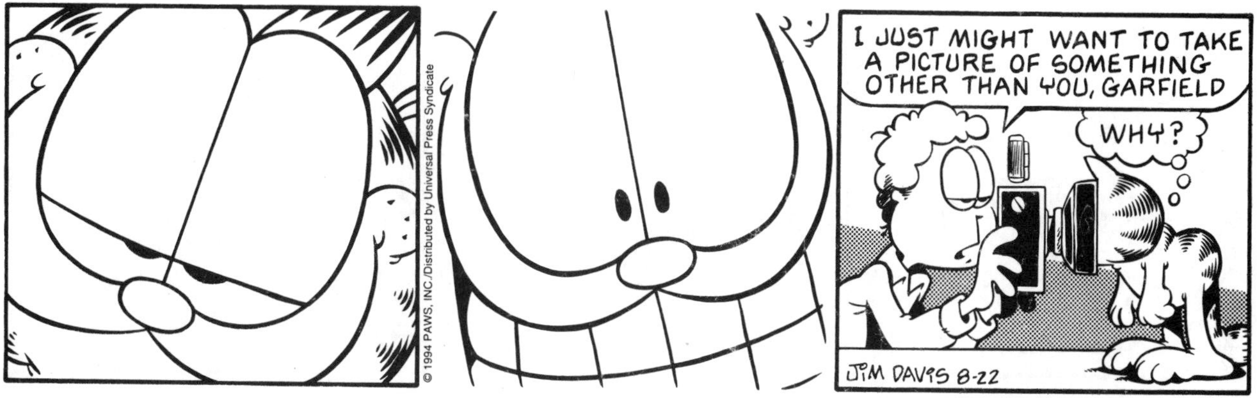
© 1994 PAWS, INC./Distributed by Universal Press Syndicate
I JUST MIGHT WANT TO TAKE A PICTURE OF SOMETHING OTHER THAN YOU, GARFIELD
WHY?
JIM DAVIS 8-22

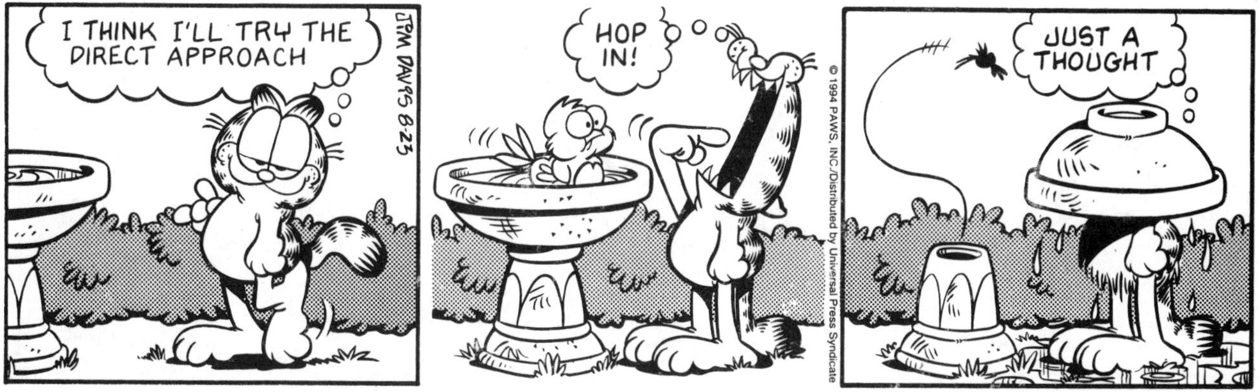
I THINK I'LL TRY THE DIRECT APPROACH
JIM DAVIS 8-23
HOP IN!
© 1994 PAWS, INC./Distributed by Universal Press Syndicate
JUST A THOUGHT

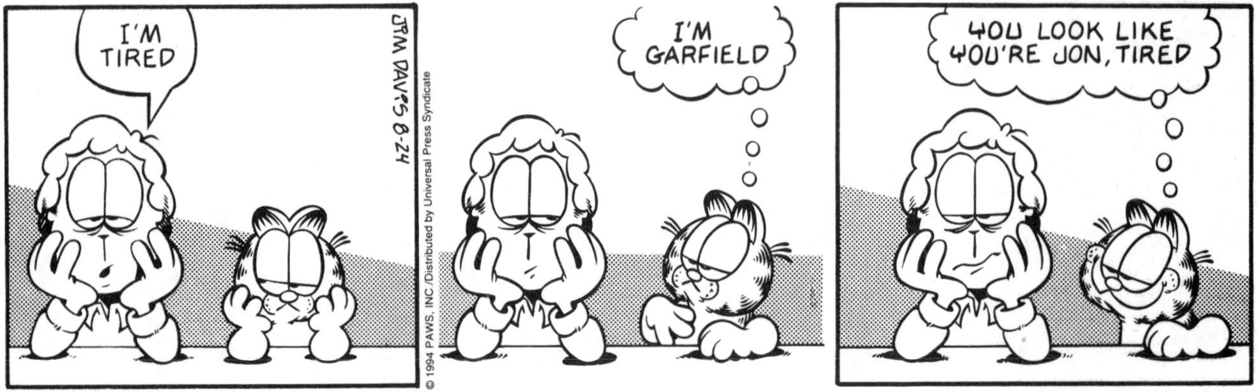
I'M TIRED
JIM DAVIS 8-24
I'M GARFIELD
YOU LOOK LIKE YOU'RE JON, TIRED

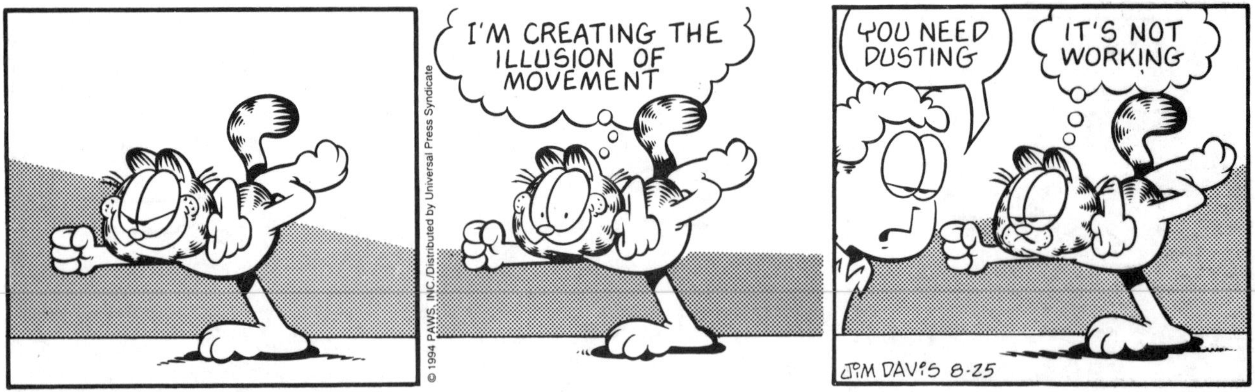
I'M CREATING THE ILLUSION OF MOVEMENT
YOU NEED DUSTING
IT'S NOT WORKING
JIM DAVIS 8-25

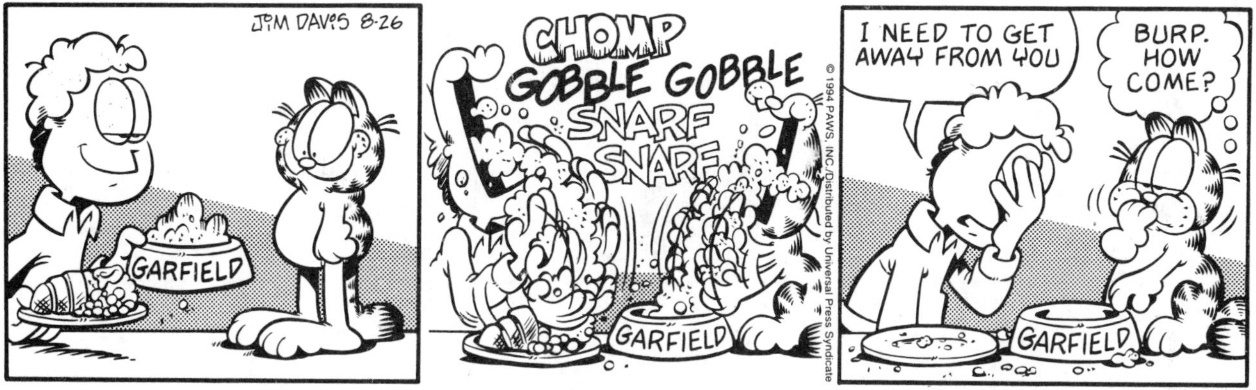
JIM DAVIS 8-26
CHOMP
GOBBLE GOBBLE
SNARF
SNARF
GARFIELD
© 1994 PAWS, INC./Distributed by Universal Press Syndicate
I NEED TO GET AWAY FROM YOU
BURP. HOW COME?
GARFIELD

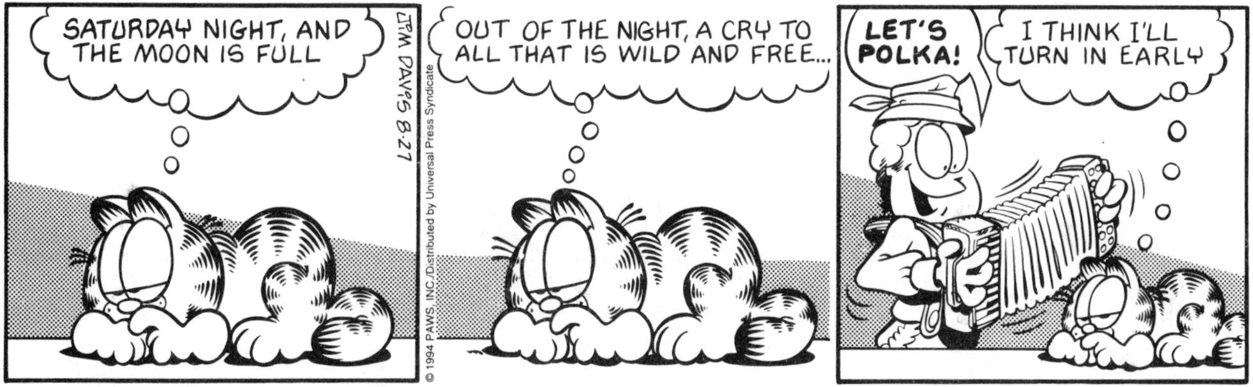
SATURDAY NIGHT, AND THE MOON IS FULL
JIM DAVIS 8-27
© 1994 PAWS, INC./Distributed by Universal Press Syndicate
OUT OF THE NIGHT, A CRY TO ALL THAT IS WILD AND FREE...
LET'S POLKA!
I THINK I'LL TURN IN EARLY

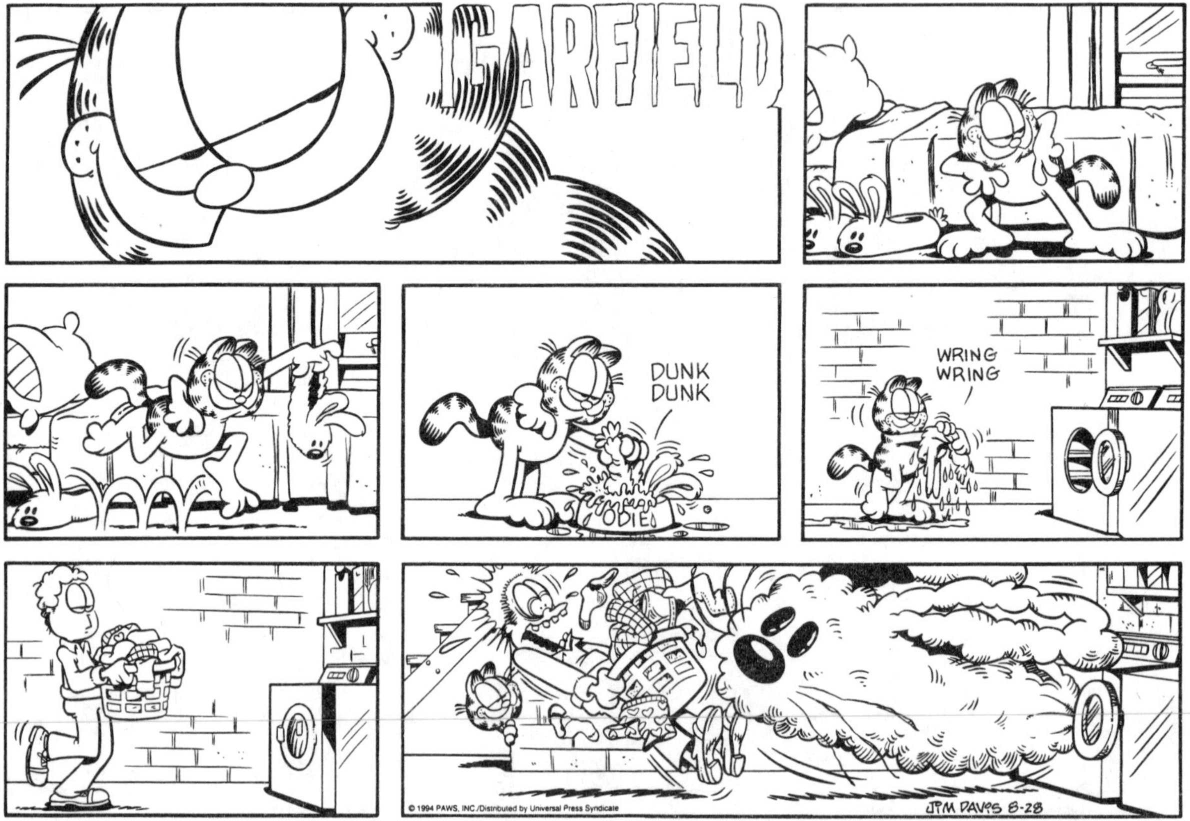
GARFIELD
DUNK
DUNK
WRING
WRING
ODIE
© 1994 PAWS, INC./Distributed by Universal Press Syndicate
JIM DAVIS 8-28

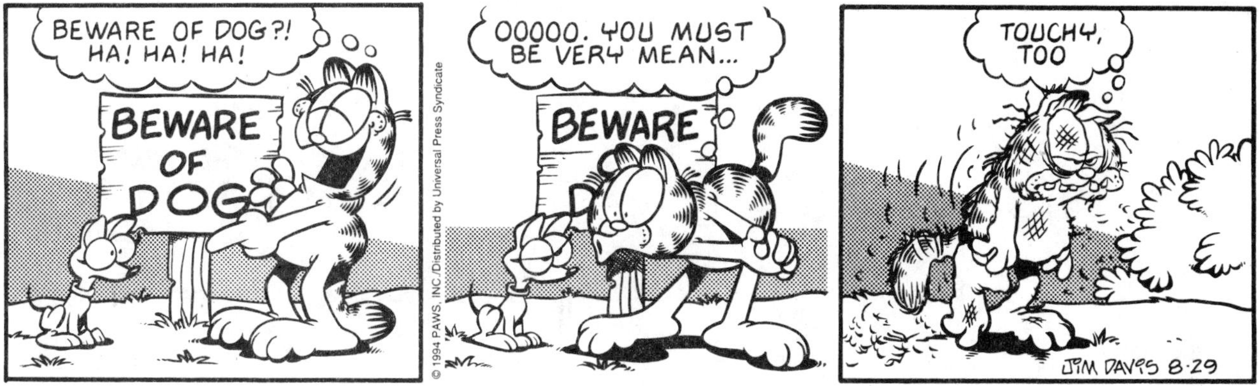
BEWARE OF DOG?! HA! HA! HA!
BEWARE OF DOG
OOOOO. YOU MUST BE VERY MEAN...
BEWARE
TOUCHY, TOO
JIM DAVIS 8-29

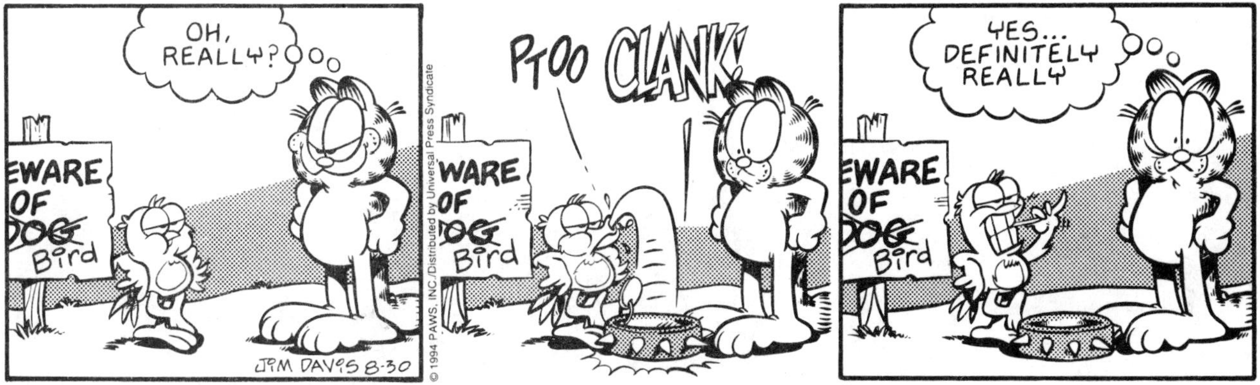
OH, REALLY?
EWARE OF DOG Bird
JIM DAVIS 8-30
PTOO
CLANK!
YES... DEFINITELY REALLY

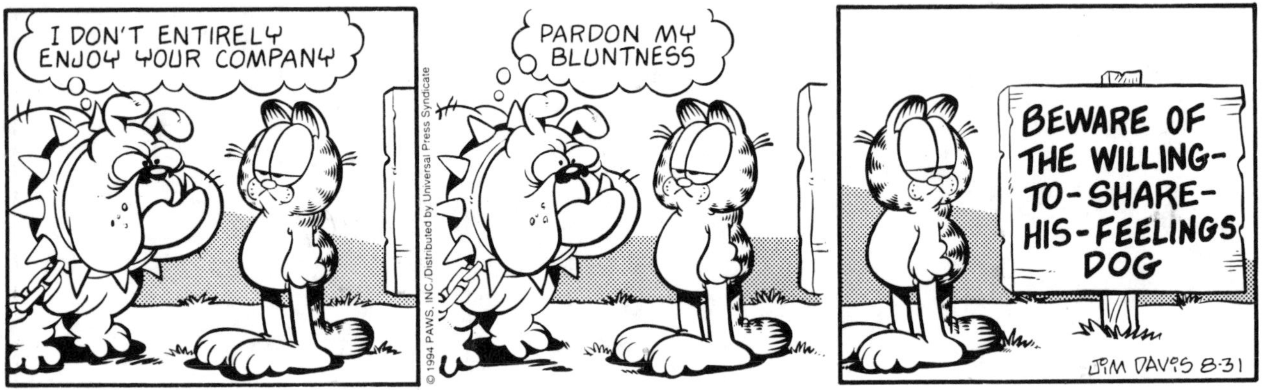
I DON'T ENTIRELY ENJOY YOUR COMPANY
PARDON MY BLUNTNESS
BEWARE OF THE WILLING-TO-SHARE-HIS-FEELINGS DOG
JIM DAVIS 8-31

© 1994 PAWS, INC./Distributed by Universal Press Syndicate

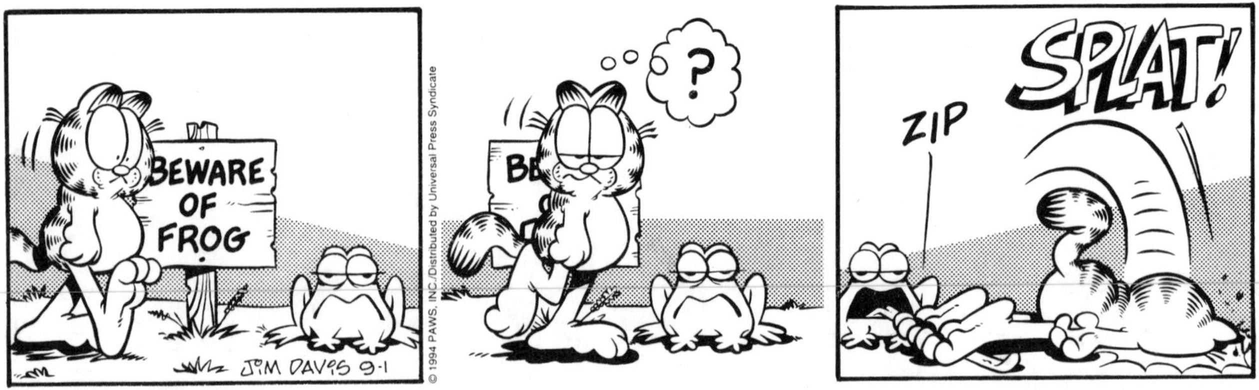
BEWARE OF FROG
JIM DAVIS 9-1
?
ZIP
SPLAT!

© 1994 PAWS, INC./Distributed by Universal Press Syndicate

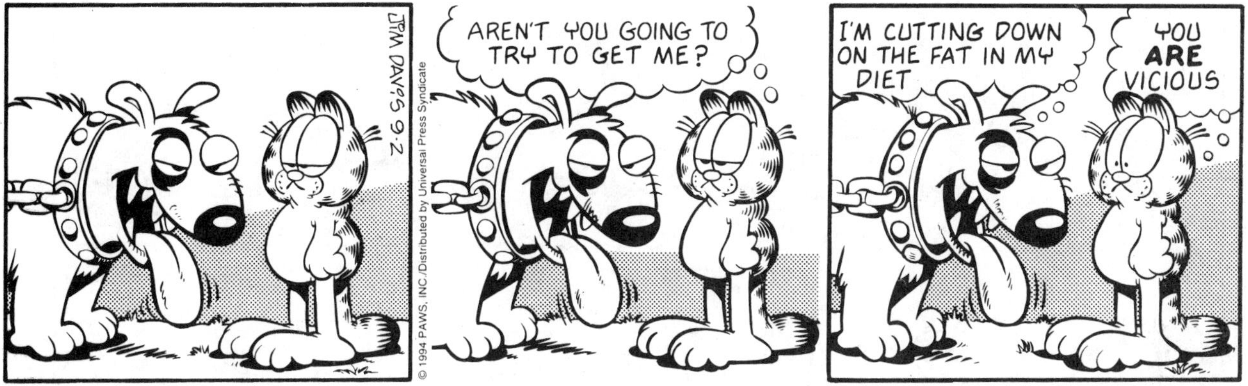

JIM DAVIS 9-2
© 1994 PAWS, INC./Distributed by Universal Press Syndicate
AREN'T YOU GOING TO TRY TO GET ME?
I'M CUTTING DOWN ON THE FAT IN MY DIET
YOU **ARE** VICIOUS

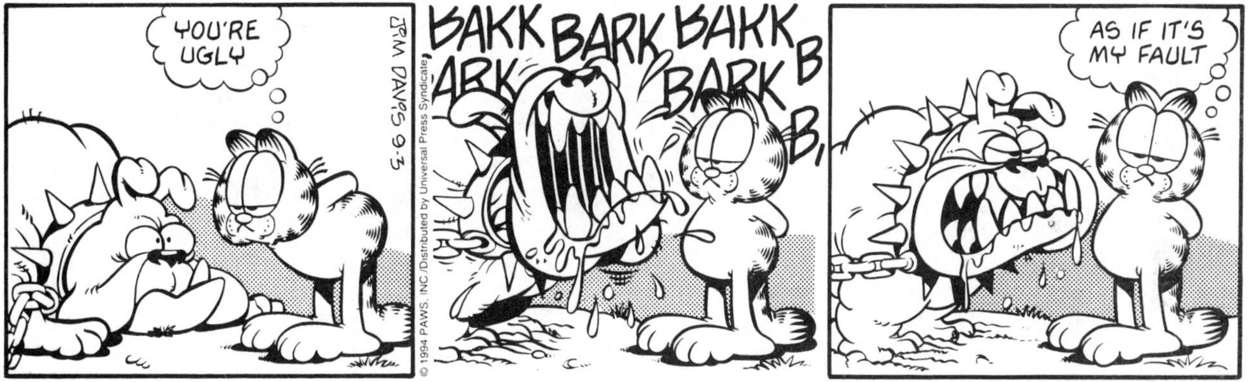

JIM DAVIS 9-3
© 1994 PAWS, INC./Distributed by Universal Press Syndicate
YOU'RE UGLY
BARK BARK BARK
ARK
BARK
B
B,
AS IF IT'S MY FAULT

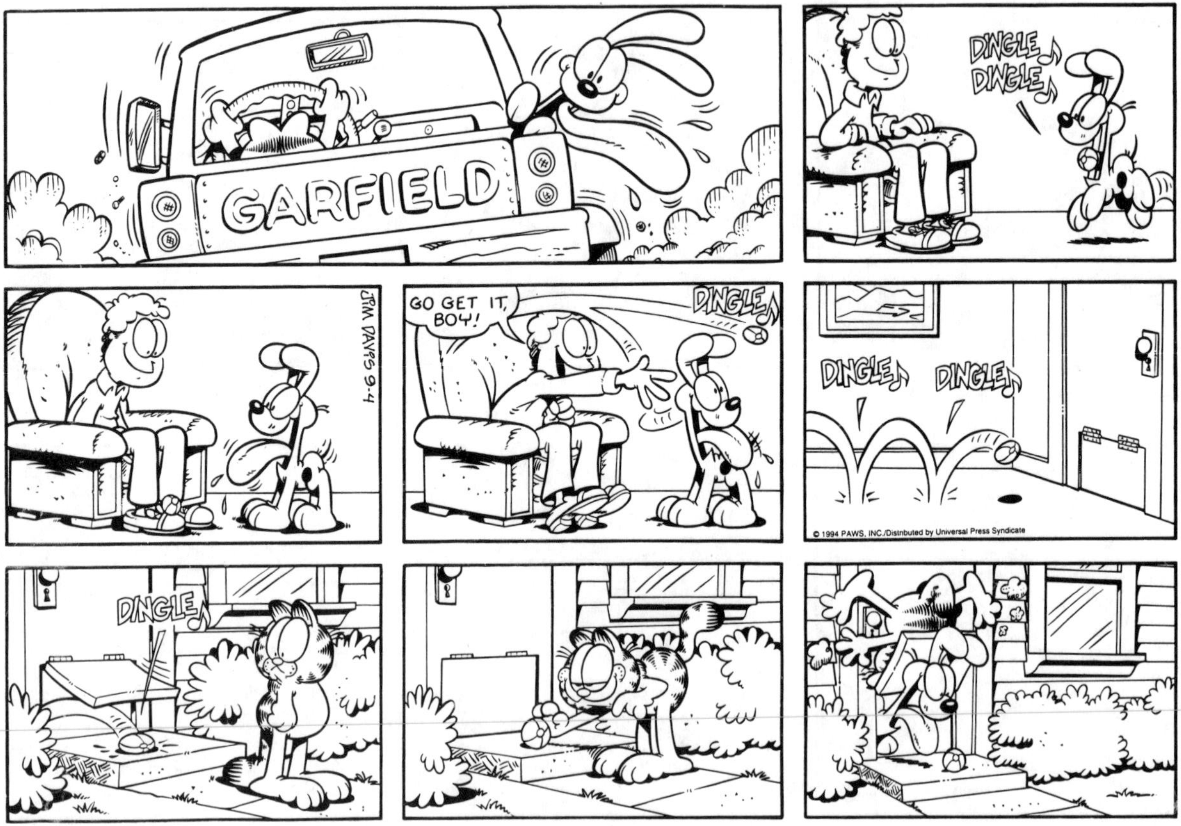
GARFIELD
DINGLE DINGLE
JIM DAVIS 9-4
GO GET IT, BOY!
DINGLE
DINGLE DINGLE
© 1994 PAWS, INC./Distributed by Universal Press Syndicate
DINGLE

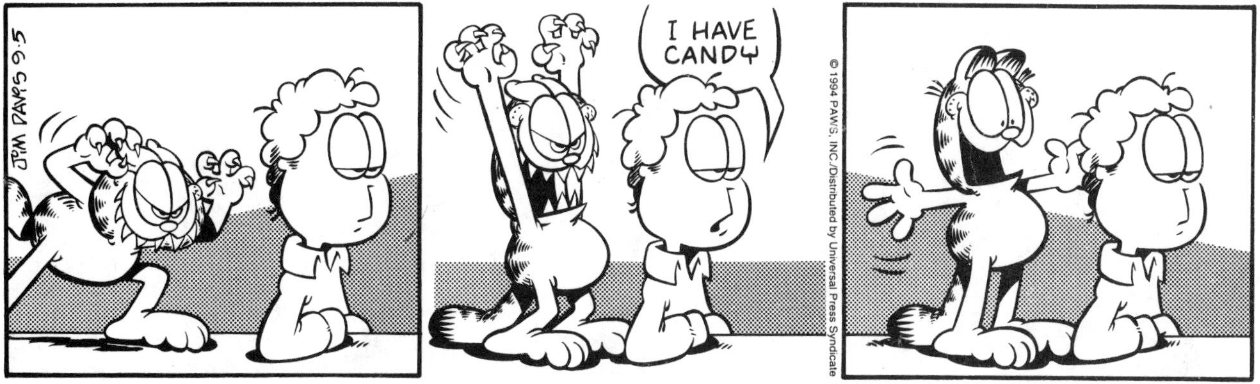
JIM DAVIS 9·5
I HAVE CANDY
© 1994 PAWS, INC./Distributed by Universal Press Syndicate

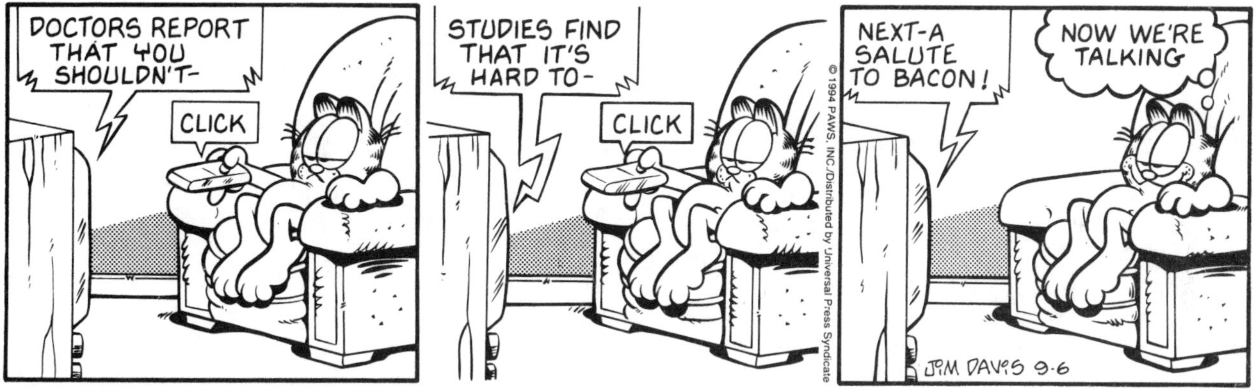
DOCTORS REPORT THAT YOU SHOULDN'T-
CLICK
STUDIES FIND THAT IT'S HARD TO-
CLICK
© 1994 PAWS, INC./Distributed by Universal Press Syndicate
NEXT-A SALUTE TO BACON!
NOW WE'RE TALKING
JIM DAVIS 9·6

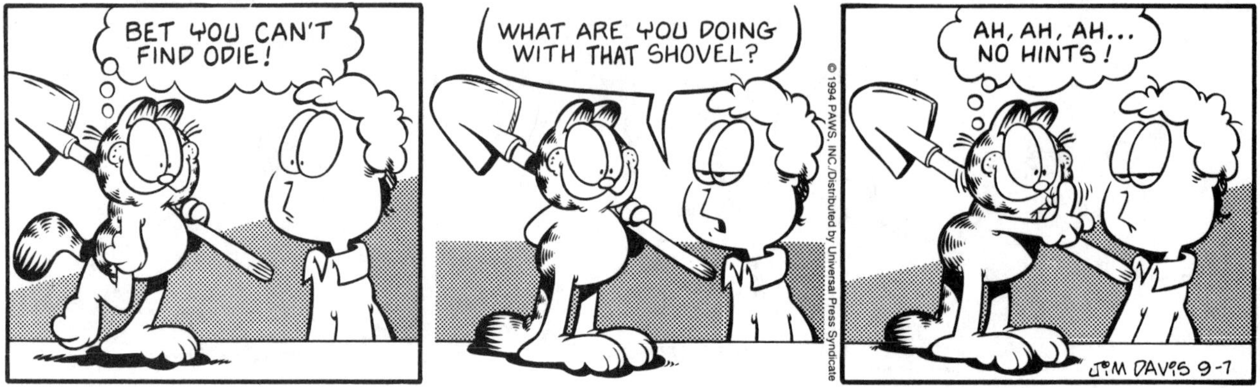
BET YOU CAN'T FIND ODIE!
WHAT ARE YOU DOING WITH THAT SHOVEL?
AH, AH, AH... NO HINTS!
© 1994 PAWS, INC./Distributed by Universal Press Syndicate
JIM DAVIS 9-7

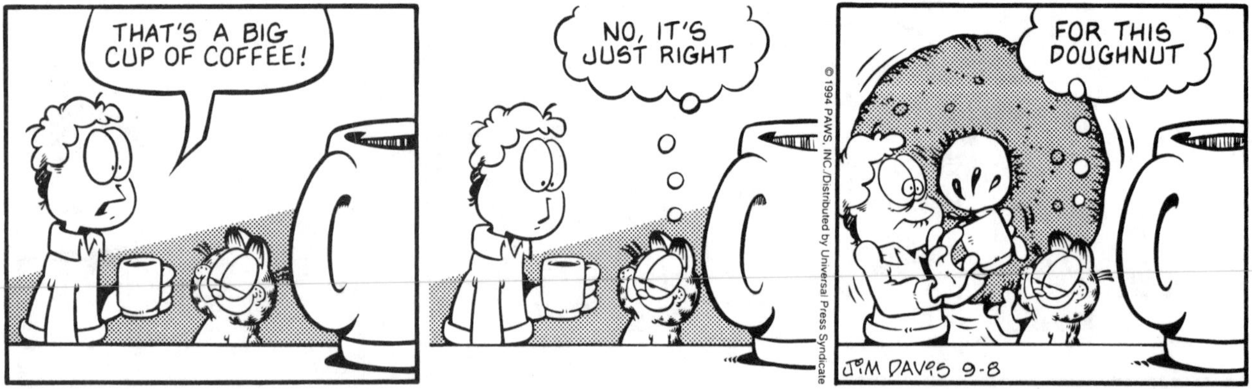
THAT'S A BIG CUP OF COFFEE!
NO, IT'S JUST RIGHT
FOR THIS DOUGHNUT
© 1994 PAWS, INC./Distributed by Universal Press Syndicate
JIM DAVIS 9-8

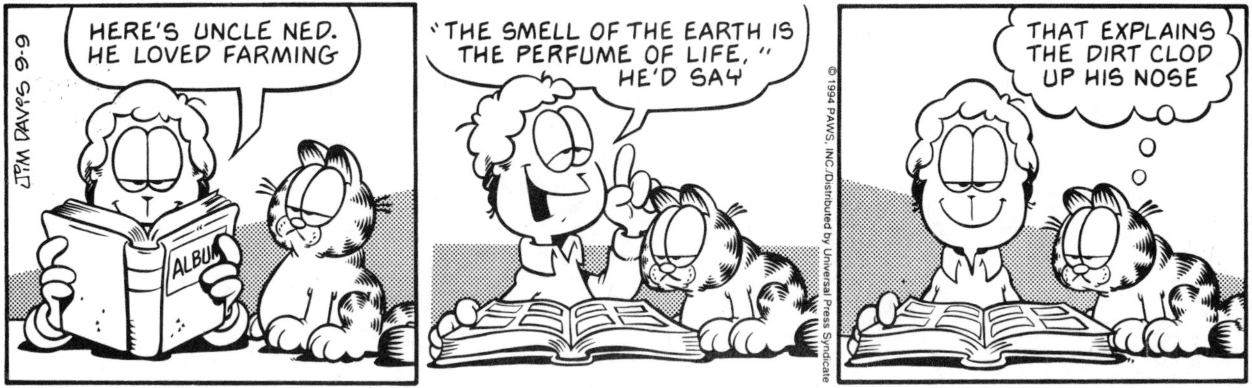
JIM DAVIS 9-9
HERE'S UNCLE NED. HE LOVED FARMING
ALBUM
"THE SMELL OF THE EARTH IS THE PERFUME OF LIFE," HE'D SAY
© 1994 PAWS, INC./Distributed by Universal Press Syndicate
THAT EXPLAINS THE DIRT CLOD UP HIS NOSE

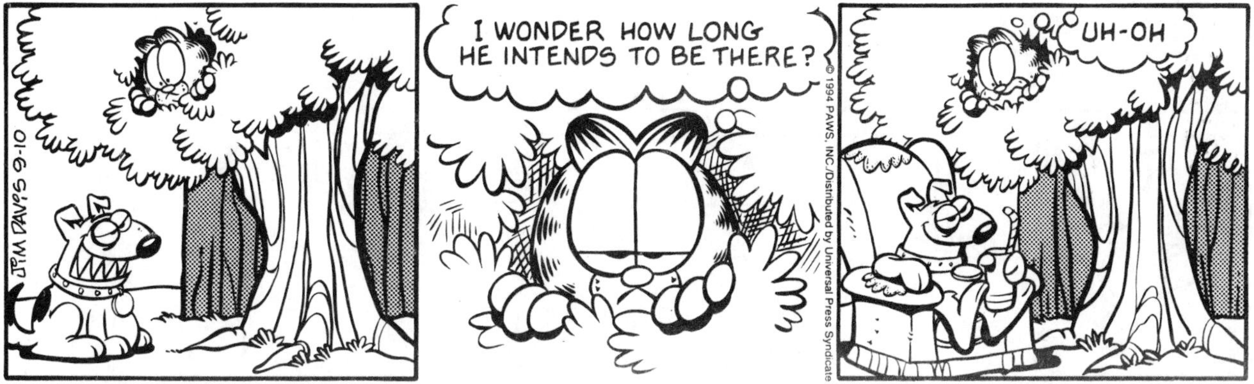
JIM DAVIS 9-10
I WONDER HOW LONG HE INTENDS TO BE THERE?
© 1994 PAWS, INC./Distributed by Universal Press Syndicate
UH-OH

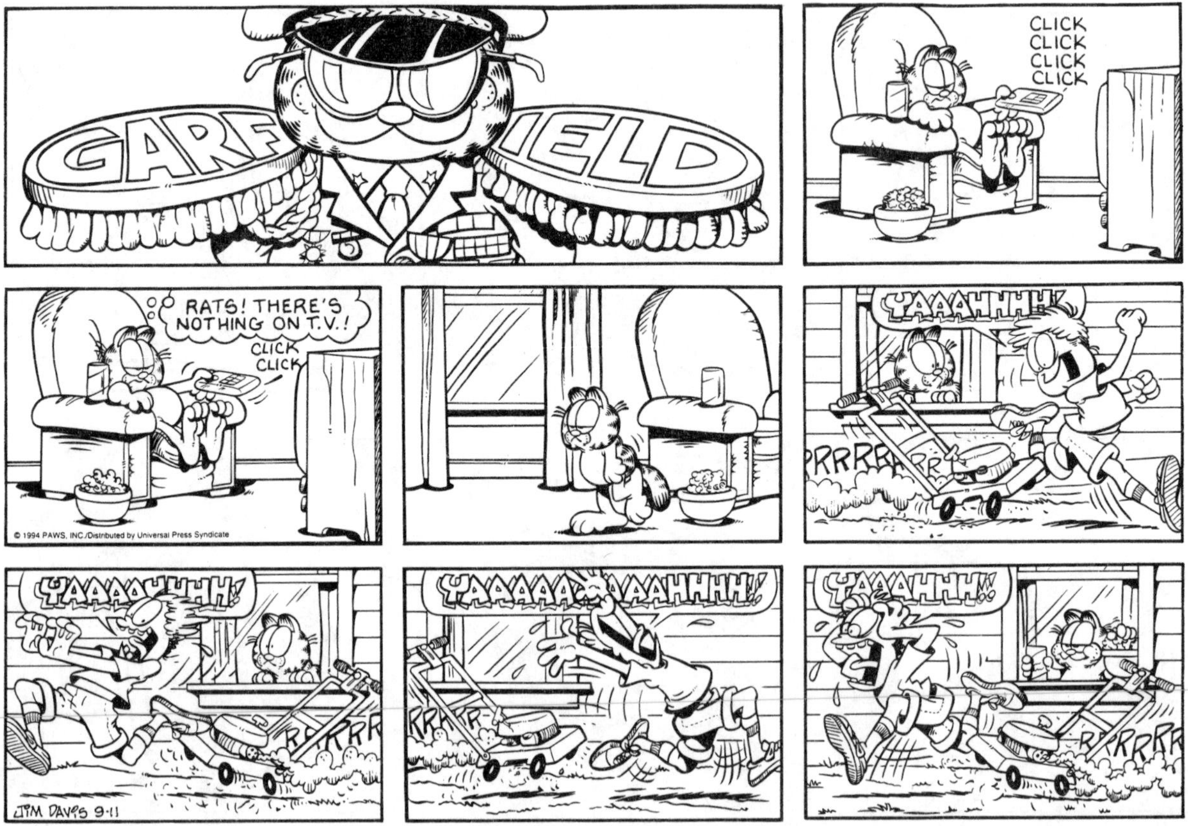
GARFIELD
CLICK
CLICK
CLICK
CLICK
RATS! THERE'S NOTHING ON T.V.!
CLICK
CLICK
© 1994 PAWS, INC./Distributed by Universal Press Syndicate
YAAAHHHH!
YAAAAHHHH!
YAAAAAAAAAHHHH!!
YAAAHHH!!
JIM DAVIS 9-11

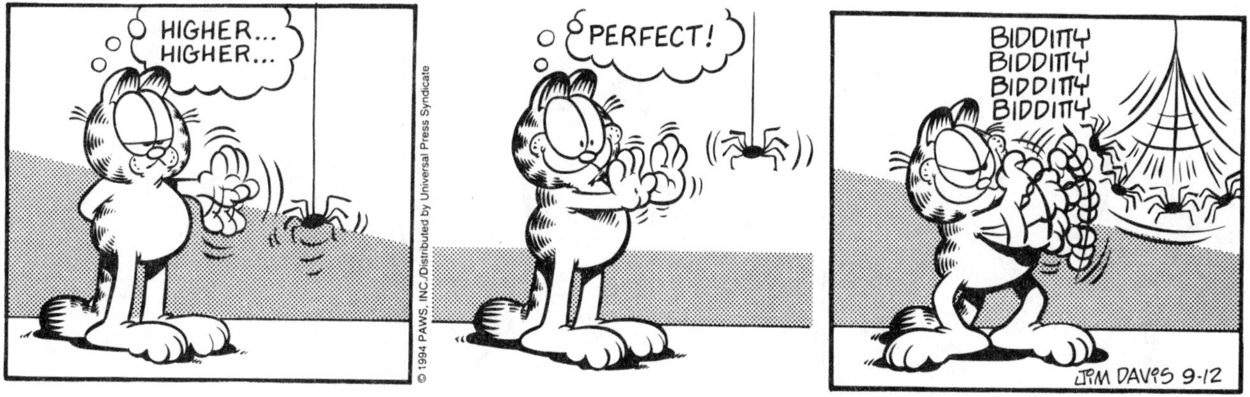
HIGHER... HIGHER...
PERFECT!
BIDDITTY BIDDITTY BIDDITTY BIDDITTY
JIM DAVIS 9-12
© 1994 PAWS, INC./Distributed by Universal Press Syndicate

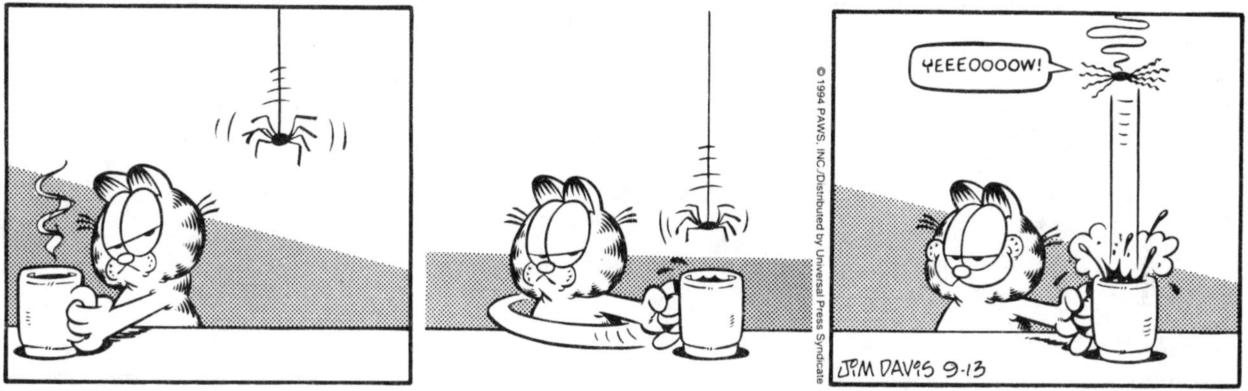
YEEEOOOOW!
JIM DAVIS 9-13
© 1994 PAWS, INC./Distributed by Universal Press Syndicate

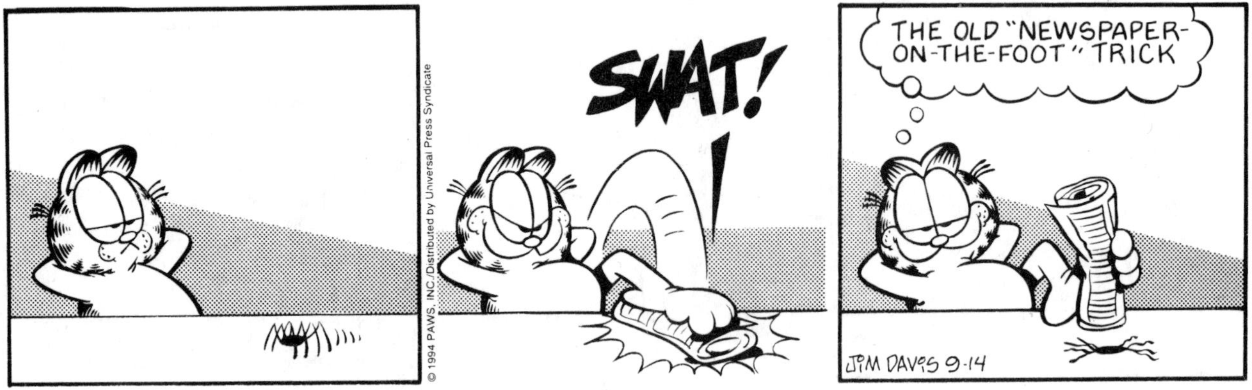
SWAT!
THE OLD "NEWSPAPER-ON-THE-FOOT" TRICK
JIM DAVIS 9-14

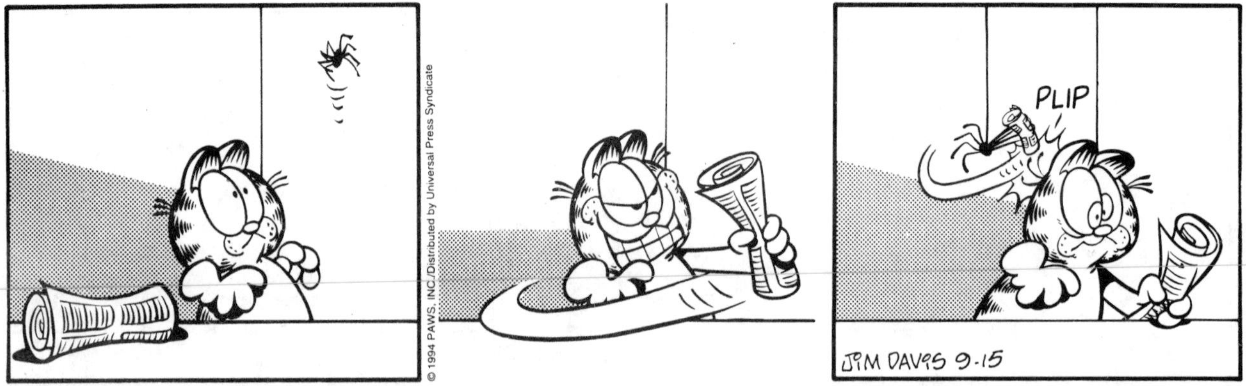
PLIP
JIM DAVIS 9-15

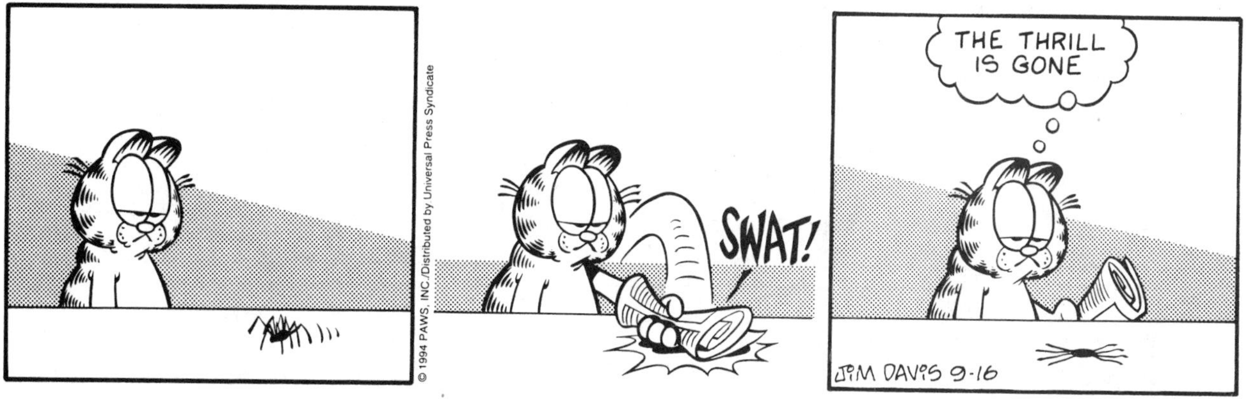
SWAT!
THE THRILL IS GONE
JIM DAVIS 9-16
© 1994 PAWS, INC./Distributed by Universal Press Syndicate

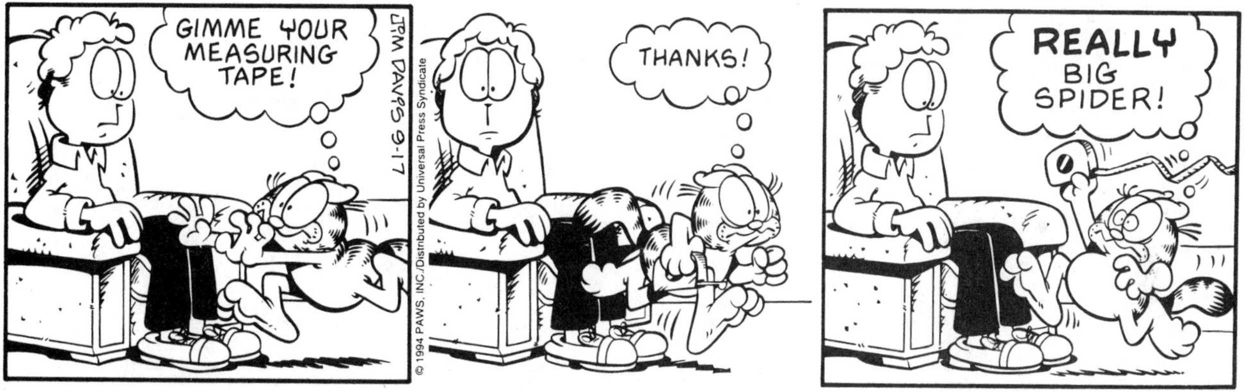
GIMME YOUR MEASURING TAPE!
JIM DAVIS 9-17
THANKS!
REALLY BIG SPIDER!
© 1994 PAWS, INC./Distributed by Universal Press Syndicate

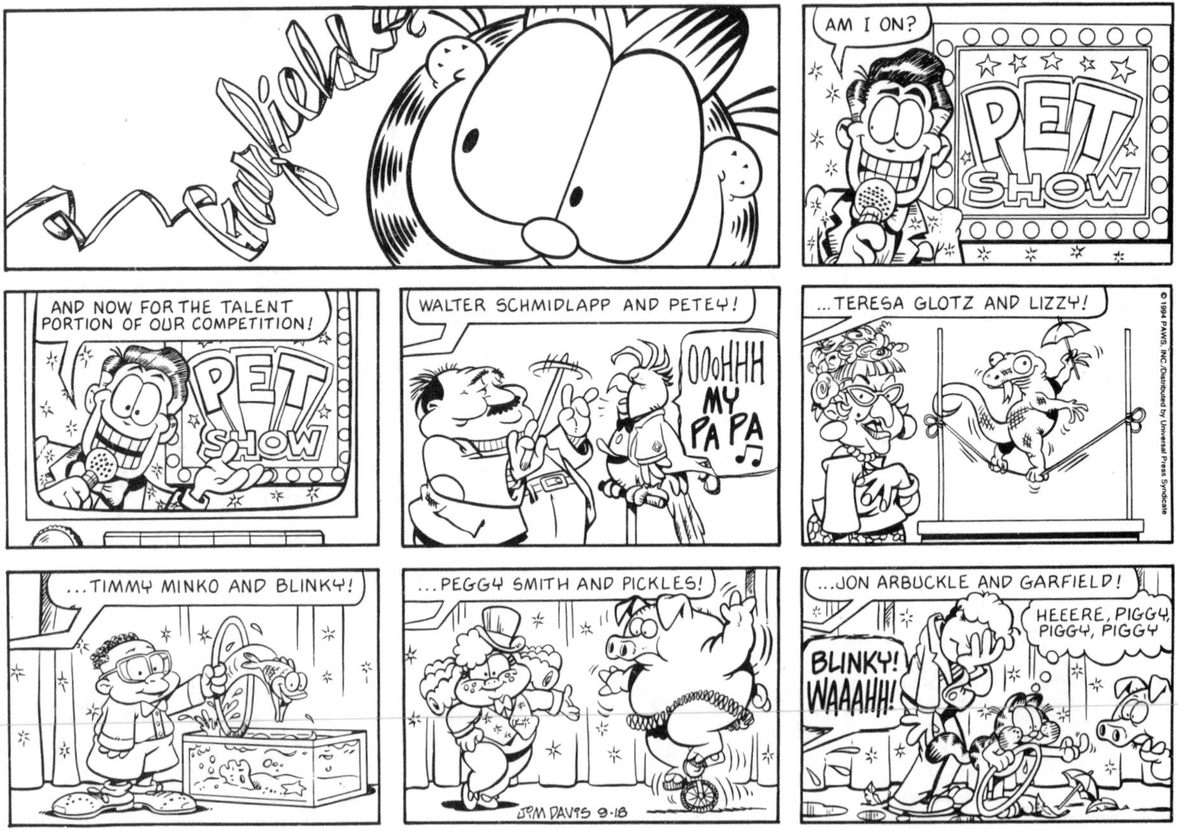
Garfield
AM I ON?
PET SHOW
AND NOW FOR THE TALENT PORTION OF OUR COMPETITION!
WALTER SCHMIDLAPP AND PETEY!
OOOHHH MY PA PA
...TERESA GLOTZ AND LIZZY!
© 1994 PAWS, INC./Distributed by Universal Press Syndicate
...TIMMY MINKO AND BLINKY!
...PEGGY SMITH AND PICKLES!
JIM DAVIS 9-18
...JON ARBUCKLE AND GARFIELD!
HEEERE, PIGGY, PIGGY, PIGGY
BLINKY! WAAAHH!

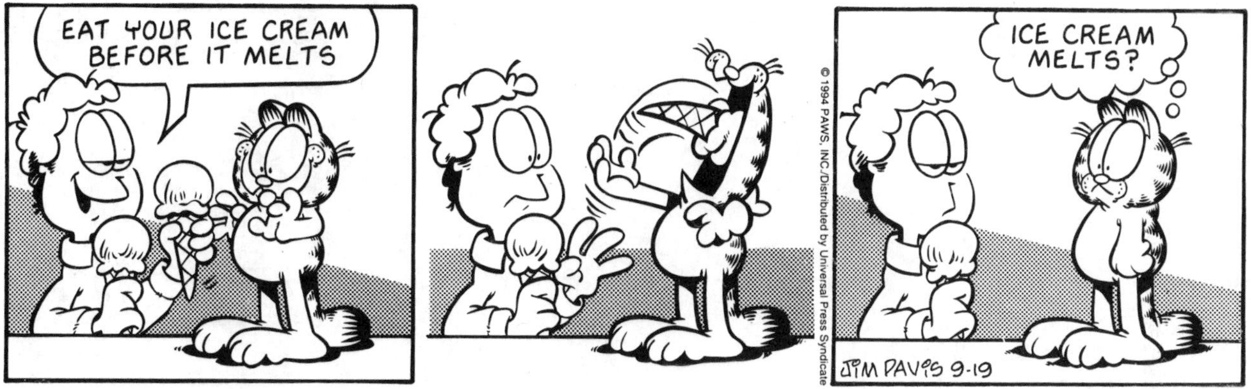
EAT YOUR ICE CREAM BEFORE IT MELTS
ICE CREAM MELTS?
© 1994 PAWS, INC./Distributed by Universal Press Syndicate
JIM DAVIS 9-19

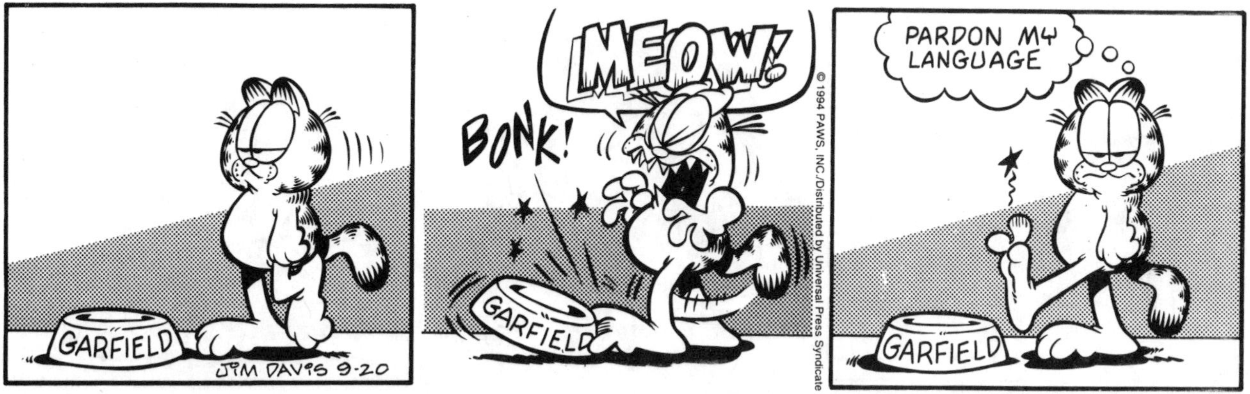
GARFIELD
JIM DAVIS 9-20
BONK!
MEOW!
GARFIELD
© 1994 PAWS, INC./Distributed by Universal Press Syndicate
PARDON MY LANGUAGE
GARFIELD

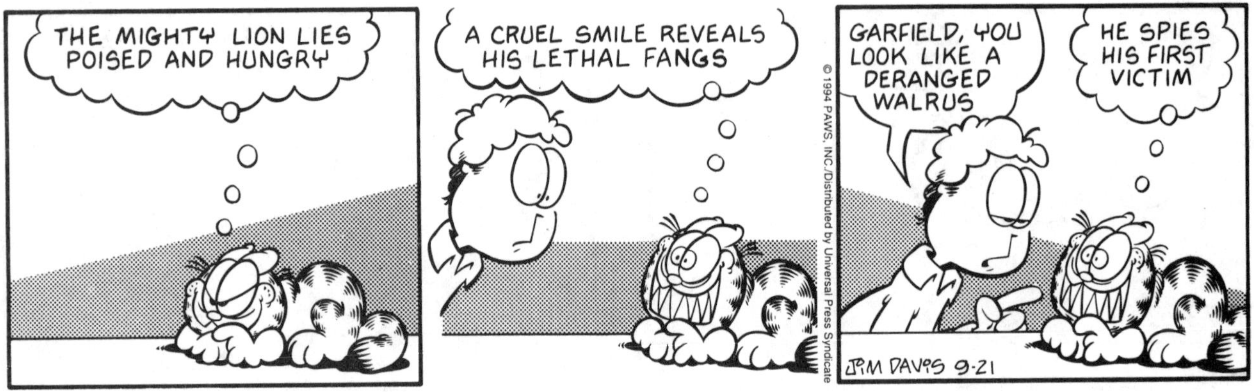
THE MIGHTY LION LIES POISED AND HUNGRY
A CRUEL SMILE REVEALS HIS LETHAL FANGS
GARFIELD, YOU LOOK LIKE A DERANGED WALRUS
HE SPIES HIS FIRST VICTIM
JIM DAVIS 9-21
© 1994 PAWS, INC./Distributed by Universal Press Syndicate

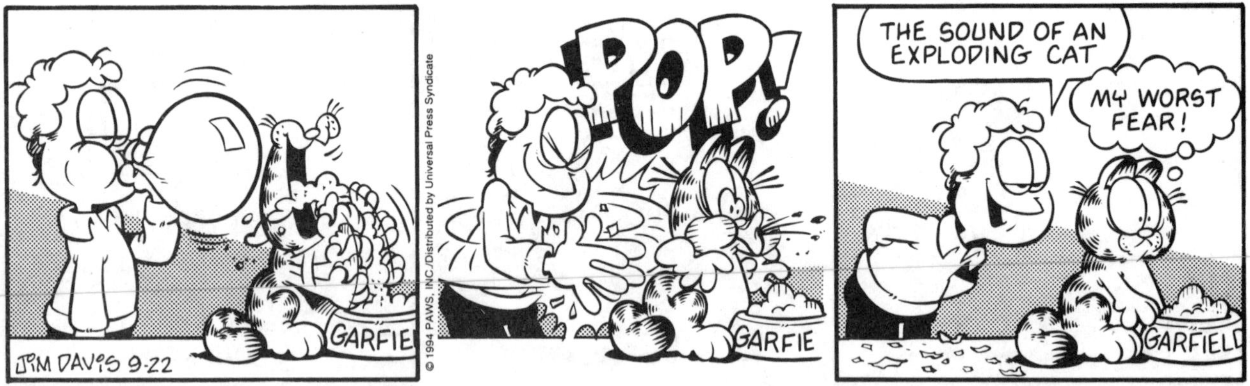
JIM DAVIS 9-22
© 1994 PAWS, INC./Distributed by Universal Press Syndicate
POP!
THE SOUND OF AN EXPLODING CAT
MY WORST FEAR!
GARFIELD

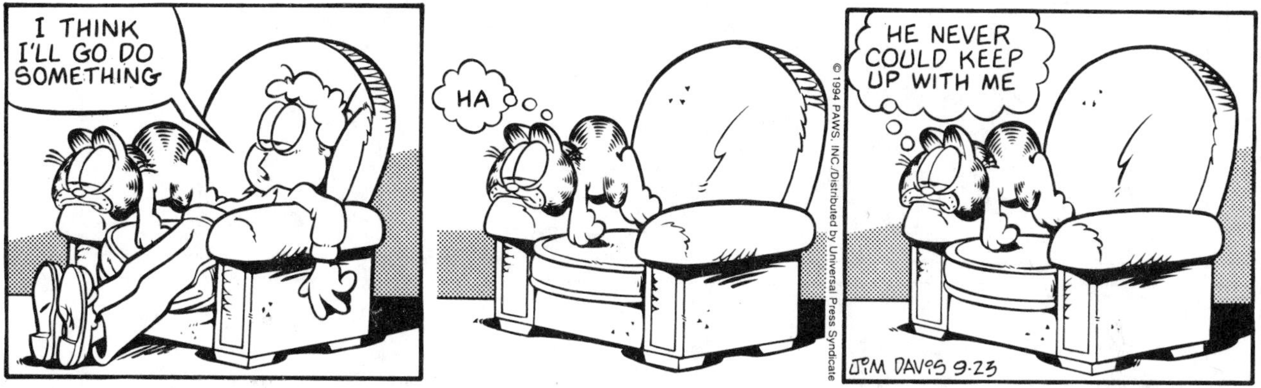
I THINK I'LL GO DO SOMETHING
HA
HE NEVER COULD KEEP UP WITH ME
JIM DAVIS 9-23

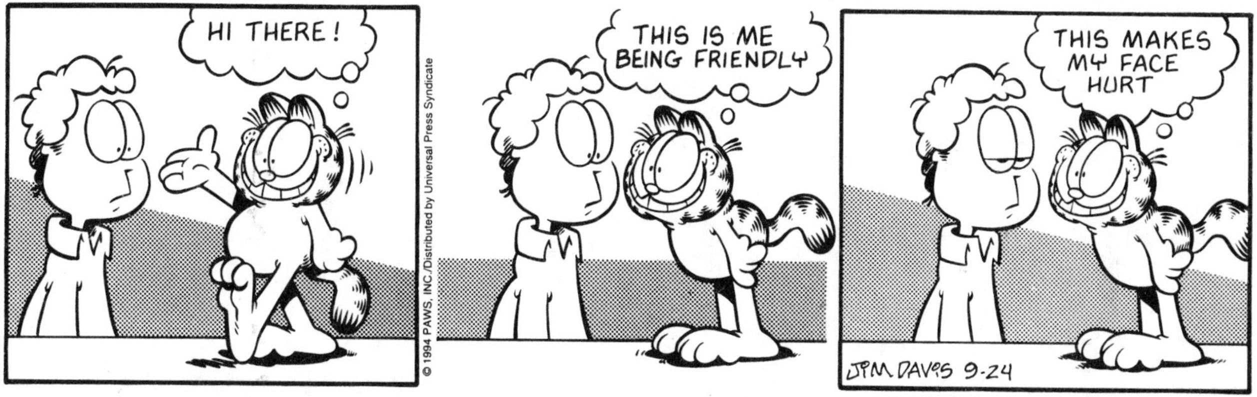
HI THERE!
THIS IS ME BEING FRIENDLY
THIS MAKES MY FACE HURT
JIM DAVIS 9-24

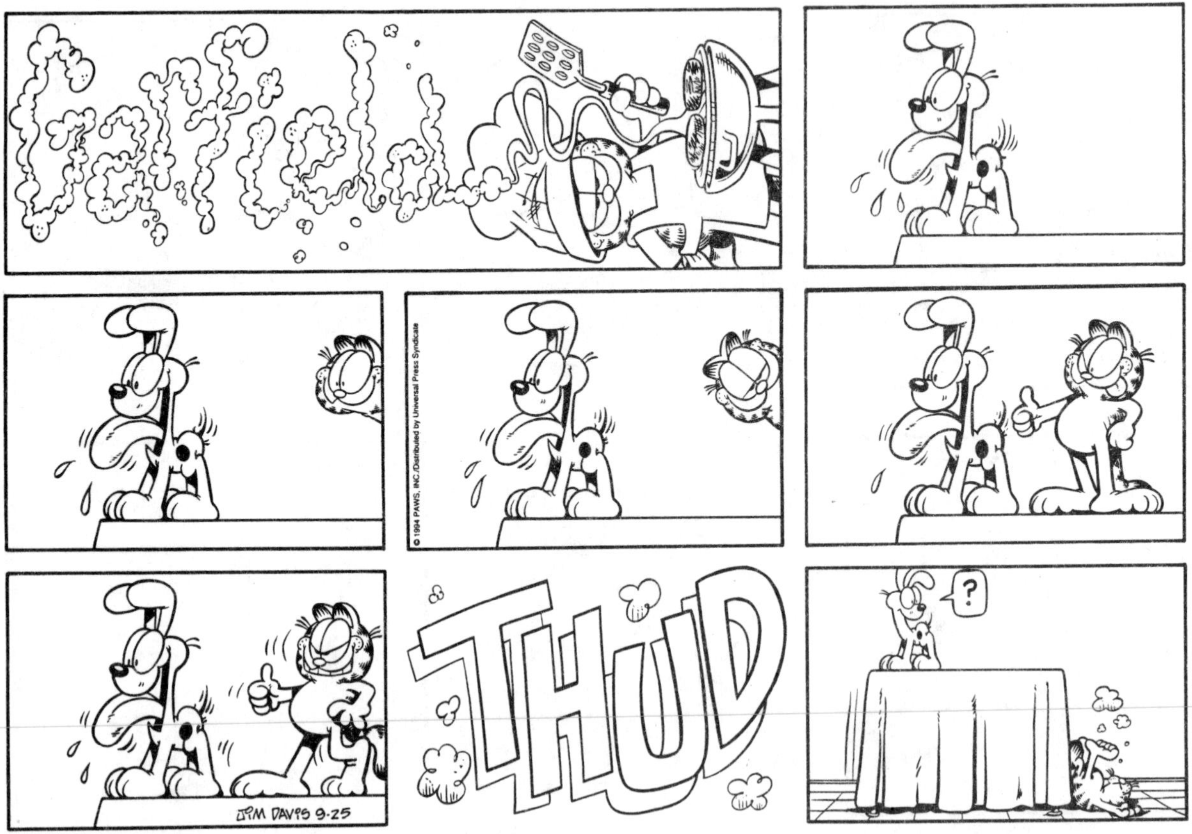
Garfield
© 1994 PAWS, INC./Distributed by Universal Press Syndicate
JIM DAVIS 9-25
THUD
?

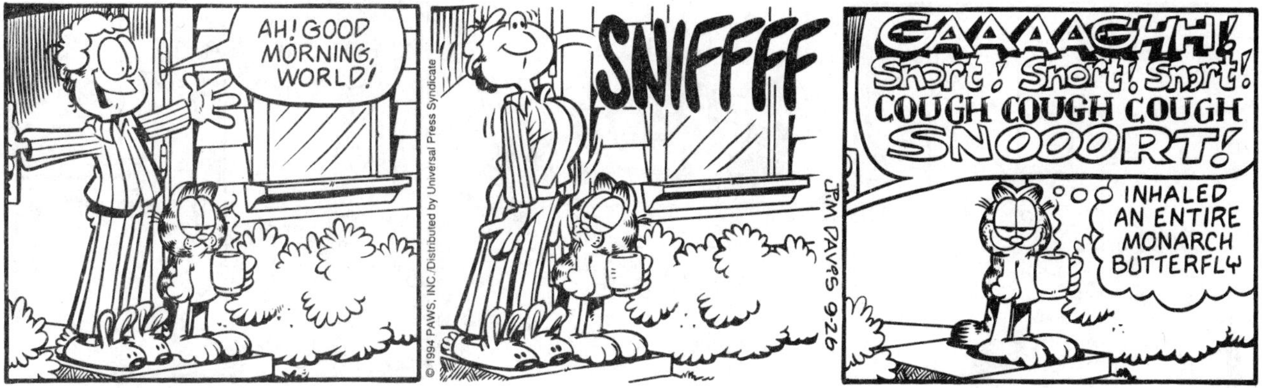
AH! GOOD MORNING, WORLD!
SNIFFFF
GAAAAGHH! Snort! Snort! Snort! COUGH COUGH COUGH SNOOORT!
INHALED AN ENTIRE MONARCH BUTTERFLY
© 1994 PAWS, INC./Distributed by Universal Press Syndicate
JIM DAVIS 9-26

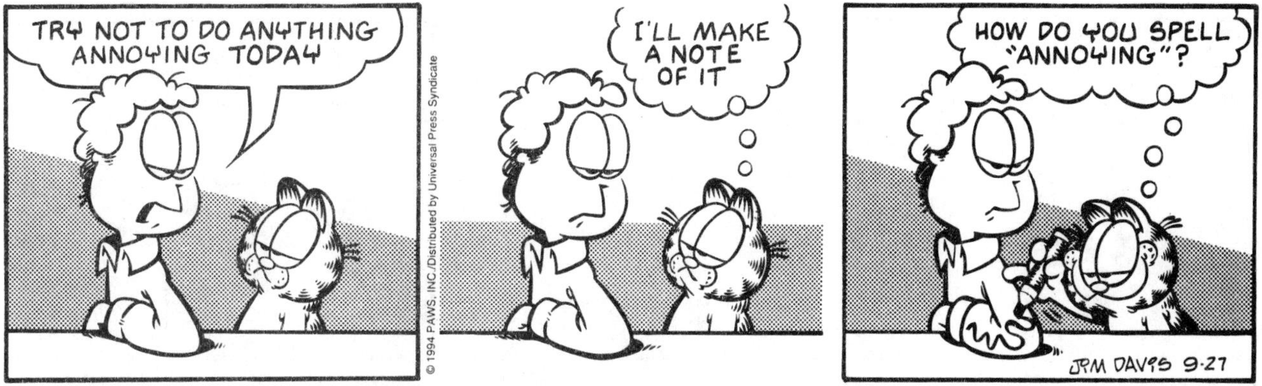
TRY NOT TO DO ANYTHING ANNOYING TODAY
I'LL MAKE A NOTE OF IT
HOW DO YOU SPELL "ANNOYING"?
© 1994 PAWS, INC./Distributed by Universal Press Syndicate
JIM DAVIS 9-27

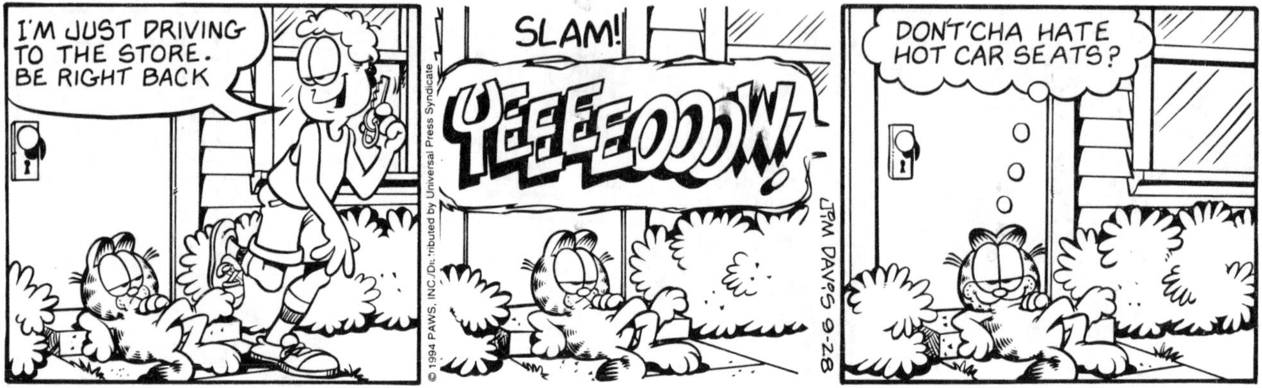
I'M JUST DRIVING TO THE STORE. BE RIGHT BACK
SLAM!
YEEEEOOOOW!
DON'T'CHA HATE HOT CAR SEATS?
© 1994 PAWS, INC./Distributed by Universal Press Syndicate
JIM DAVIS 9-28

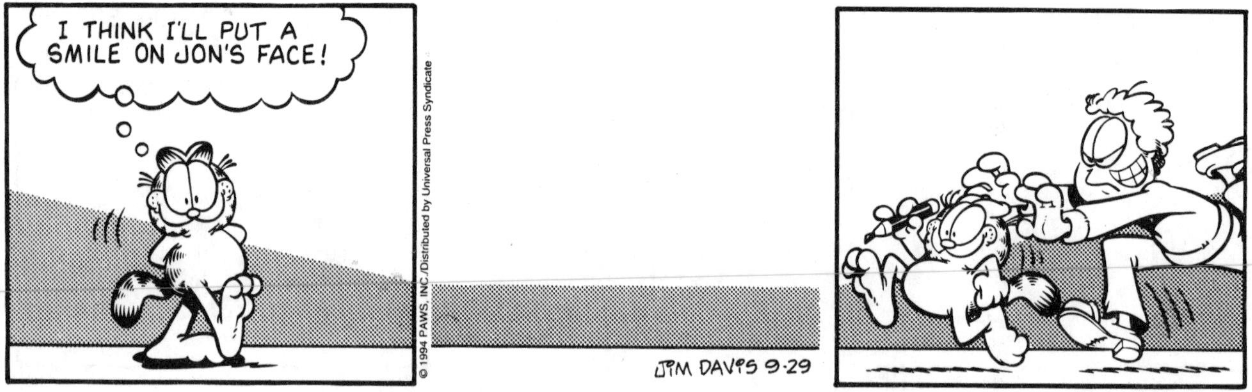
I THINK I'LL PUT A SMILE ON JON'S FACE!
© 1994 PAWS, INC./Distributed by Universal Press Syndicate
JIM DAVIS 9-29

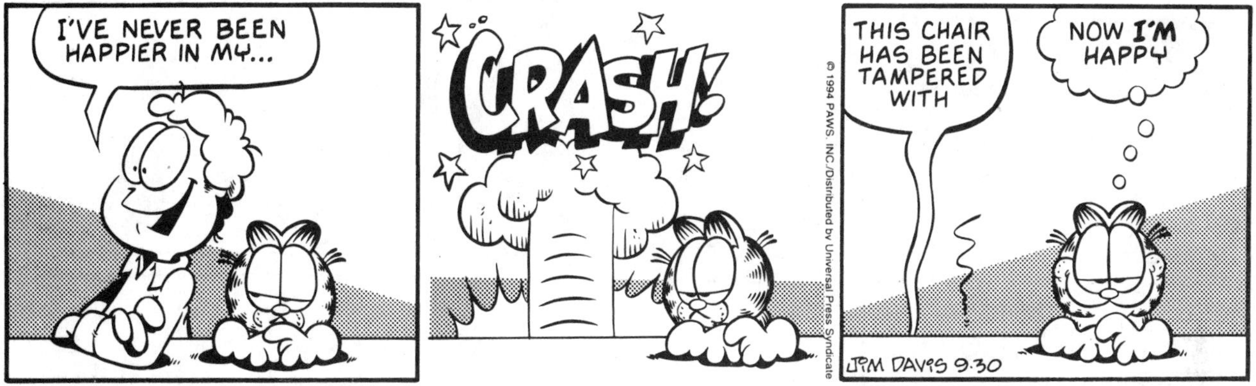
I'VE NEVER BEEN HAPPIER IN MY...
CRASH!
THIS CHAIR HAS BEEN TAMPERED WITH
NOW **I'M** HAPPY
JIM DAVIS 9-30
© 1994 PAWS, INC./Distributed by Universal Press Syndicate

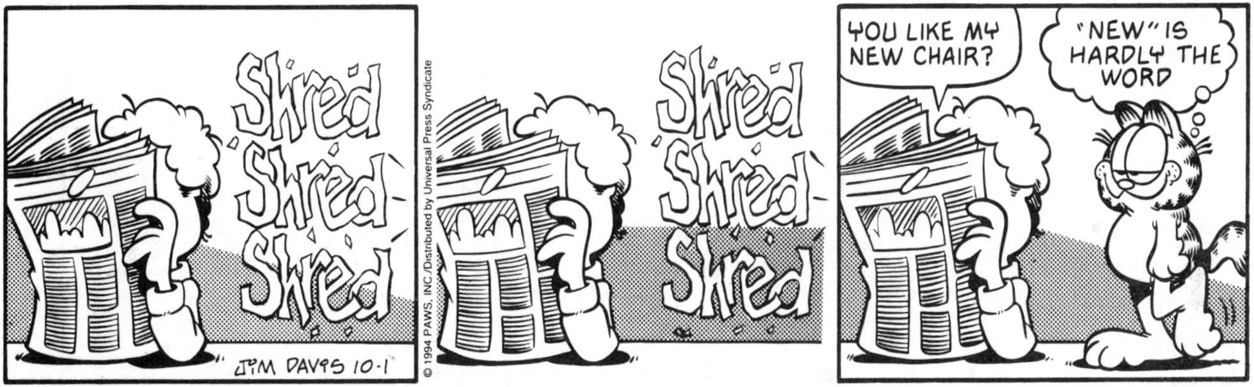
Shred Shred Shred
JIM DAVIS 10-1
Shred Shred Shred
YOU LIKE MY NEW CHAIR?
"NEW" IS HARDLY THE WORD
© 1994 PAWS, INC./Distributed by Universal Press Syndicate

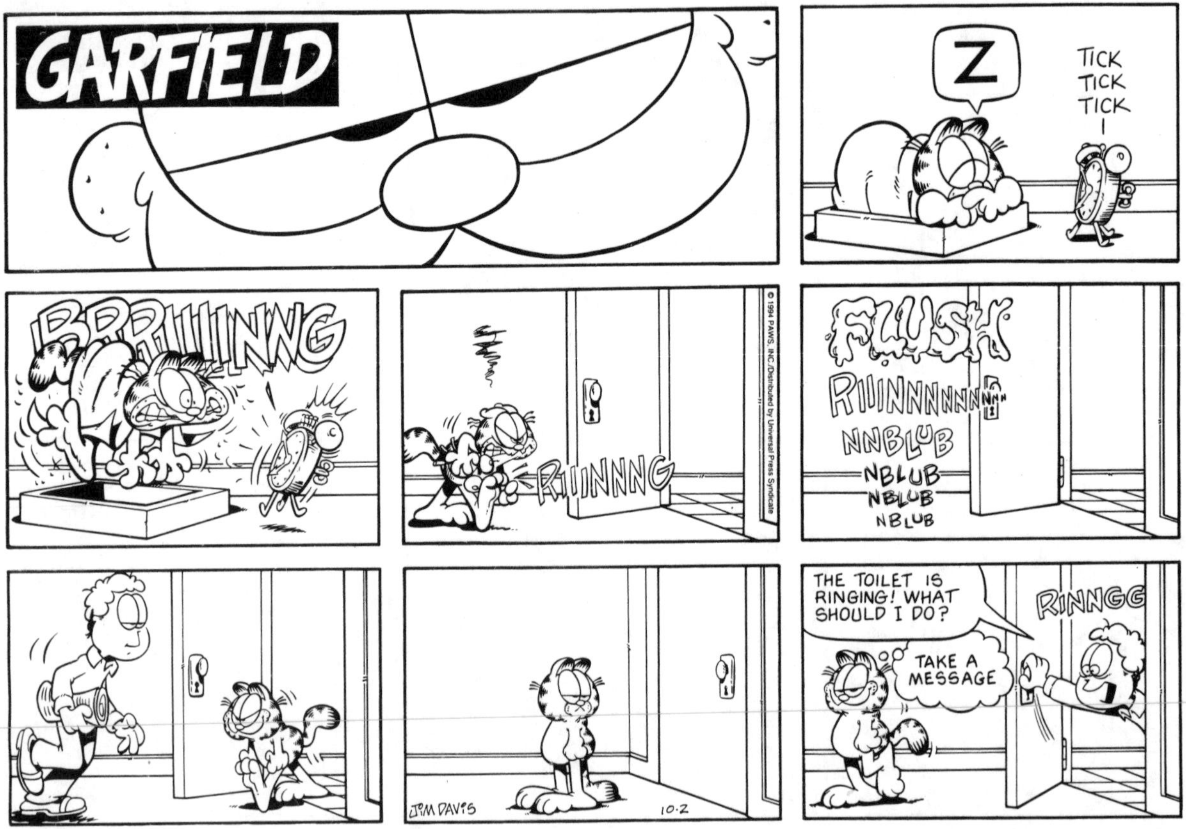
GARFIELD
Z
TICK
TICK
TICK
BRRIIIINNG
© 1994 PAWS, INC./Distributed by Universal Press Syndicate
RIIINNNG
FLUSH
RIIINNNNNNNNN
NNBLUB
NBLUB
NBLUB
NBLUB
JIM DAVIS
10-2
THE TOILET IS RINGING! WHAT SHOULD I DO?
RINNGG
TAKE A MESSAGE

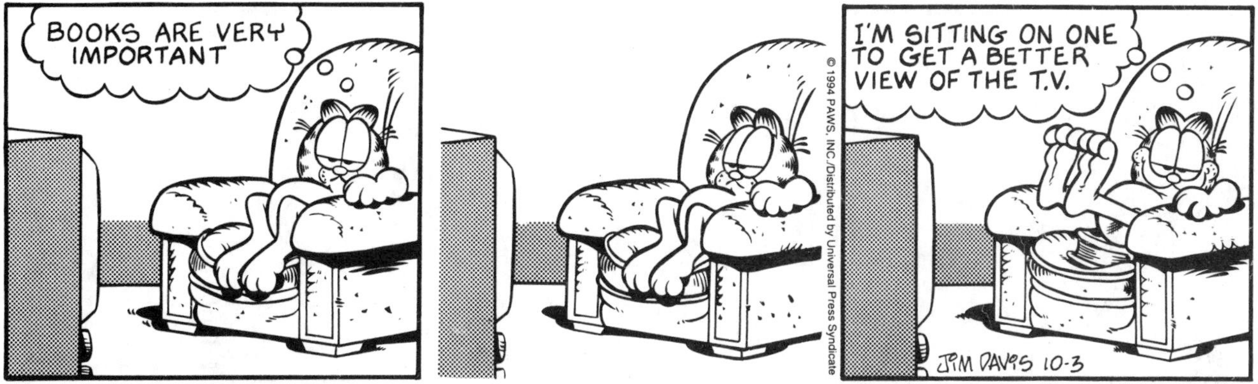
BOOKS ARE VERY IMPORTANT
I'M SITTING ON ONE TO GET A BETTER VIEW OF THE T.V.
© 1994 PAWS, INC./Distributed by Universal Press Syndicate
JIM DAVIS 10-3

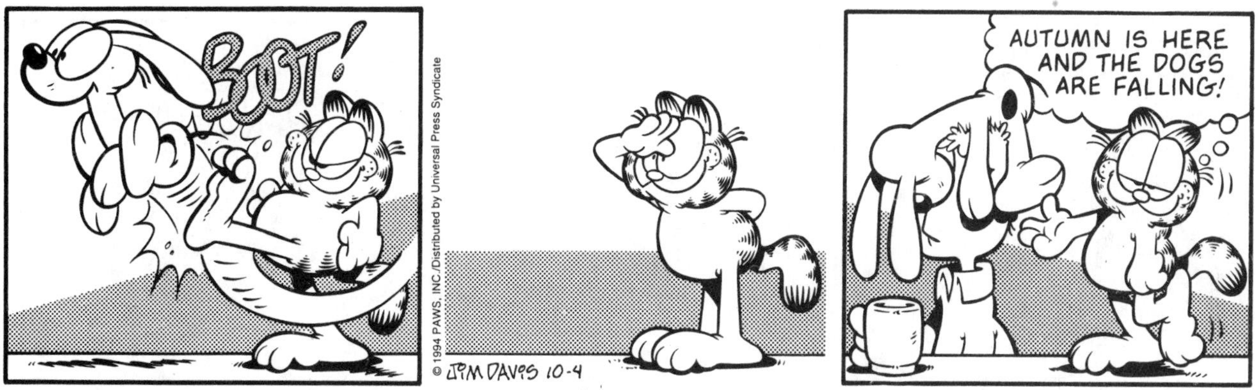
BOOT!
© 1994 PAWS, INC./Distributed by Universal Press Syndicate
JIM DAVIS 10-4
AUTUMN IS HERE AND THE DOGS ARE FALLING!

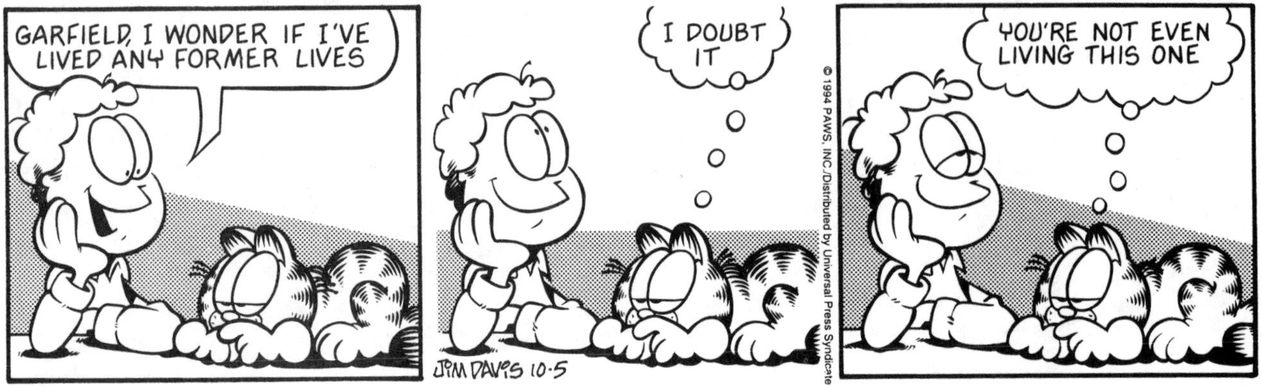
GARFIELD, I WONDER IF I'VE LIVED ANY FORMER LIVES
I DOUBT IT
YOU'RE NOT EVEN LIVING THIS ONE
JIM DAVIS 10-5

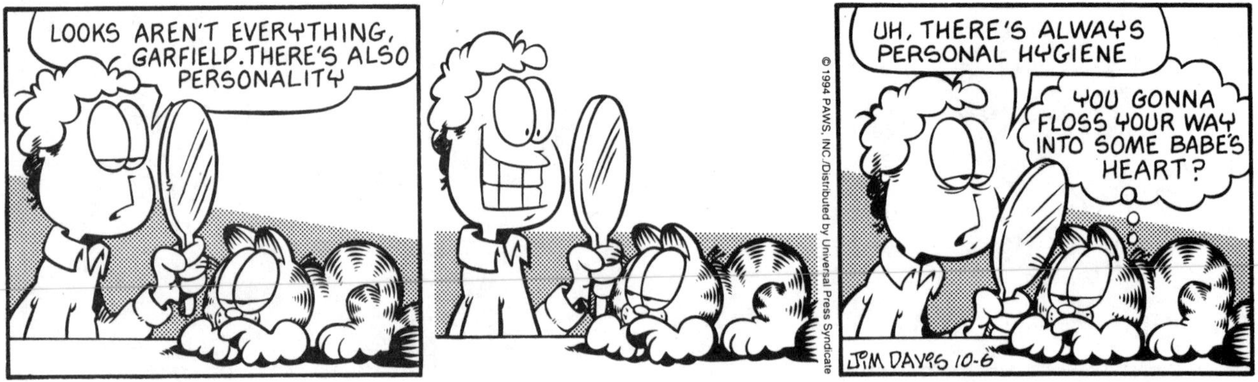
LOOKS AREN'T EVERYTHING, GARFIELD. THERE'S ALSO PERSONALITY
UH, THERE'S ALWAYS PERSONAL HYGIENE
YOU GONNA FLOSS YOUR WAY INTO SOME BABE'S HEART?
JIM DAVIS 10-6

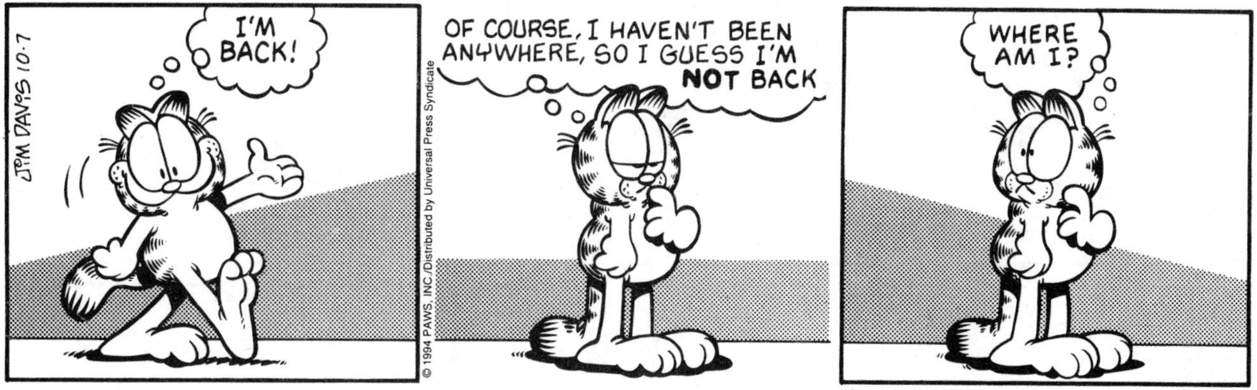
JIM DAVIS 10-7
I'M BACK!
OF COURSE, I HAVEN'T BEEN ANYWHERE, SO I GUESS I'M **NOT** BACK
WHERE AM I?

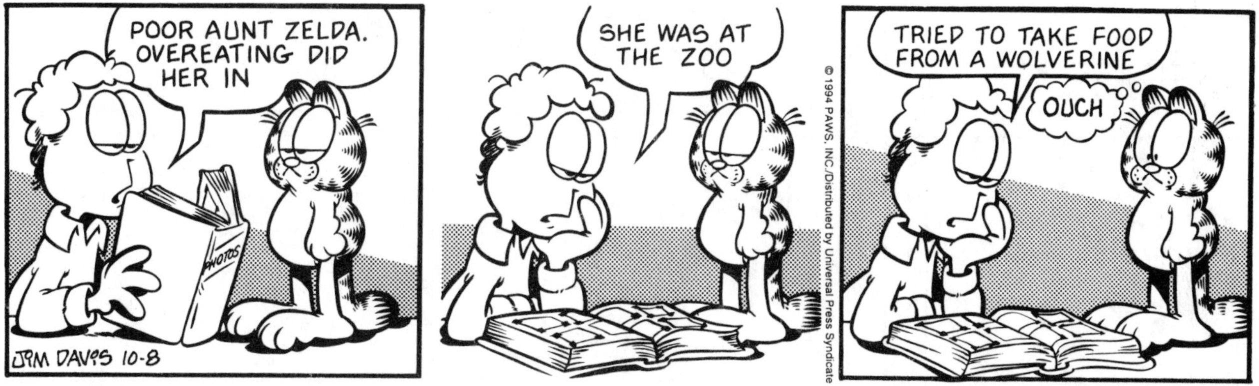
POOR AUNT ZELDA. OVEREATING DID HER IN
PHOTOS
JIM DAVIS 10-8
SHE WAS AT THE ZOO
TRIED TO TAKE FOOD FROM A WOLVERINE
OUCH

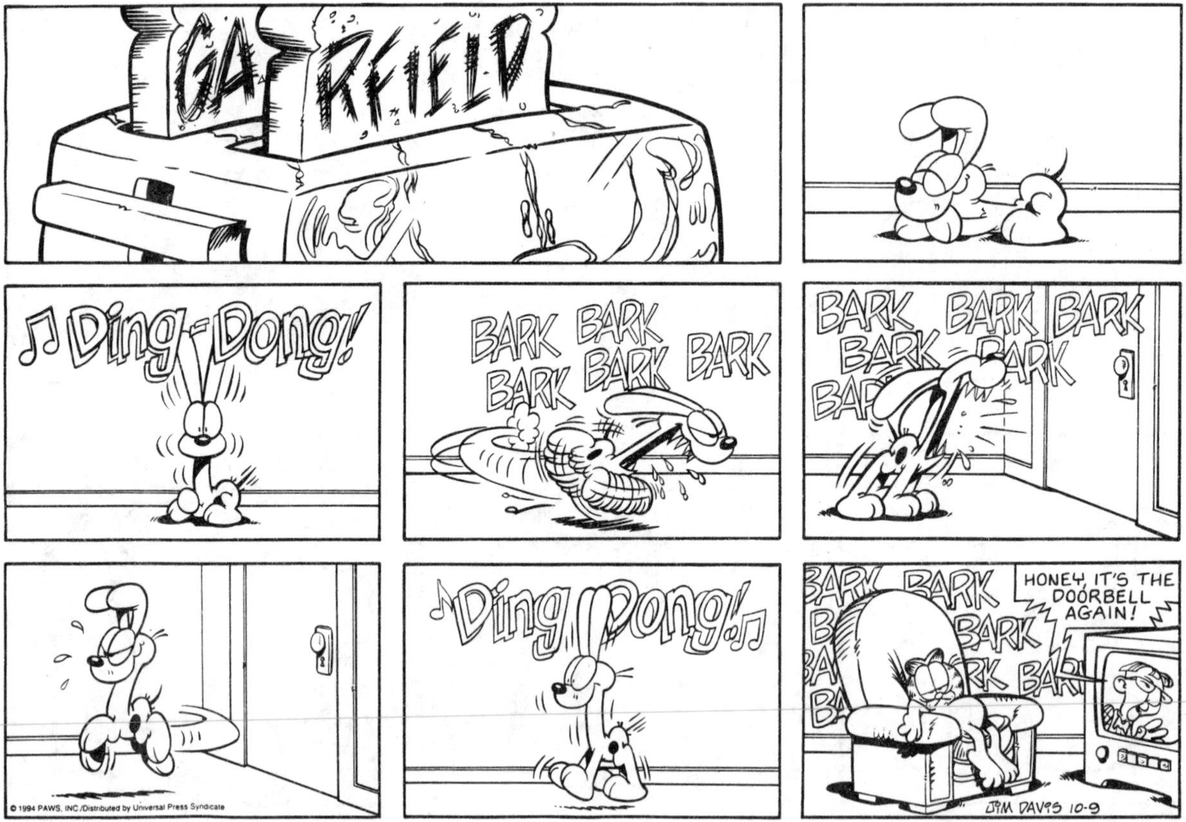
GARFIELD
Ding-Dong!
BARK BARK BARK BARK BARK BARK
BARK BARK BARK
Ding Dong!
HONEY, IT'S THE DOORBELL AGAIN!
BARK BARK BARK
JIM DAVIS 10-9

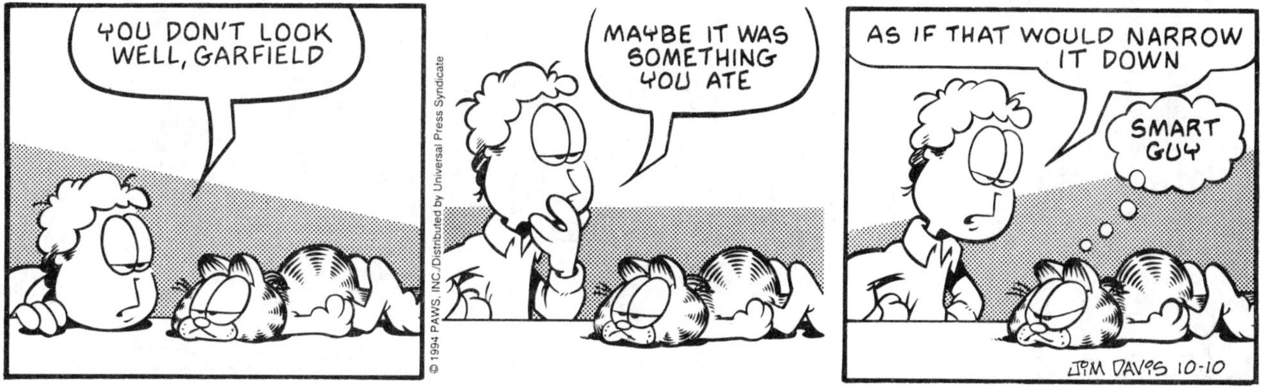
YOU DON'T LOOK WELL, GARFIELD
MAYBE IT WAS SOMETHING YOU ATE
AS IF THAT WOULD NARROW IT DOWN
SMART GUY
JIM DAVIS 10-10

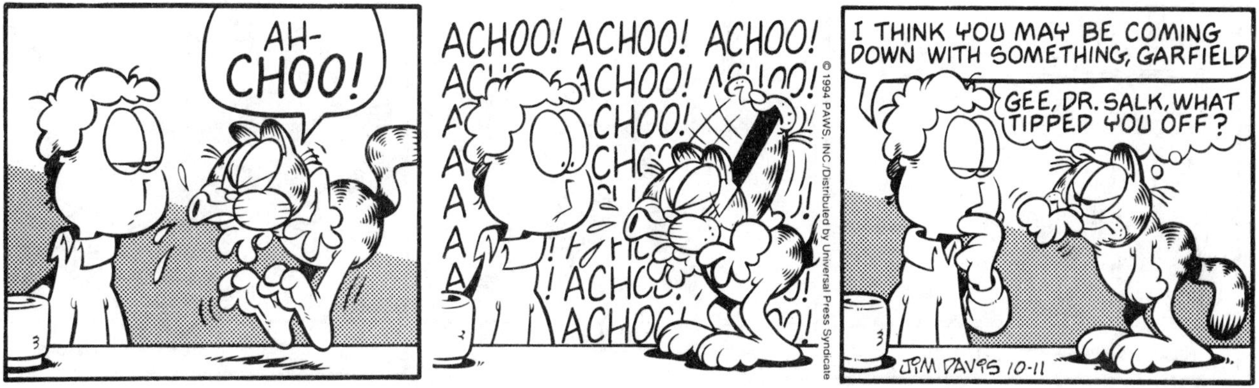
AH-CHOO!
ACHOO! ACHOO! ACHOO!
ACHOO!
CHOO!
I THINK YOU MAY BE COMING DOWN WITH SOMETHING, GARFIELD
GEE, DR. SALK, WHAT TIPPED YOU OFF?
JIM DAVIS 10-11

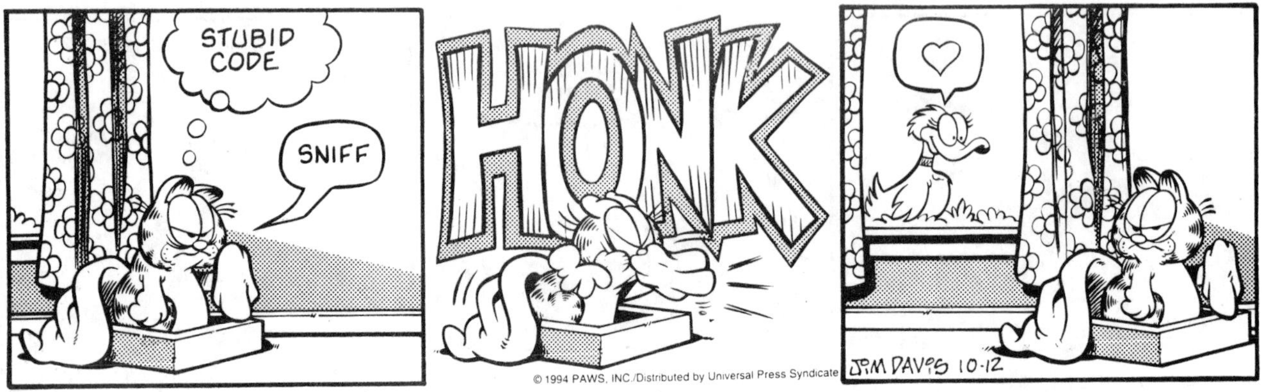
STUBID
CODE
SNIFF
HONK
JIM DAVIS 10-12

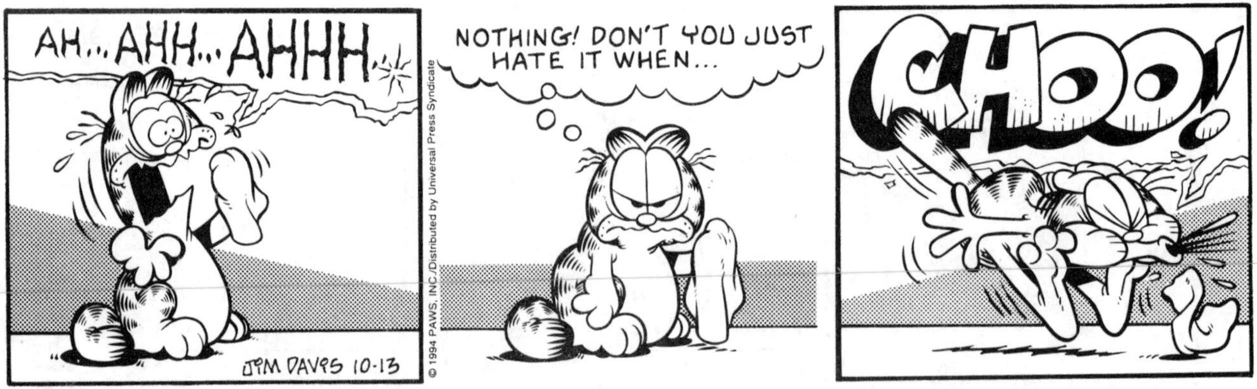
AH... AHH... AHHH...
JIM DAVIS 10-13
NOTHING! DON'T YOU JUST
HATE IT WHEN...
CHOO!

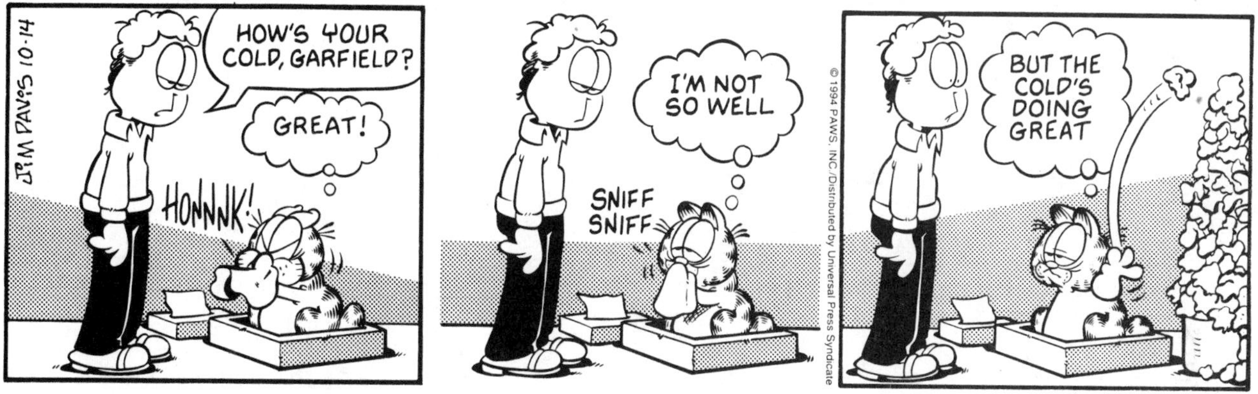
JIM DAVIS 10·14
HOW'S YOUR COLD, GARFIELD?
GREAT!
HONNNK!
I'M NOT SO WELL
SNIFF SNIFF
BUT THE COLD'S DOING GREAT

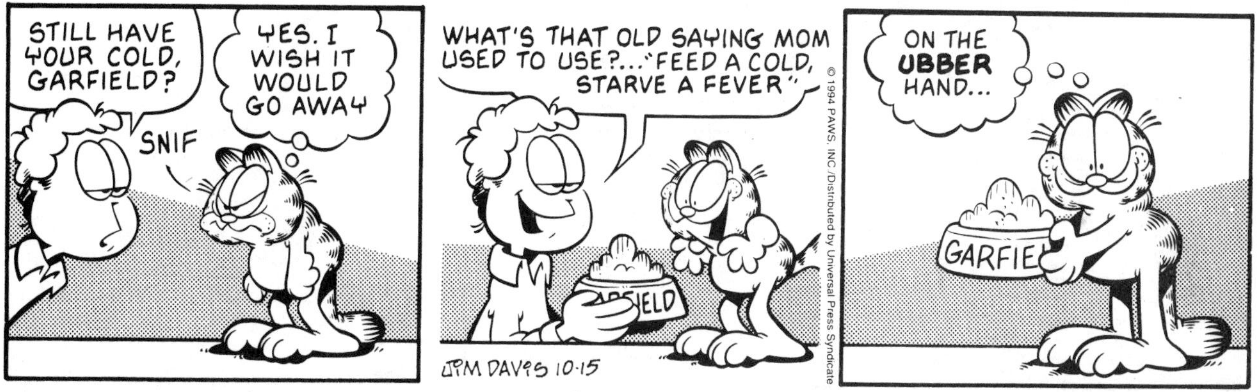
STILL HAVE YOUR COLD, GARFIELD?
YES. I WISH IT WOULD GO AWAY
SNIF
WHAT'S THAT OLD SAYING MOM USED TO USE?... "FEED A COLD, STARVE A FEVER"
JIM DAVIS 10·15
ON THE **UBBER** HAND...

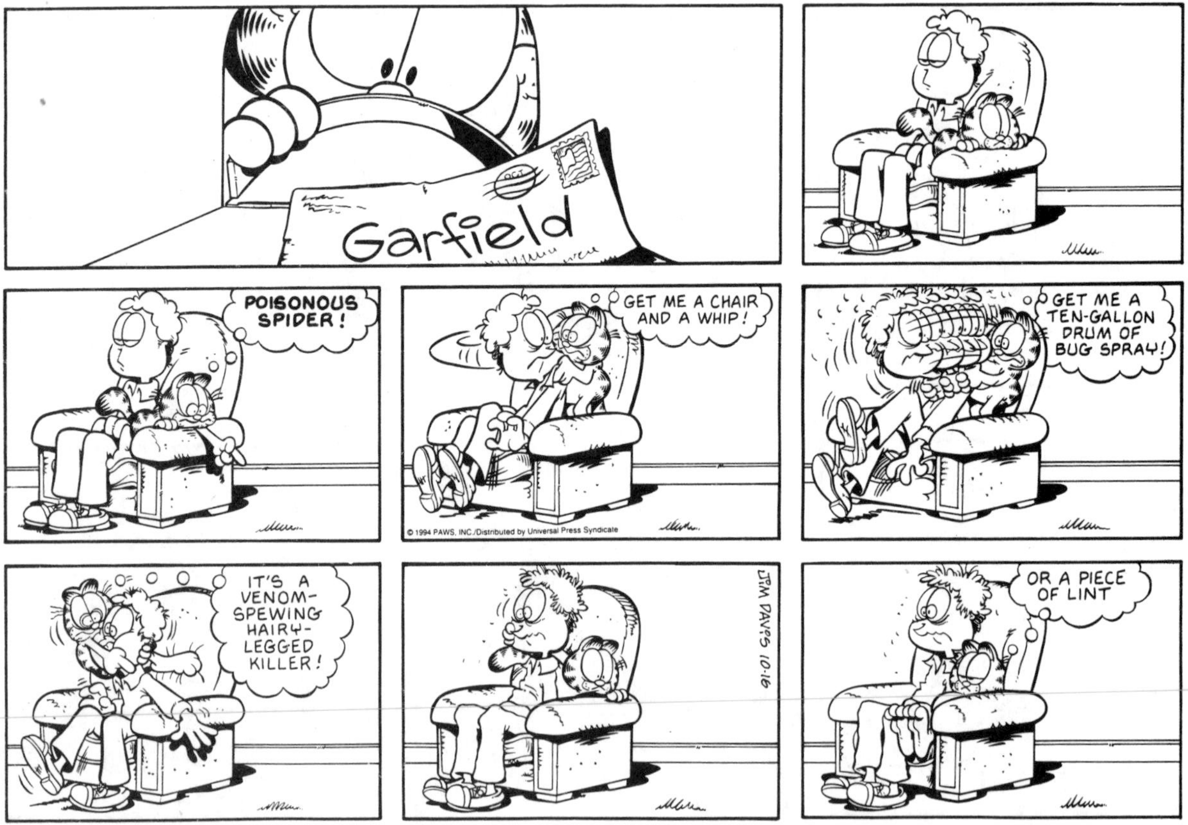
Garfield
POISONOUS SPIDER!
GET ME A CHAIR AND A WHIP!
© 1994 PAWS, INC./Distributed by Universal Press Syndicate
GET ME A TEN-GALLON DRUM OF BUG SPRAY!
IT'S A VENOM-SPEWING HAIRY-LEGGED KILLER!
JIM DAVIS 10-16
OR A PIECE OF LINT

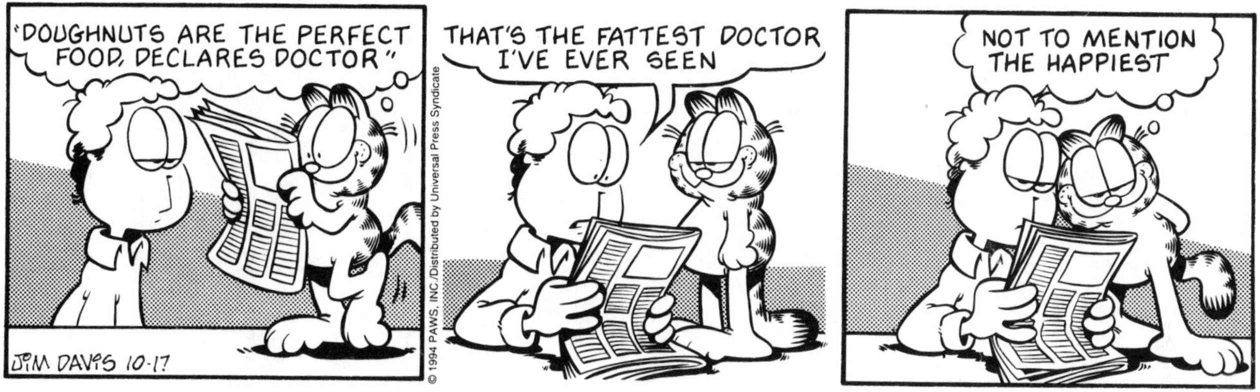
"DOUGHNUTS ARE THE PERFECT FOOD, DECLARES DOCTOR"
JIM DAVIS 10-17
© 1994 PAWS, INC./Distributed by Universal Press Syndicate
THAT'S THE FATTEST DOCTOR I'VE EVER SEEN
NOT TO MENTION THE HAPPIEST

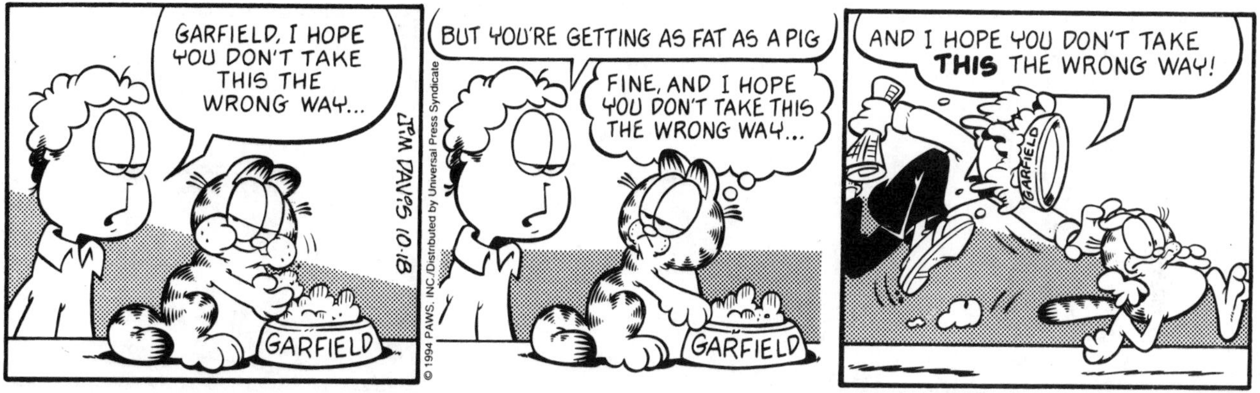
GARFIELD, I HOPE YOU DON'T TAKE THIS THE WRONG WAY...
GARFIELD
JIM DAVIS 10-18
© 1994 PAWS, INC./Distributed by Universal Press Syndicate
BUT YOU'RE GETTING AS FAT AS A PIG
FINE, AND I HOPE YOU DON'T TAKE THIS THE WRONG WAY...
GARFIELD
AND I HOPE YOU DON'T TAKE **THIS** THE WRONG WAY!
GARFIELD

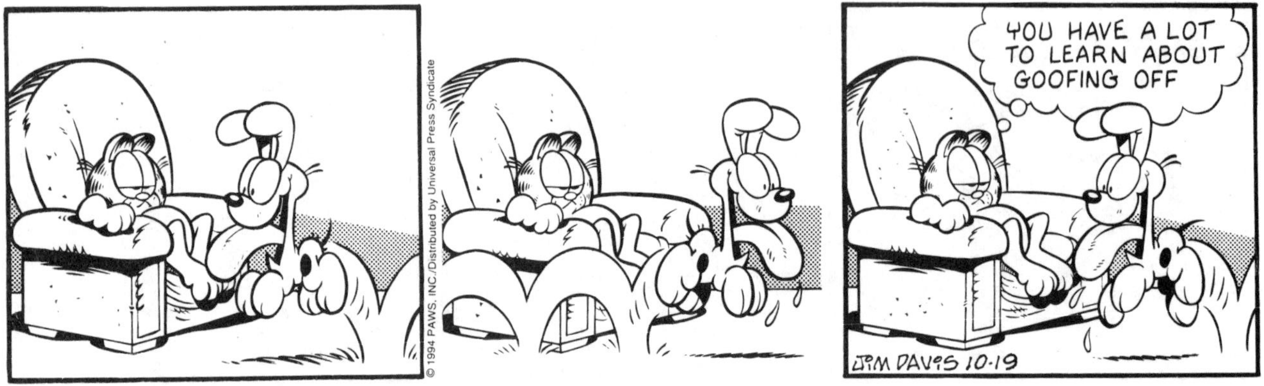
YOU HAVE A LOT TO LEARN ABOUT GOOFING OFF
JIM DAVIS 10-19

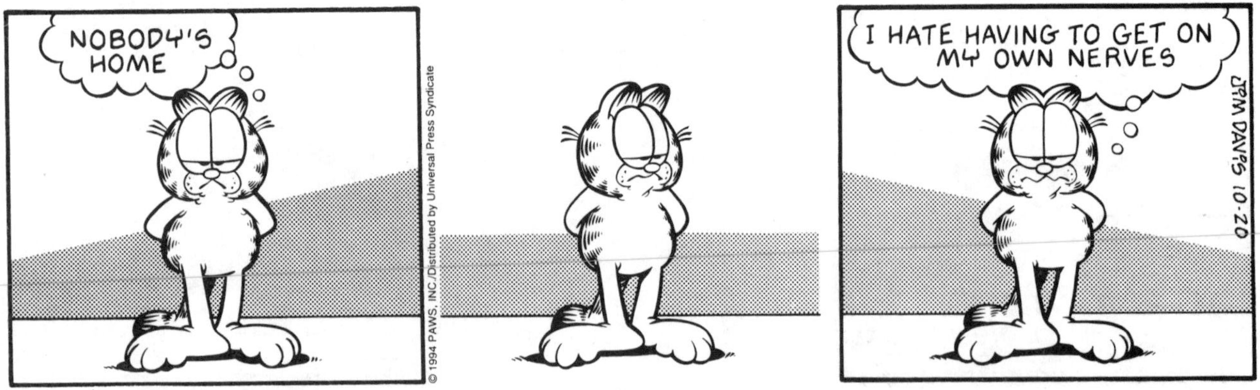
NOBODY'S HOME
I HATE HAVING TO GET ON MY OWN NERVES
JIM DAVIS 10-20

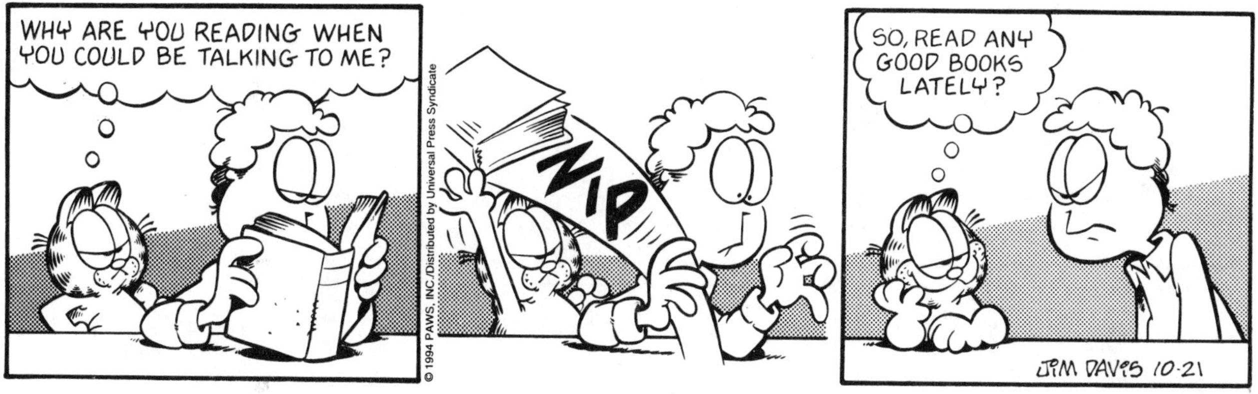
WHY ARE YOU READING WHEN YOU COULD BE TALKING TO ME?
ZIP
SO, READ ANY GOOD BOOKS LATELY?
JIM DAVIS 10-21

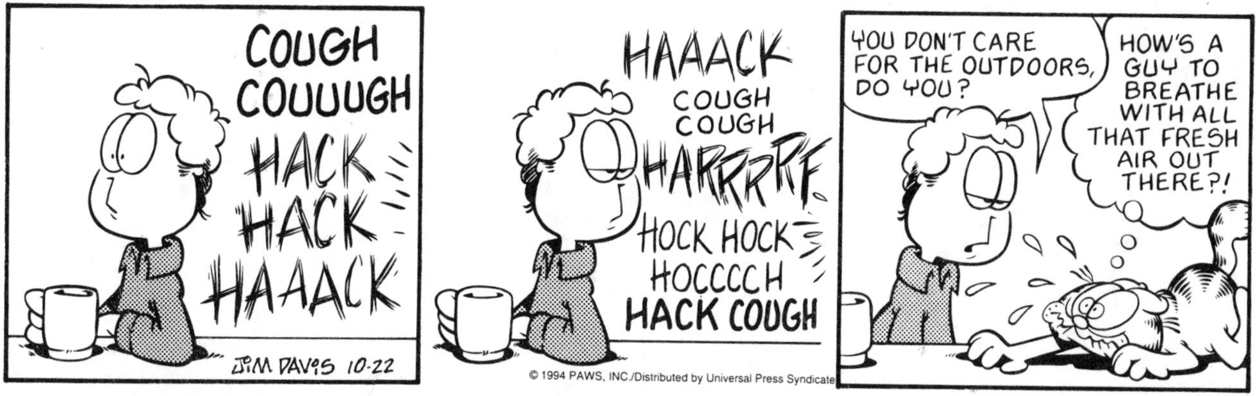
COUGH COUUUGH
HACK HACK HAAACK
JIM DAVIS 10-22
HAAACK
COUGH COUGH
HARRRRRF
HOCK HOCK
HOCCCCH
HACK COUGH
YOU DON'T CARE FOR THE OUTDOORS, DO YOU?
HOW'S A GUY TO BREATHE WITH ALL THAT FRESH AIR OUT THERE?!

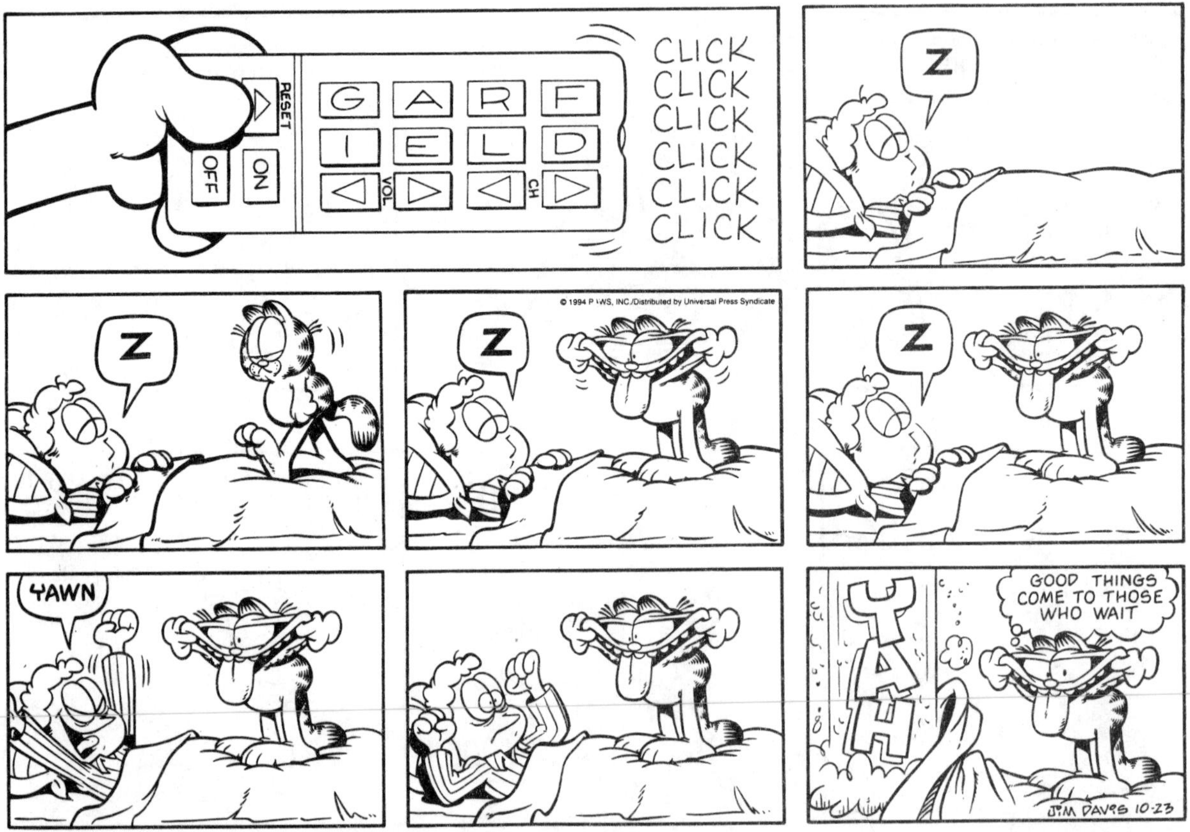
RESET
OFF
ON
G A R F
I E L D
VOL
CH
CLICK CLICK CLICK CLICK CLICK CLICK
Z
Z
© 1994 PAWS, INC./Distributed by Universal Press Syndicate
Z
Z
YAWN
YAAH
GOOD THINGS COME TO THOSE WHO WAIT
JIM DAVIS 10-23

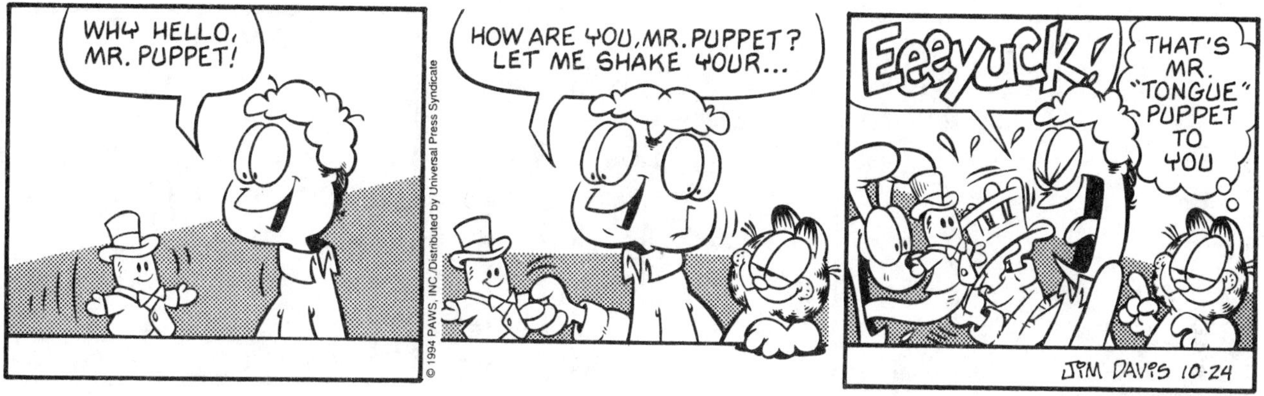
WHY HELLO, MR. PUPPET!
HOW ARE YOU, MR. PUPPET? LET ME SHAKE YOUR...
EEEYUCK!
THAT'S MR. "TONGUE" PUPPET TO YOU
JIM DAVIS 10-24

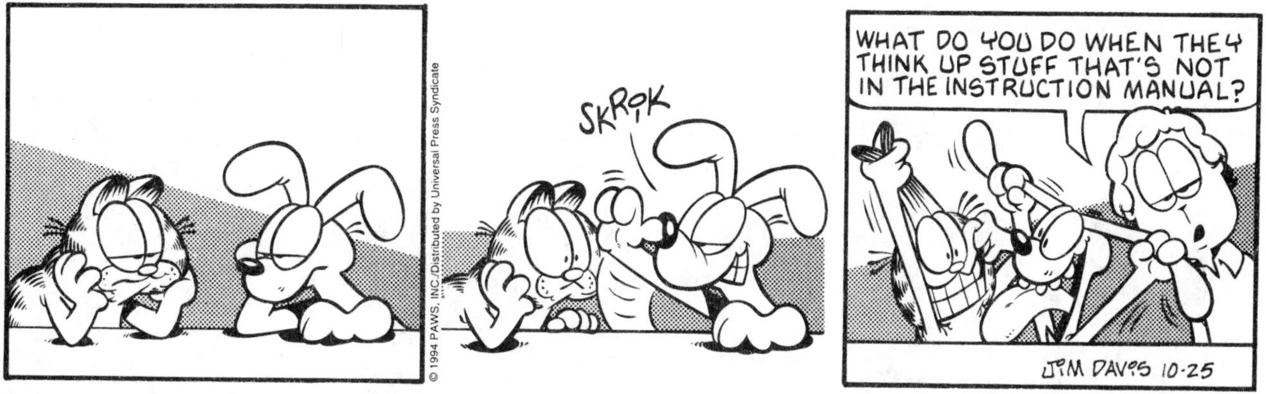
SKROIK
WHAT DO YOU DO WHEN THEY THINK UP STUFF THAT'S NOT IN THE INSTRUCTION MANUAL?
JIM DAVIS 10-25

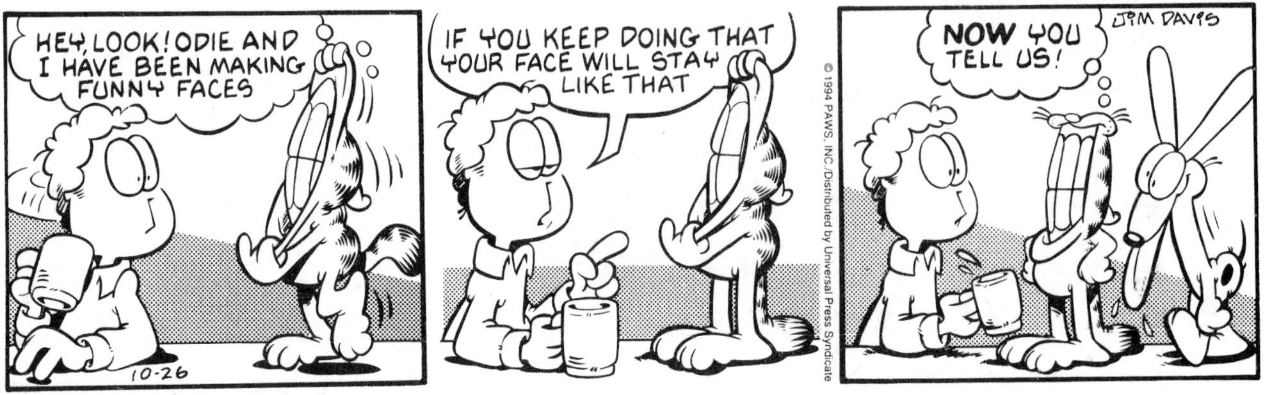
HEY, LOOK! ODIE AND I HAVE BEEN MAKING FUNNY FACES
10-26
IF YOU KEEP DOING THAT YOUR FACE WILL STAY LIKE THAT
© 1994 PAWS, INC./Distributed by Universal Press Syndicate
NOW YOU TELL US!
JIM DAVIS

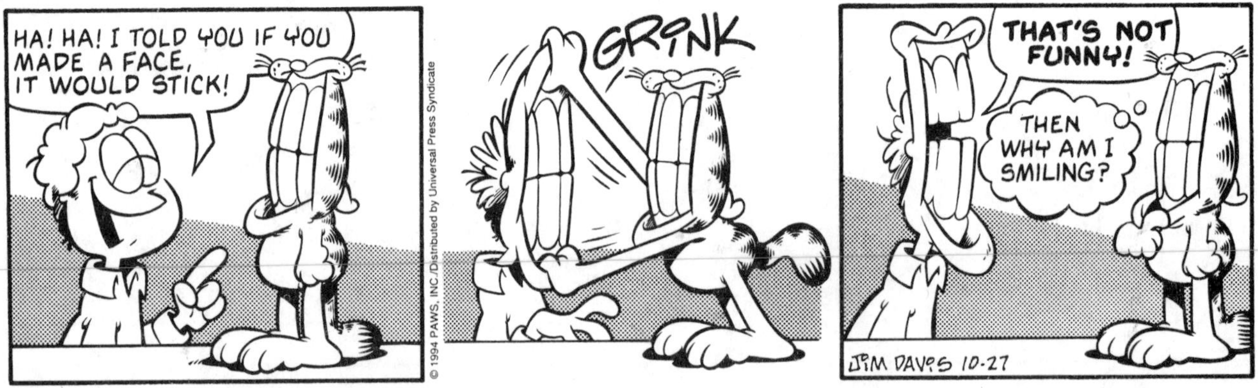
HA! HA! I TOLD YOU IF YOU MADE A FACE, IT WOULD STICK!
© 1994 PAWS, INC./Distributed by Universal Press Syndicate
GRINK
THAT'S NOT FUNNY!
THEN WHY AM I SMILING?
JIM DAVIS 10-27

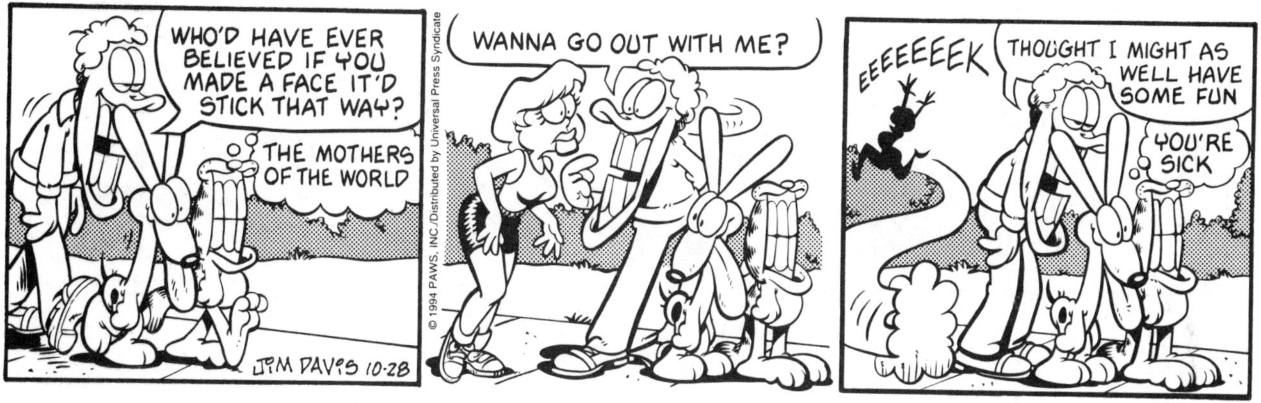
WHO'D HAVE EVER BELIEVED IF YOU MADE A FACE IT'D STICK THAT WAY?
THE MOTHERS OF THE WORLD
JIM DAVIS 10-28
© 1994 PAWS, INC./Distributed by Universal Press Syndicate
WANNA GO OUT WITH ME?
EEEEEEEEK
THOUGHT I MIGHT AS WELL HAVE SOME FUN
YOU'RE SICK

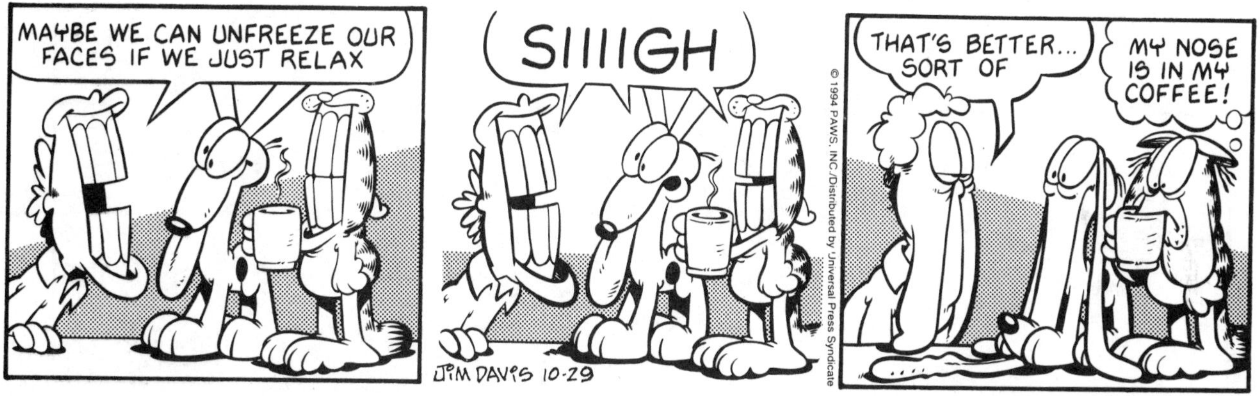
MAYBE WE CAN UNFREEZE OUR FACES IF WE JUST RELAX
SIIIIGH
JIM DAVIS 10-29
© 1994 PAWS, INC./Distributed by Universal Press Syndicate
THAT'S BETTER... SORT OF
MY NOSE IS IN MY COFFEE!

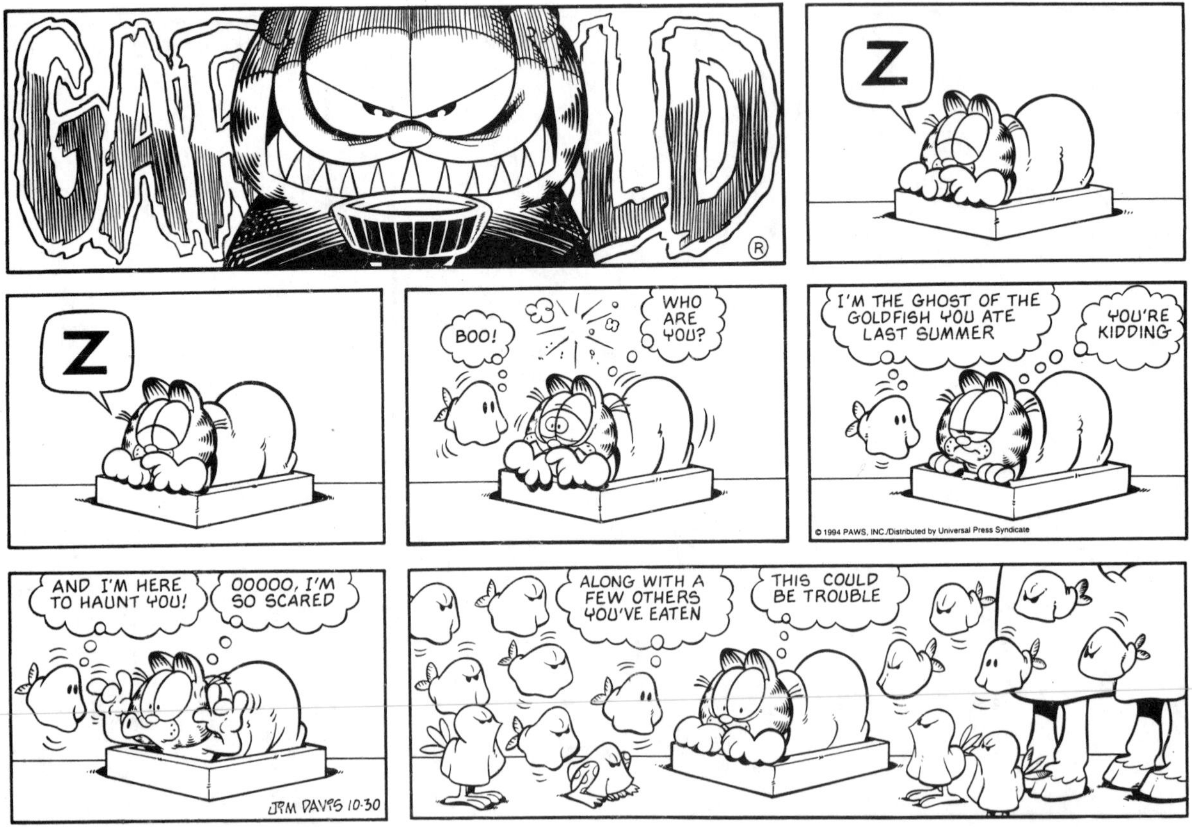
GARFIELD
Z
Z
BOO!
WHO ARE YOU?
I'M THE GHOST OF THE GOLDFISH YOU ATE LAST SUMMER
YOU'RE KIDDING
© 1994 PAWS, INC./Distributed by Universal Press Syndicate
AND I'M HERE TO HAUNT YOU!
OOOOO, I'M SO SCARED
JIM DAVIS 10-30
ALONG WITH A FEW OTHERS YOU'VE EATEN
THIS COULD BE TROUBLE

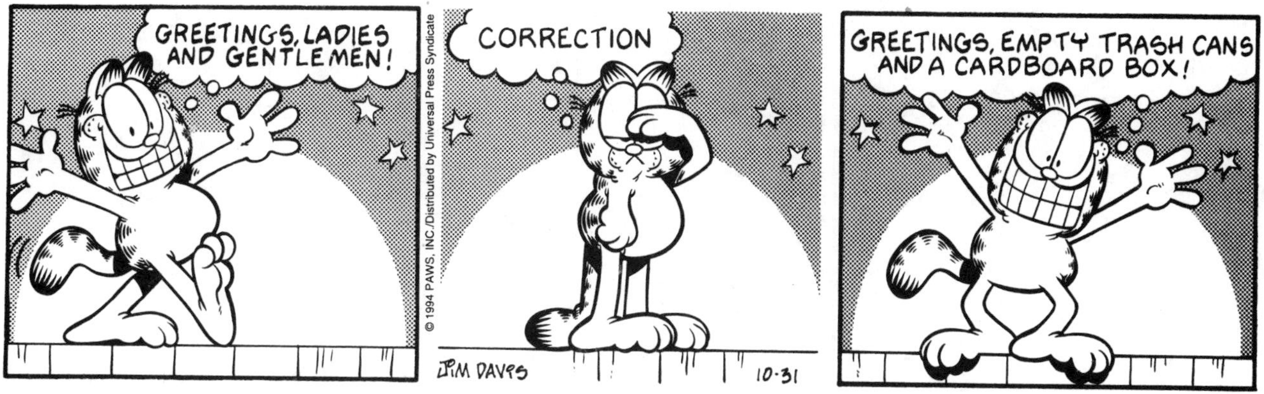
GREETINGS, LADIES AND GENTLEMEN!
CORRECTION
GREETINGS, EMPTY TRASH CANS AND A CARDBOARD BOX!
JIM DAVIS
10-31

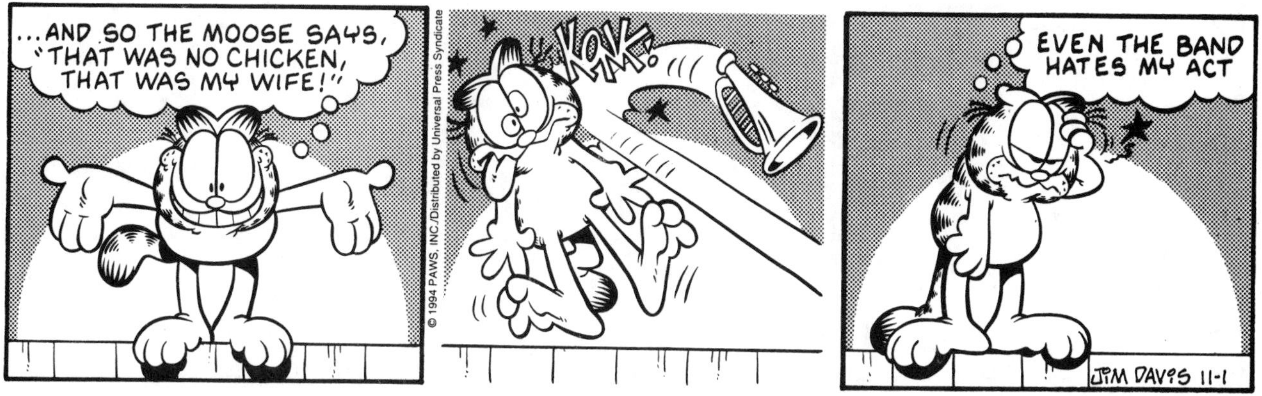
...AND SO THE MOOSE SAYS, "THAT WAS NO CHICKEN, THAT WAS MY WIFE!"
KONK!
EVEN THE BAND HATES MY ACT
JIM DAVIS 11-1

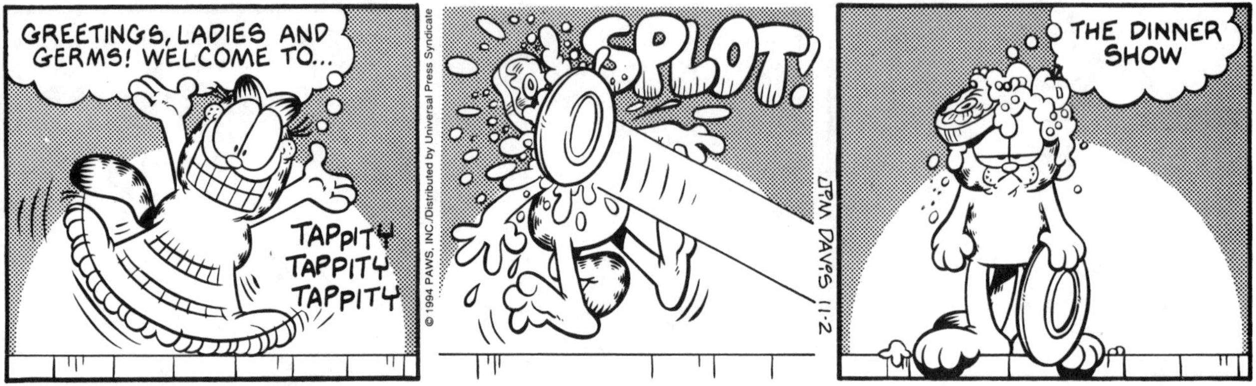
GREETINGS, LADIES AND GERMS! WELCOME TO...
TAPPITY
TAPPITY
TAPPITY
© 1994 PAWS, INC./Distributed by Universal Press Syndicate
SPLOT!
JIM DAVIS 11-2
THE DINNER SHOW

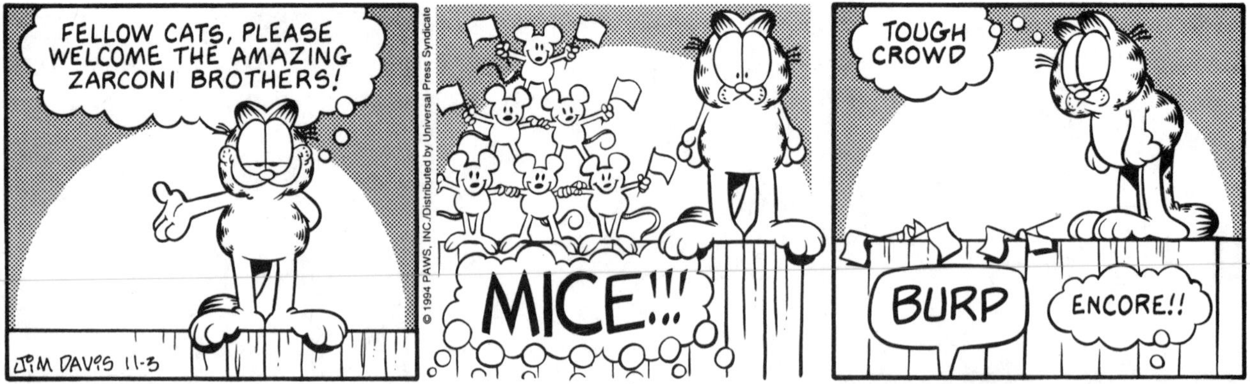
FELLOW CATS, PLEASE WELCOME THE AMAZING ZARCONI BROTHERS!
JIM DAVIS 11-3
© 1994 PAWS, INC./Distributed by Universal Press Syndicate
MICE!!!
TOUGH CROWD
BURP
ENCORE!!

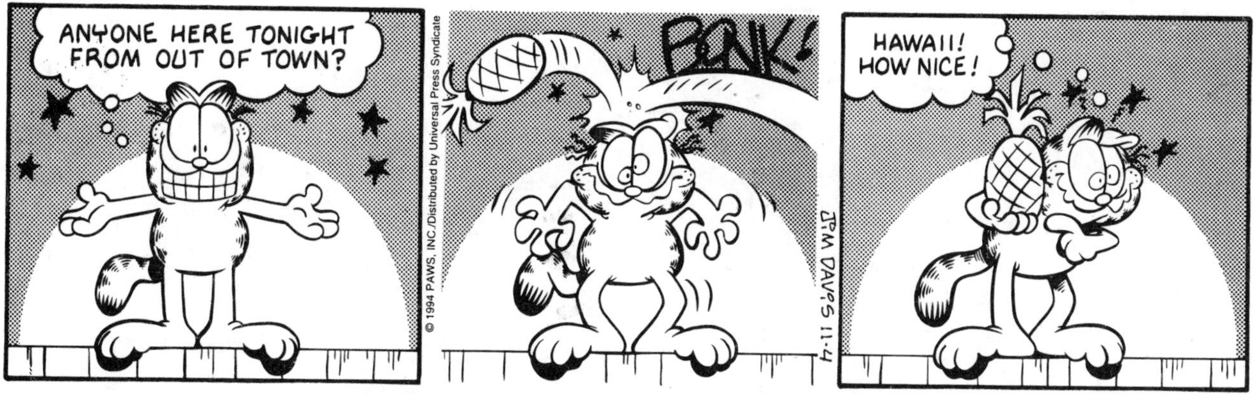

ANYONE HERE TONIGHT FROM OUT OF TOWN?
BONK!
© 1994 PAWS, INC./Distributed by Universal Press Syndicate
JIM DAVIS 11-4
HAWAII! HOW NICE!

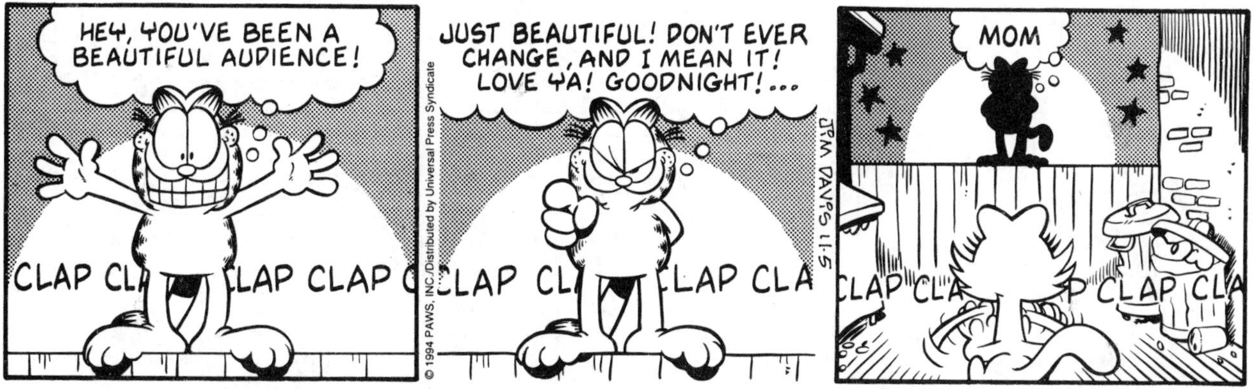

HEY, YOU'VE BEEN A BEAUTIFUL AUDIENCE!
CLAP CLA CLAP CLAP C
© 1994 PAWS, INC./Distributed by Universal Press Syndicate
JUST BEAUTIFUL! DON'T EVER CHANGE, AND I MEAN IT! LOVE YA! GOODNIGHT!...
CLAP CL CLAP CLA
JIM DAVIS 11-5
MOM
CLAP CLA CLAP CLA

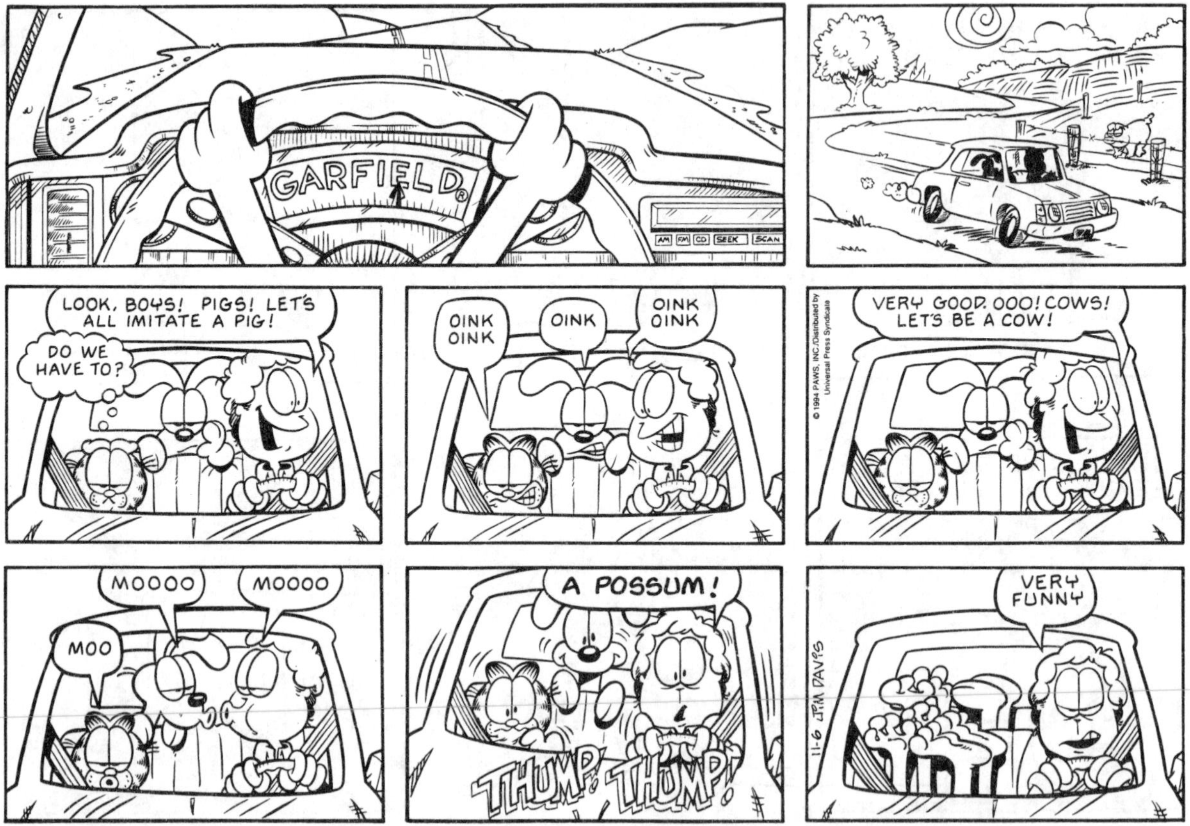
GARFIELD®
AM FM CD SEEK SCAN
LOOK, BOYS! PIGS! LET'S ALL IMITATE A PIG!
DO WE HAVE TO?
OINK OINK
OINK
OINK OINK
© 1994 PAWS, INC./Distributed by Universal Press Syndicate
VERY GOOD. OOO! COWS! LET'S BE A COW!
MOOOO
MOOOO
MOO
A POSSUM!
THUMP! THUMP!
11-6 JIM DAVIS
VERY FUNNY

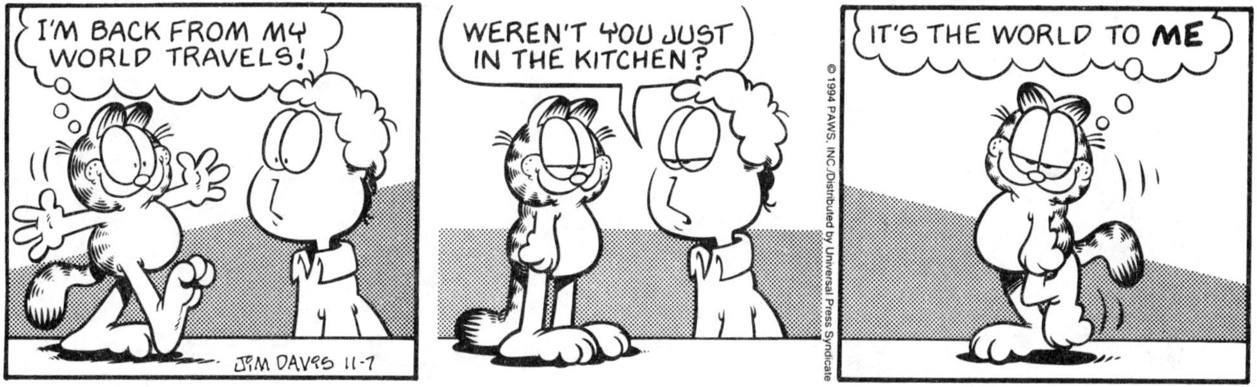
I'M BACK FROM MY WORLD TRAVELS!
JIM DAVIS 11-7
WEREN'T YOU JUST IN THE KITCHEN?
© 1994 PAWS, INC./Distributed by Universal Press Syndicate
IT'S THE WORLD TO **ME**

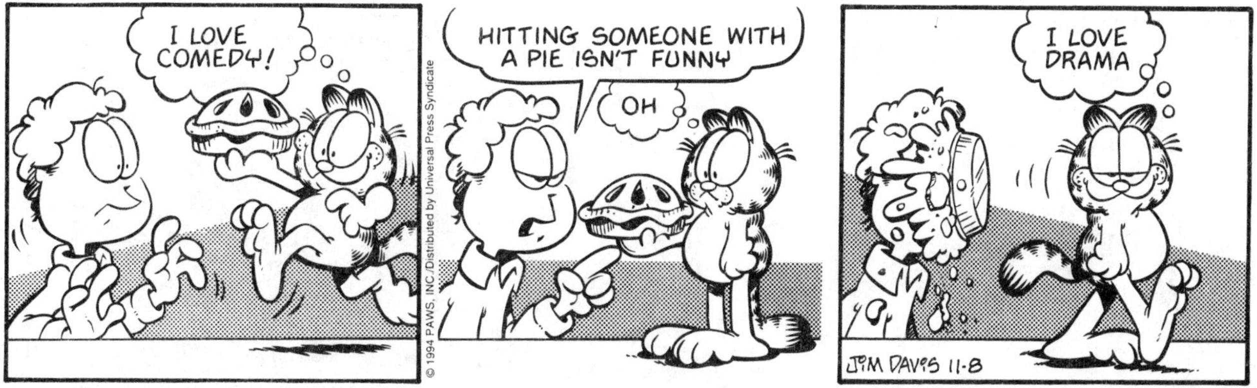
I LOVE COMEDY!
© 1994 PAWS, INC./Distributed by Universal Press Syndicate
HITTING SOMEONE WITH A PIE ISN'T FUNNY
OH
I LOVE DRAMA
JIM DAVIS 11-8

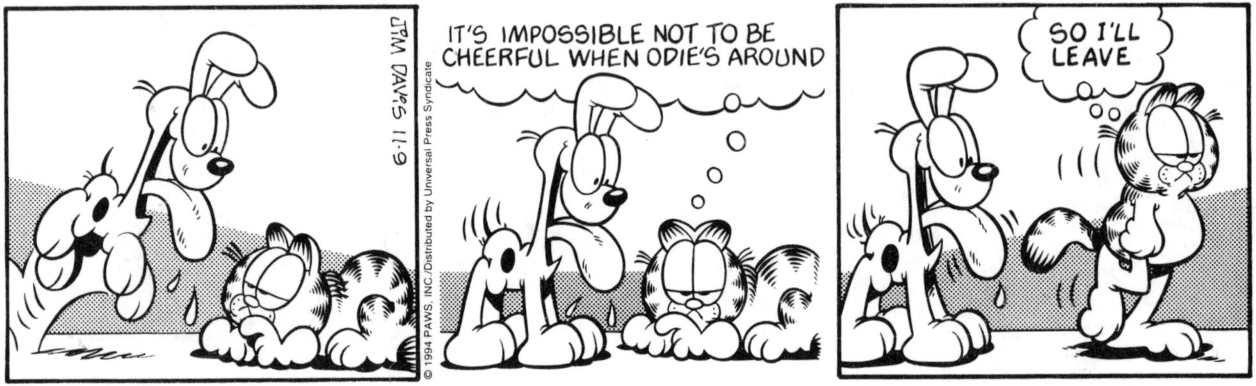
JIM DAVIS 11-9
© 1994 PAWS, INC./Distributed by Universal Press Syndicate
IT'S IMPOSSIBLE NOT TO BE CHEERFUL WHEN ODIE'S AROUND
SO I'LL LEAVE

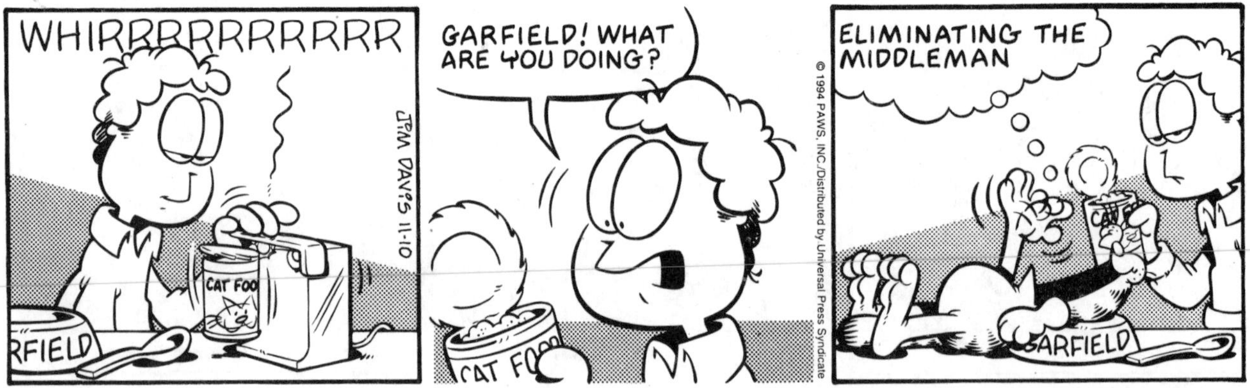
WHIRRRRRRRRRRR
JIM DAVIS 11-10
CAT FOO
RFIELD
GARFIELD! WHAT ARE YOU DOING?
CAT FO
© 1994 PAWS, INC./Distributed by Universal Press Syndicate
ELIMINATING THE MIDDLEMAN
ARFIELD

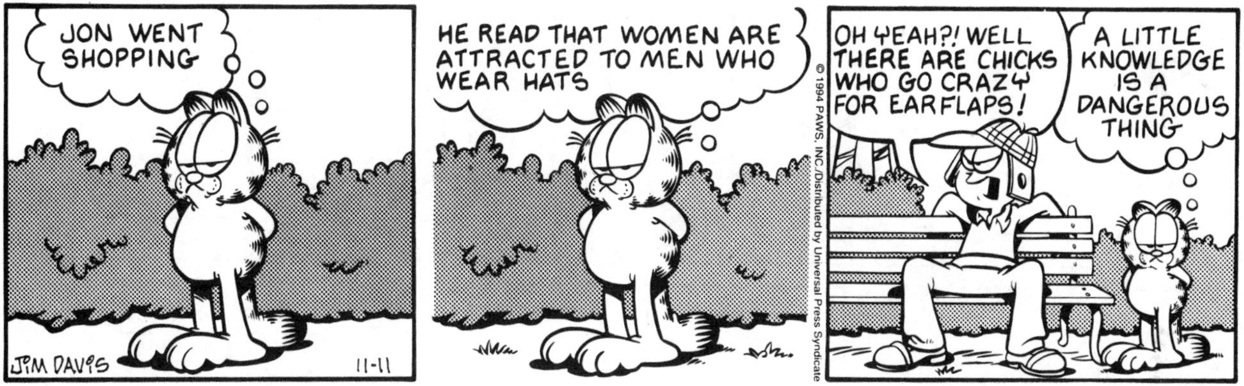
JON WENT SHOPPING
HE READ THAT WOMEN ARE ATTRACTED TO MEN WHO WEAR HATS
OH YEAH?! WELL THERE ARE CHICKS WHO GO CRAZY FOR EARFLAPS!
A LITTLE KNOWLEDGE IS A DANGEROUS THING
JIM DAVIS 11-11

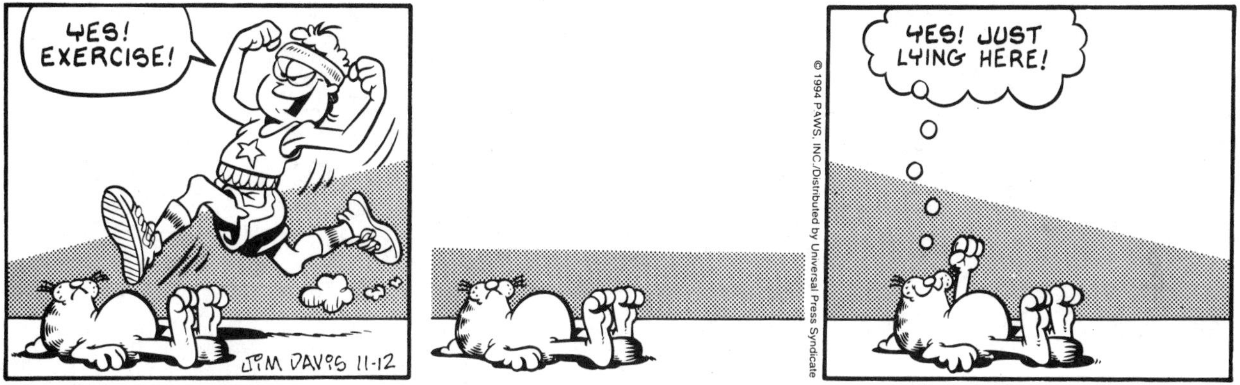
YES! EXERCISE!
YES! JUST LYING HERE!
JIM DAVIS 11-12

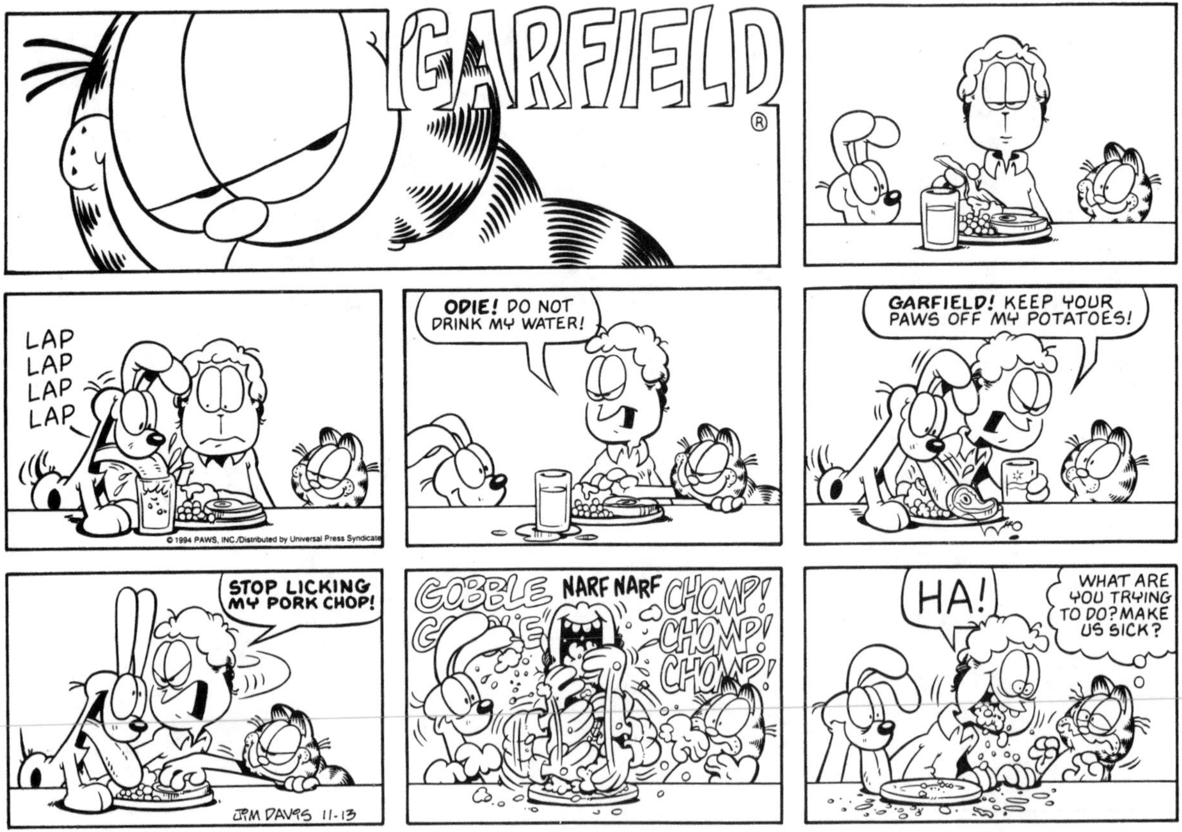
GARFIELD®
LAP
LAP
LAP
LAP
© 1994 PAWS, INC./Distributed by Universal Press Syndicate
ODIE! DO NOT DRINK MY WATER!
GARFIELD! KEEP YOUR PAWS OFF MY POTATOES!
STOP LICKING MY PORK CHOP!
JIM DAVIS 11-13
GOBBLE
GOBBLE
NARF NARF
CHOMP!
CHOMP!
CHOMP!
HA!
WHAT ARE YOU TRYING TO DO? MAKE US SICK?

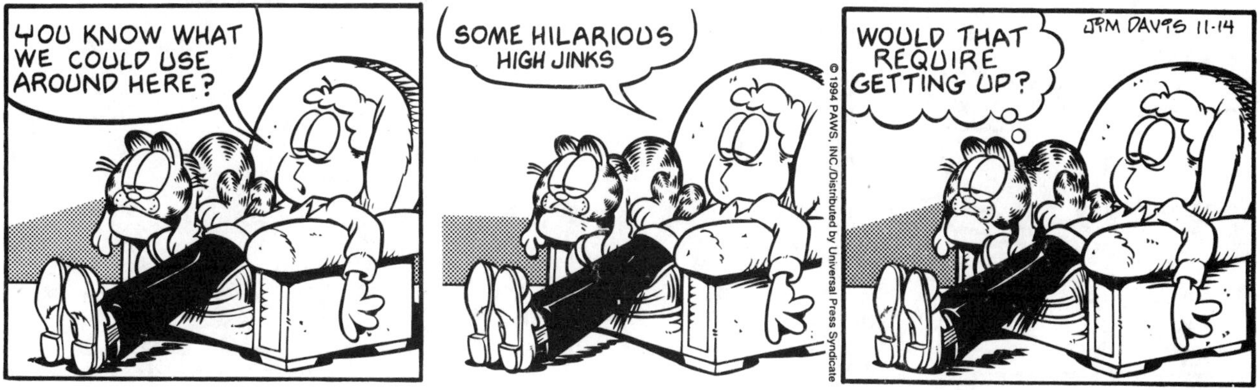
YOU KNOW WHAT WE COULD USE AROUND HERE?
SOME HILARIOUS HIGH JINKS
WOULD THAT REQUIRE GETTING UP?
JIM DAVIS 11-14
© 1994 PAWS, INC./Distributed by Universal Press Syndicate

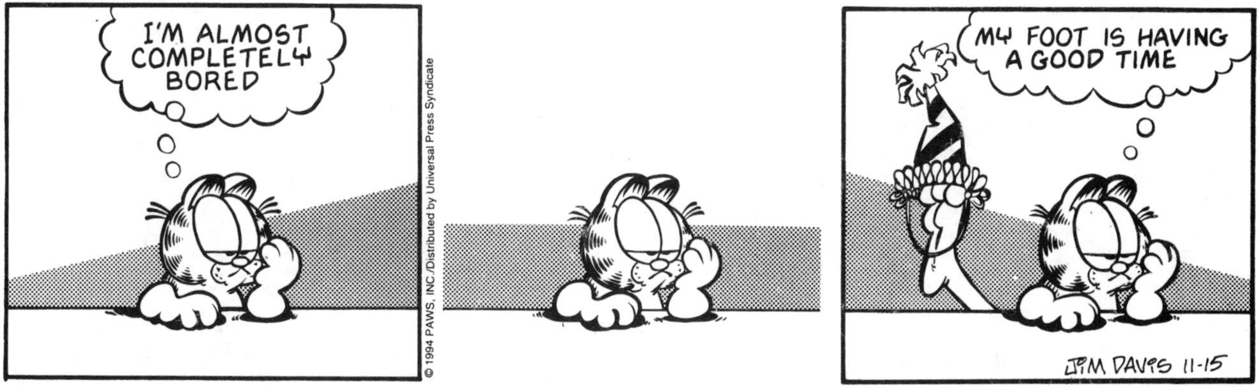
I'M ALMOST COMPLETELY BORED
MY FOOT IS HAVING A GOOD TIME
JIM DAVIS 11-15
© 1994 PAWS, INC./Distributed by Universal Press Syndicate

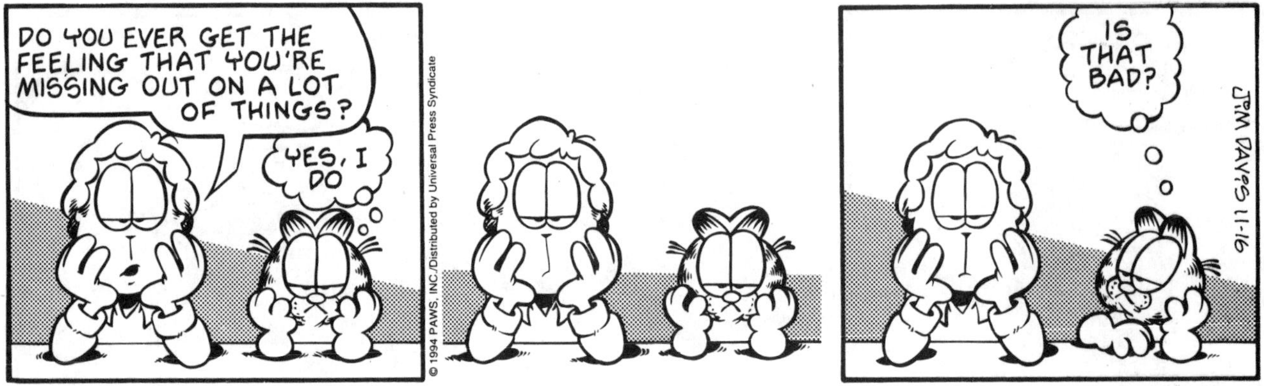
DO YOU EVER GET THE FEELING THAT YOU'RE MISSING OUT ON A LOT OF THINGS?
YES, I DO
IS THAT BAD?
JIM DAVIS 11-16
© 1994 PAWS, INC./Distributed by Universal Press Syndicate

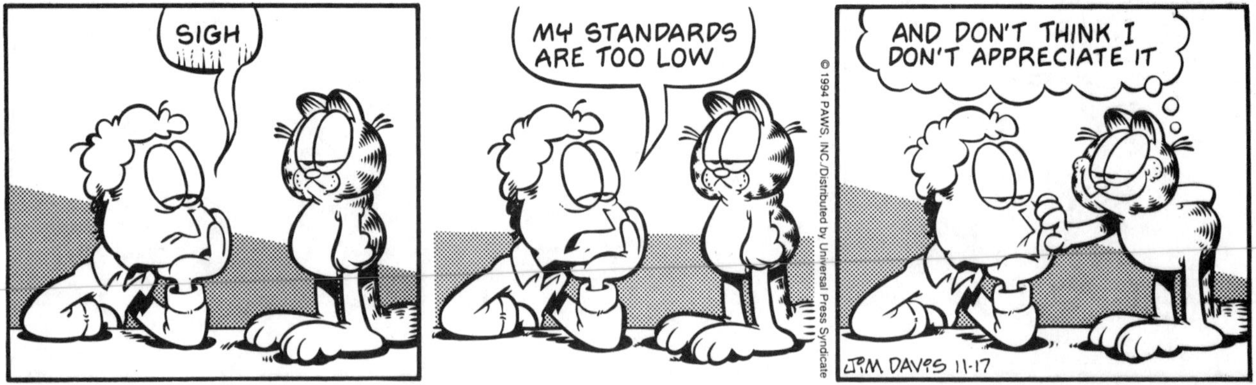
SIGH
MY STANDARDS ARE TOO LOW
AND DON'T THINK I DON'T APPRECIATE IT
JIM DAVIS 11-17
© 1994 PAWS, INC./Distributed by Universal Press Syndicate

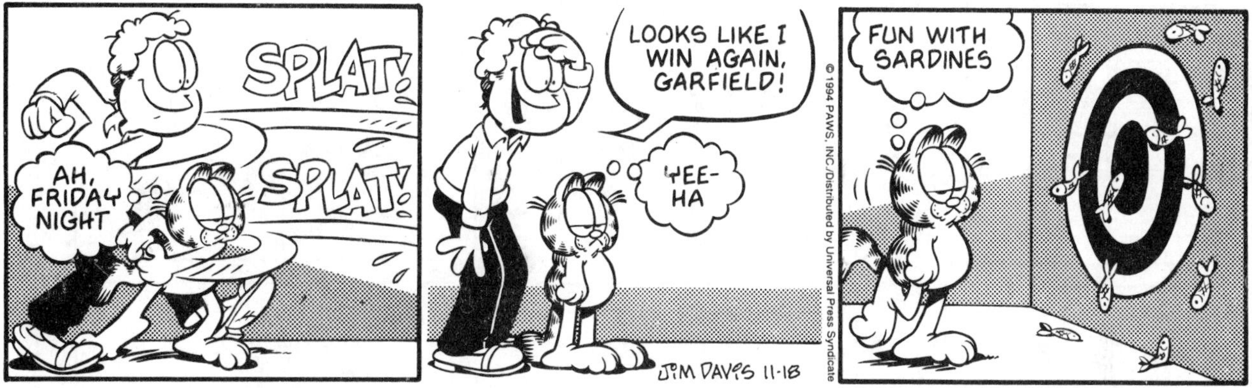
AH, FRIDAY NIGHT
SPLAT!
SPLAT!
LOOKS LIKE I WIN AGAIN, GARFIELD!
YEE-HA
JIM DAVIS 11-18
© 1994 PAWS, INC./Distributed by Universal Press Syndicate
FUN WITH SARDINES

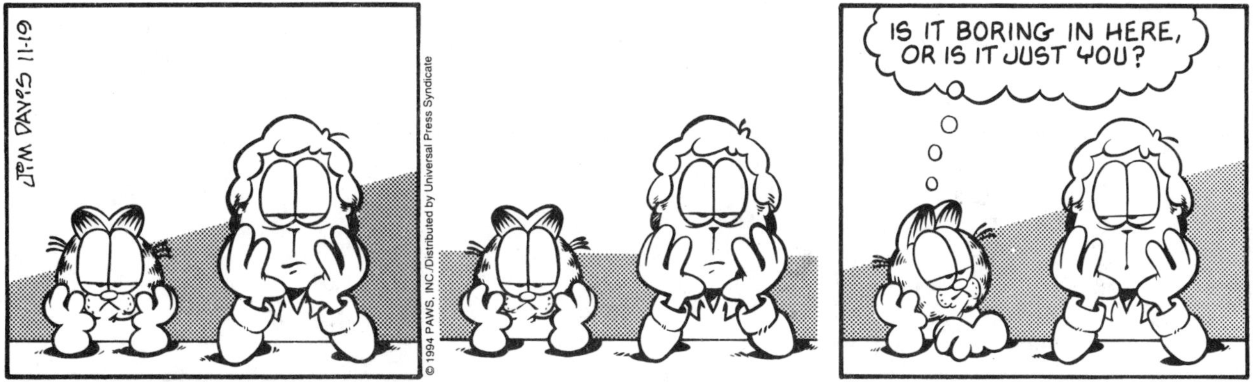
JIM DAVIS 11-19
© 1994 PAWS, INC./Distributed by Universal Press Syndicate
IS IT BORING IN HERE, OR IS IT JUST YOU?

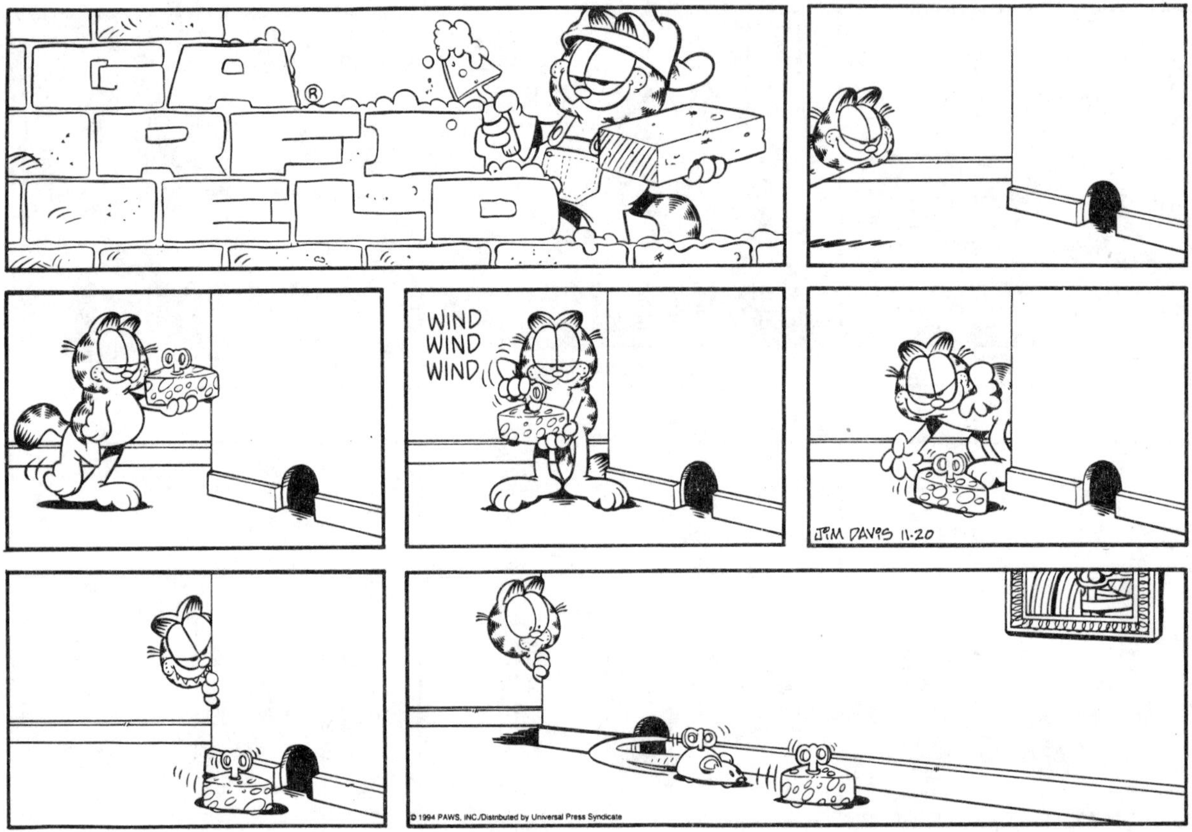
GARFIELD
WIND WIND WIND
JIM DAVIS 11-20
© 1994 PAWS, INC./Distributed by Universal Press Syndicate

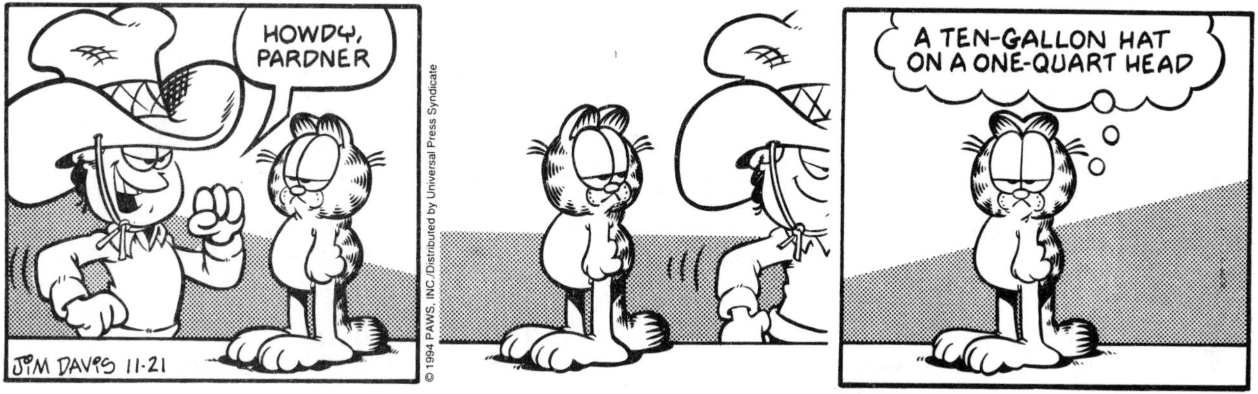
HOWDY, PARDNER
A TEN-GALLON HAT ON A ONE-QUART HEAD
JIM DAVIS 11-21

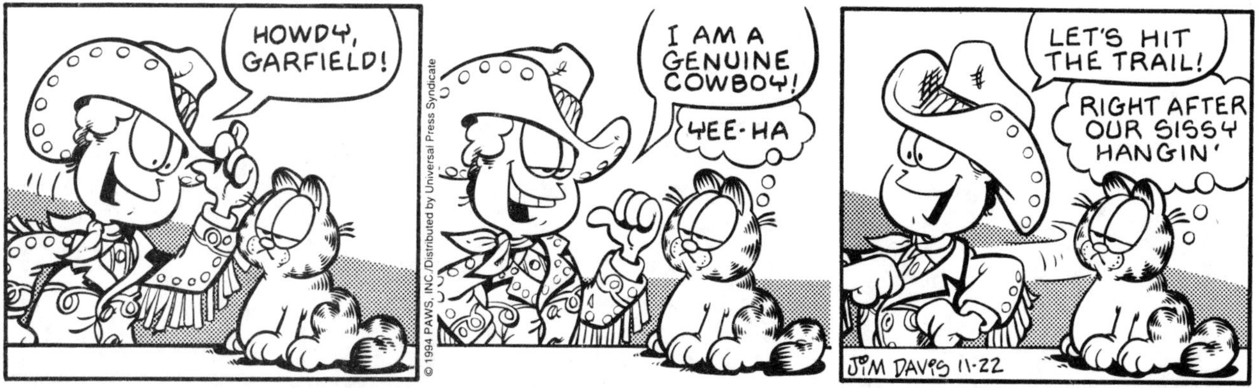
HOWDY, GARFIELD!
I AM A GENUINE COWBOY!
YEE-HA
LET'S HIT THE TRAIL!
RIGHT AFTER OUR SISSY HANGIN'
JIM DAVIS 11-22

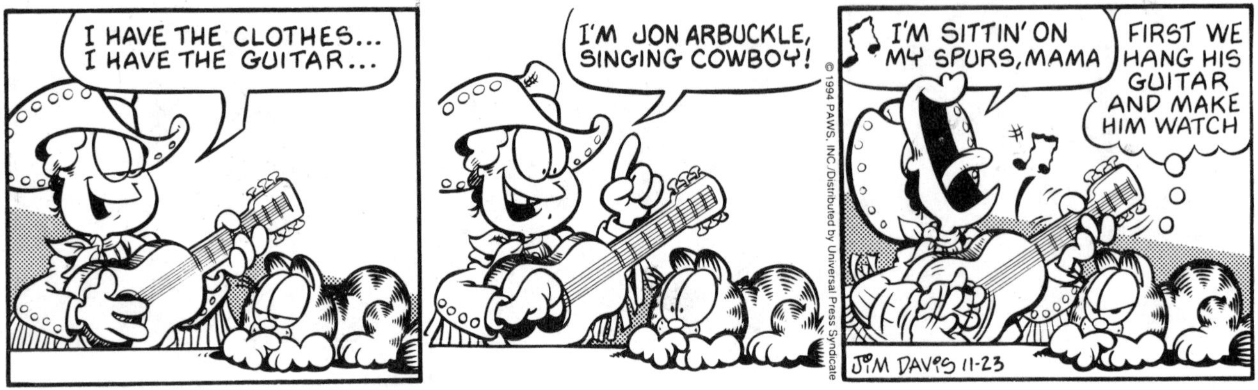
I HAVE THE CLOTHES...
I HAVE THE GUITAR...
I'M JON ARBUCKLE, SINGING COWBOY!
I'M SITTIN' ON MY SPURS, MAMA
FIRST WE HANG HIS GUITAR AND MAKE HIM WATCH
JIM DAVIS 11-23

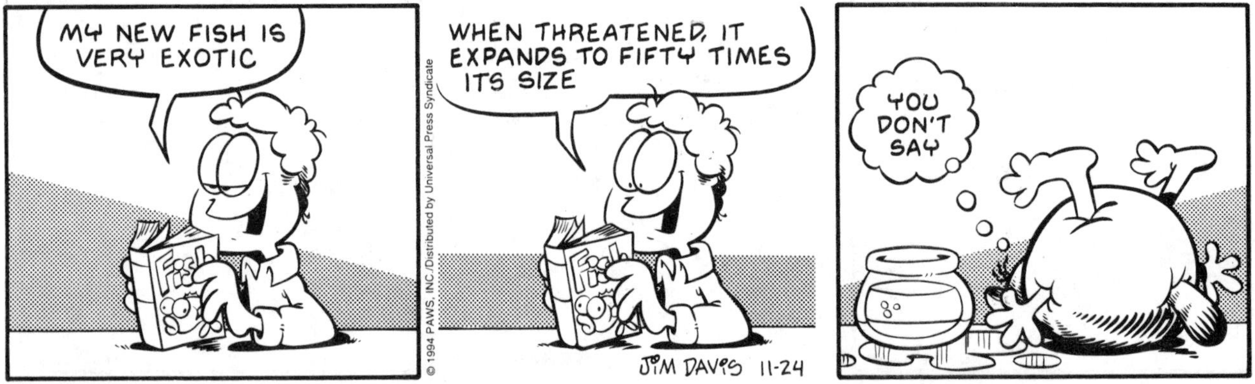
MY NEW FISH IS VERY EXOTIC
Fish
WHEN THREATENED, IT EXPANDS TO FIFTY TIMES ITS SIZE
JIM DAVIS 11-24
YOU DON'T SAY

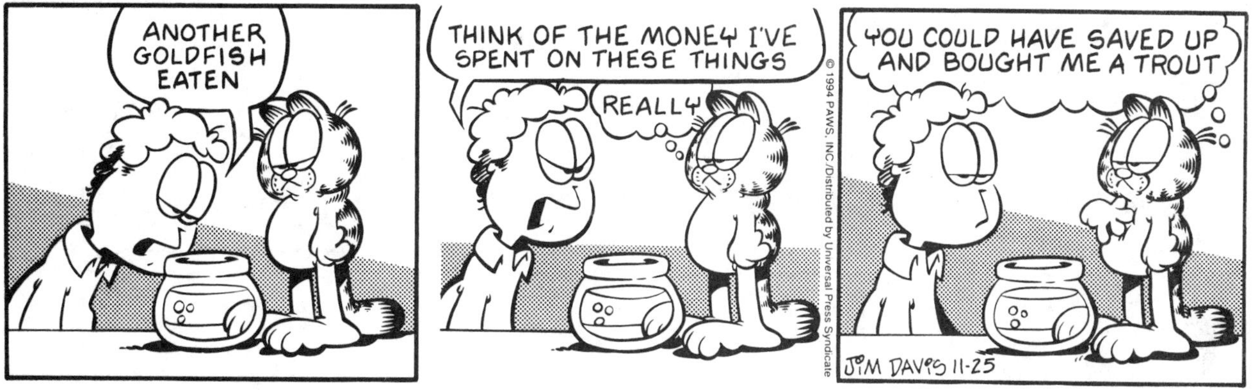
ANOTHER GOLDFISH EATEN
THINK OF THE MONEY I'VE SPENT ON THESE THINGS
REALLY
YOU COULD HAVE SAVED UP AND BOUGHT ME A TROUT
© 1994 PAWS, INC./Distributed by Universal Press Syndicate
JIM DAVIS 11-25

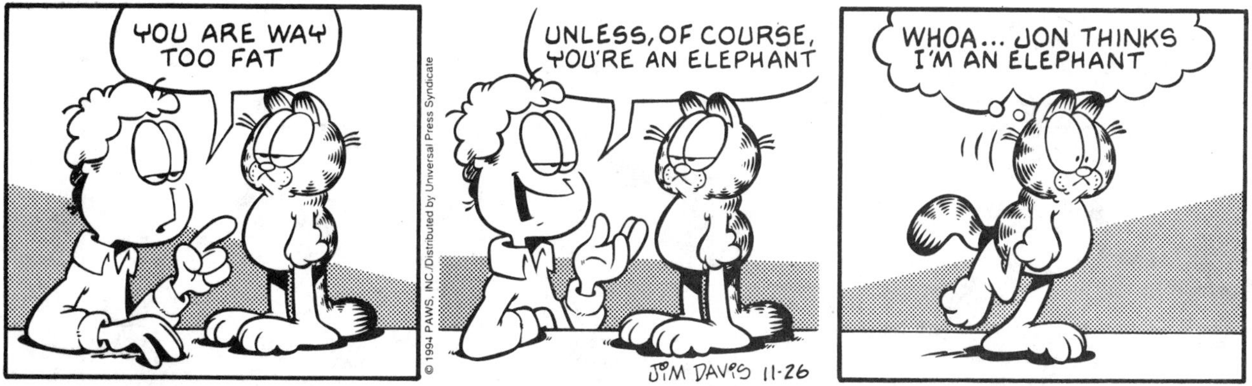
YOU ARE WAY TOO FAT
© 1994 PAWS, INC./Distributed by Universal Press Syndicate
UNLESS, OF COURSE, YOU'RE AN ELEPHANT
JIM DAVIS 11-26
WHOA... JON THINKS I'M AN ELEPHANT

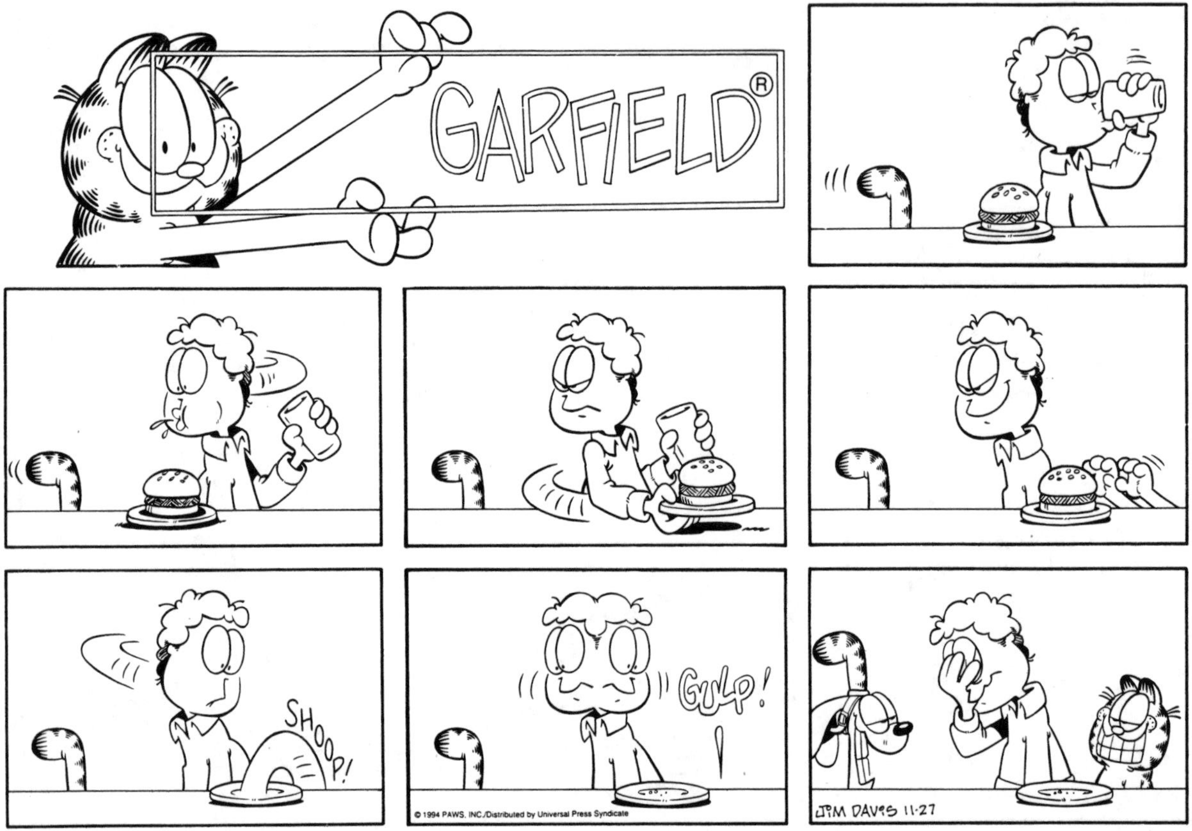
GARFIELD®
SHOOOP!
GULP!
© 1994 PAWS, INC./Distributed by Universal Press Syndicate
JIM DAVIS 11-27

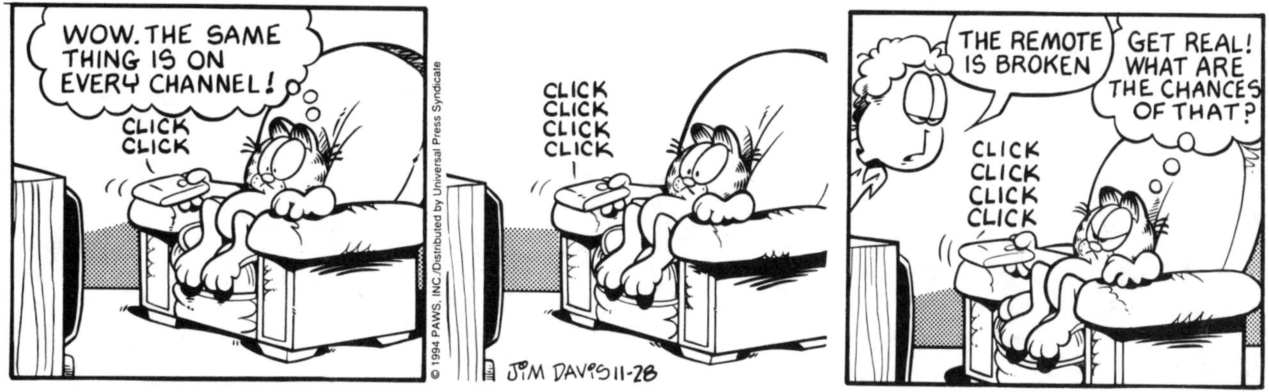
WOW. THE SAME THING IS ON EVERY CHANNEL!
CLICK CLICK
CLICK CLICK CLICK CLICK
THE REMOTE IS BROKEN
GET REAL! WHAT ARE THE CHANCES OF THAT?
CLICK CLICK CLICK CLICK
JIM DAVIS 11-28

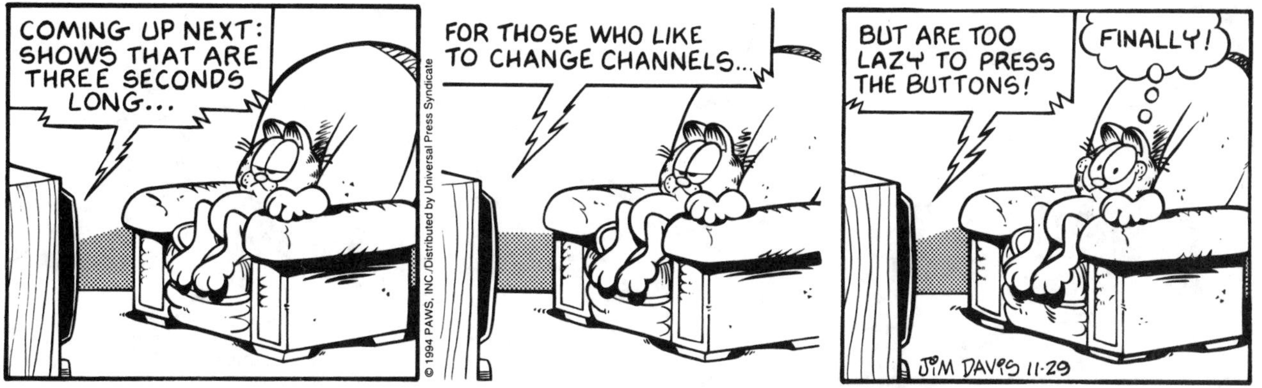
COMING UP NEXT: SHOWS THAT ARE THREE SECONDS LONG...
FOR THOSE WHO LIKE TO CHANGE CHANNELS...
BUT ARE TOO LAZY TO PRESS THE BUTTONS!
FINALLY!
JIM DAVIS 11-29

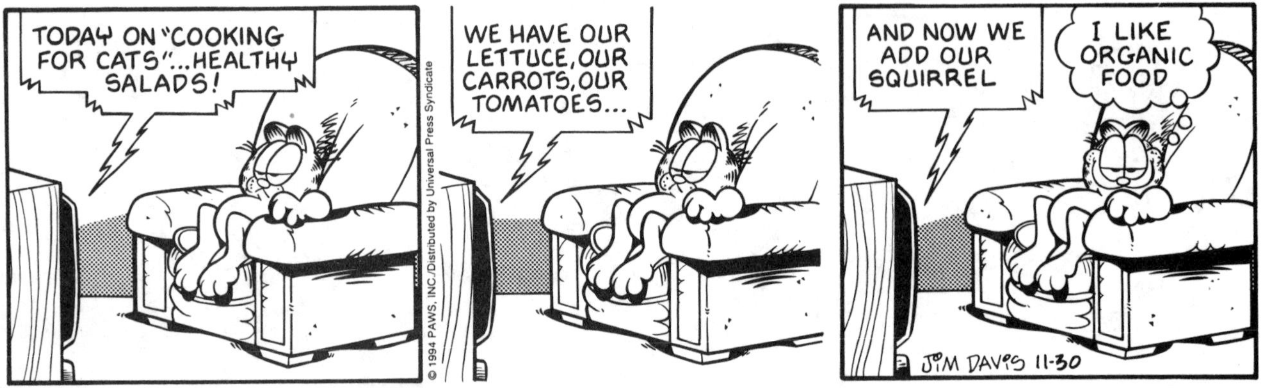
TODAY ON "COOKING FOR CATS"... HEALTHY SALADS!
WE HAVE OUR LETTUCE, OUR CARROTS, OUR TOMATOES...
AND NOW WE ADD OUR SQUIRREL
I LIKE ORGANIC FOOD
© 1994 PAWS, INC./Distributed by Universal Press Syndicate
JIM DAVIS 11-30

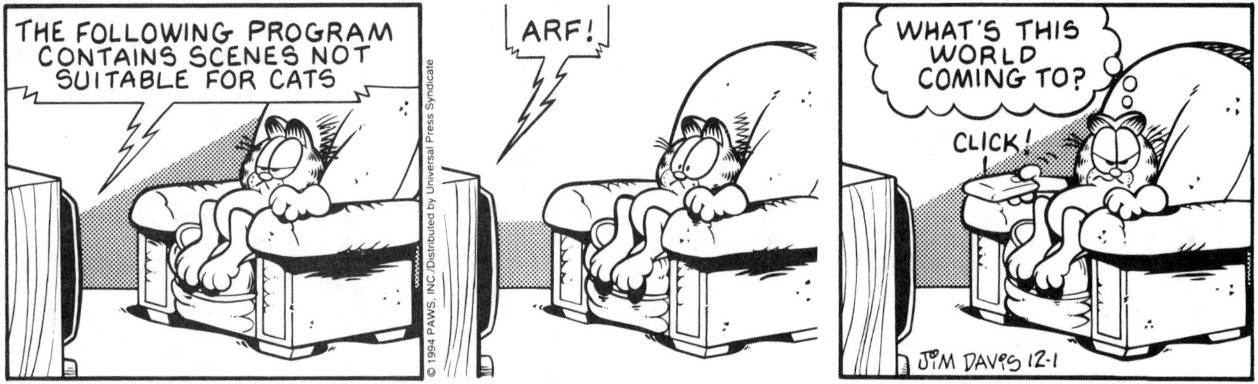
THE FOLLOWING PROGRAM CONTAINS SCENES NOT SUITABLE FOR CATS
ARF!
WHAT'S THIS WORLD COMING TO?
CLICK!
© 1994 PAWS, INC./Distributed by Universal Press Syndicate
JIM DAVIS 12-1

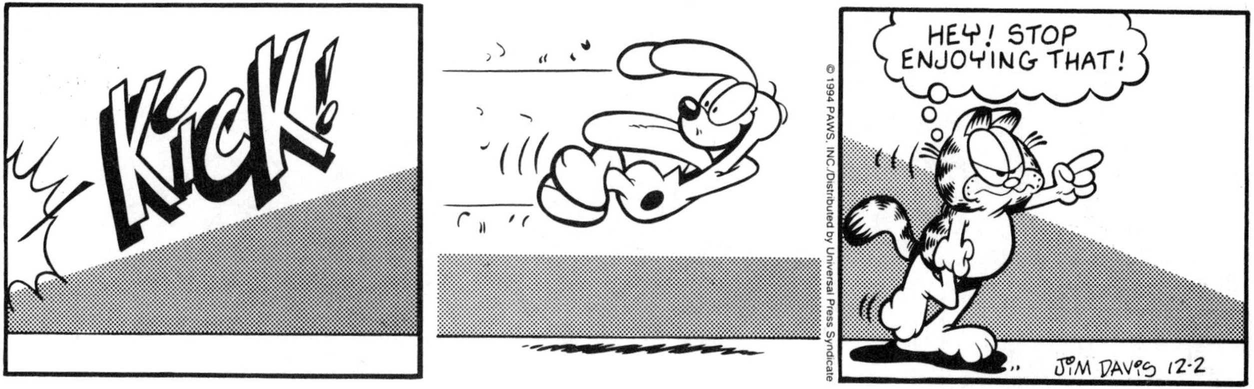
KICK!
HEY! STOP ENJOYING THAT!
JIM DAVIS 12-2
© 1994 PAWS, INC./Distributed by Universal Press Syndicate

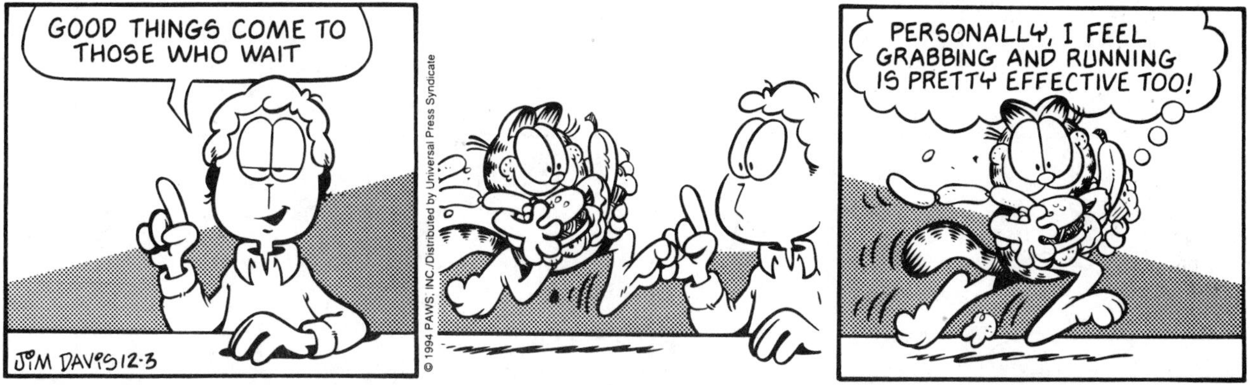
GOOD THINGS COME TO THOSE WHO WAIT
JIM DAVIS 12-3
© 1994 PAWS, INC./Distributed by Universal Press Syndicate
PERSONALLY, I FEEL GRABBING AND RUNNING IS PRETTY EFFECTIVE TOO!

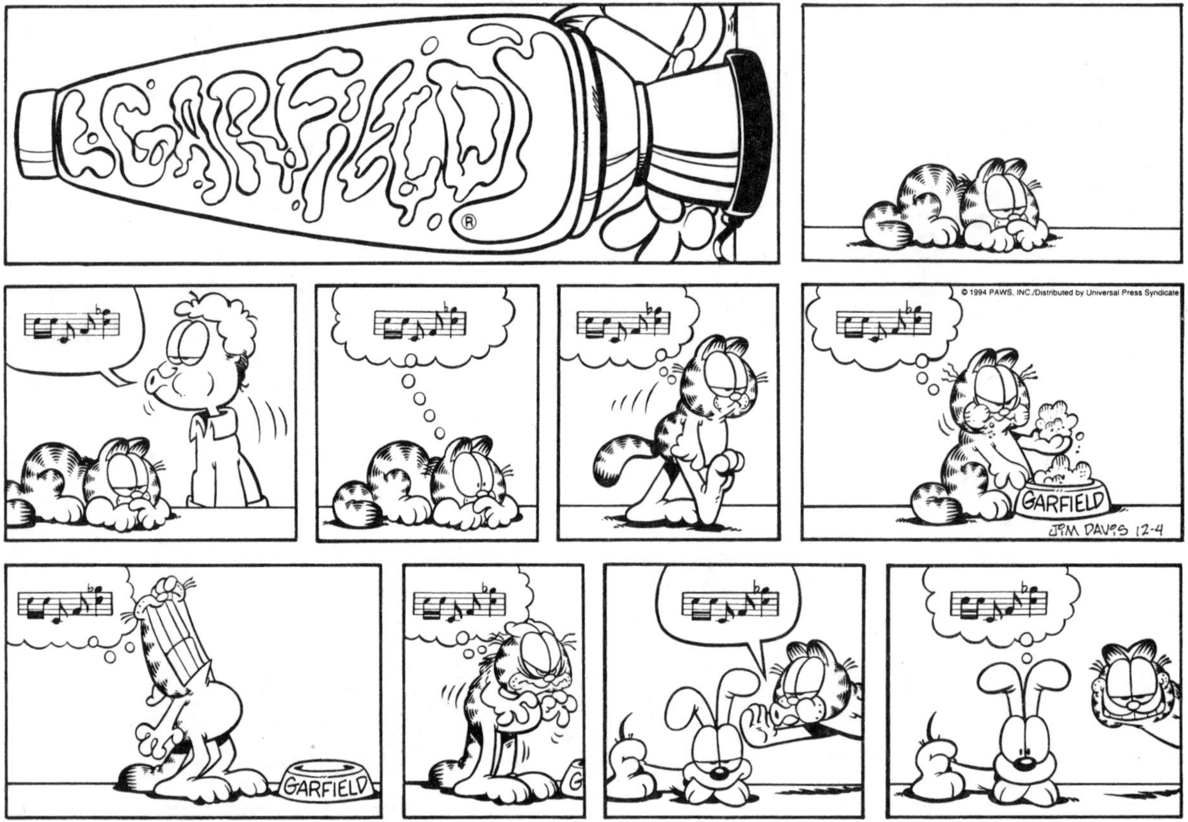
GARFIELD®
© 1994 PAWS, INC./Distributed by Universal Press Syndicate
GARFIELD
JIM DAVIS 12-4
GARFIELD
G

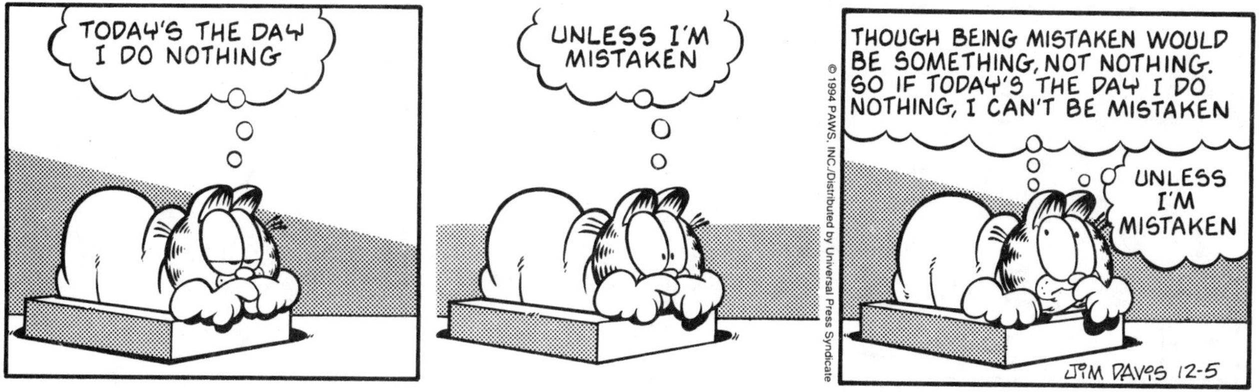
TODAY'S THE DAY I DO NOTHING
UNLESS I'M MISTAKEN
THOUGH BEING MISTAKEN WOULD BE SOMETHING, NOT NOTHING. SO IF TODAY'S THE DAY I DO NOTHING, I CAN'T BE MISTAKEN
UNLESS I'M MISTAKEN
JIM DAVIS 12-5

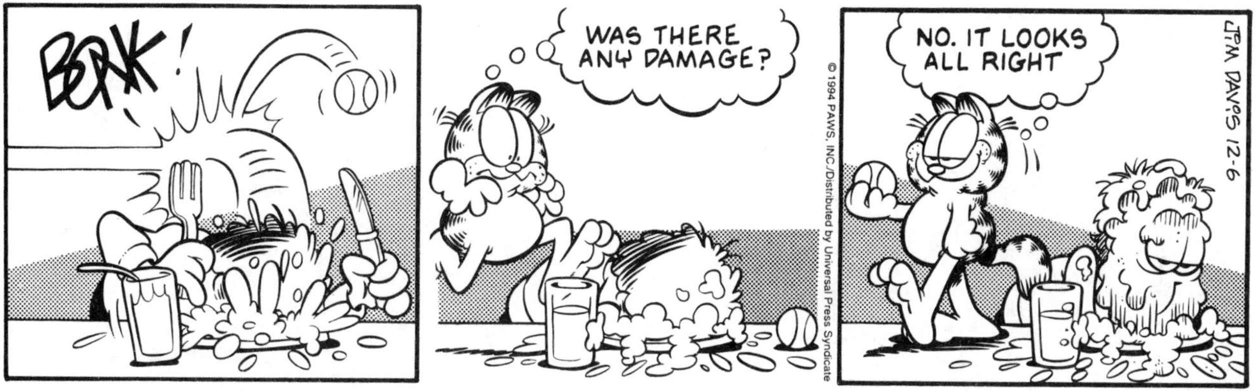
BONK!
WAS THERE ANY DAMAGE?
NO. IT LOOKS ALL RIGHT
JIM DAVIS 12-6

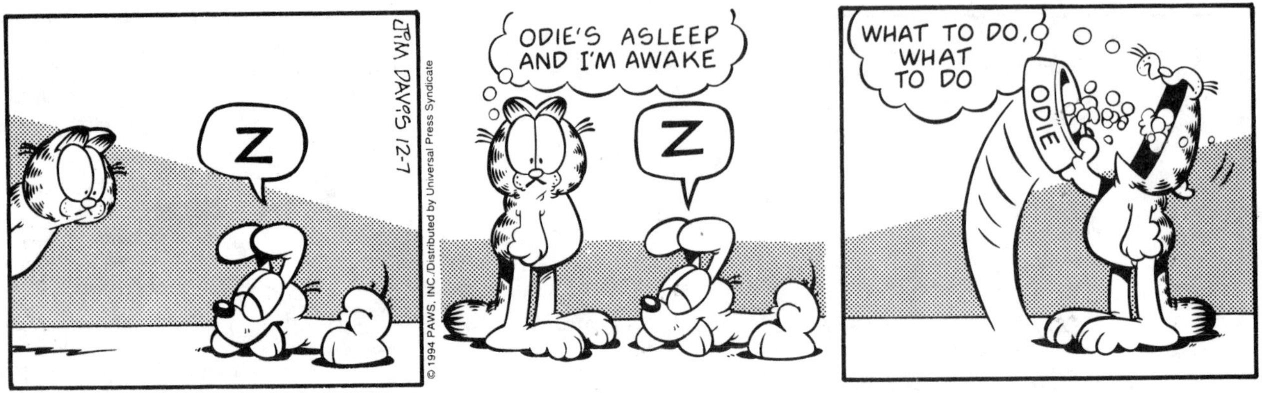
Z
JIM DAVIS 12-7
ODIE'S ASLEEP AND I'M AWAKE
Z
WHAT TO DO, WHAT TO DO
ODIE

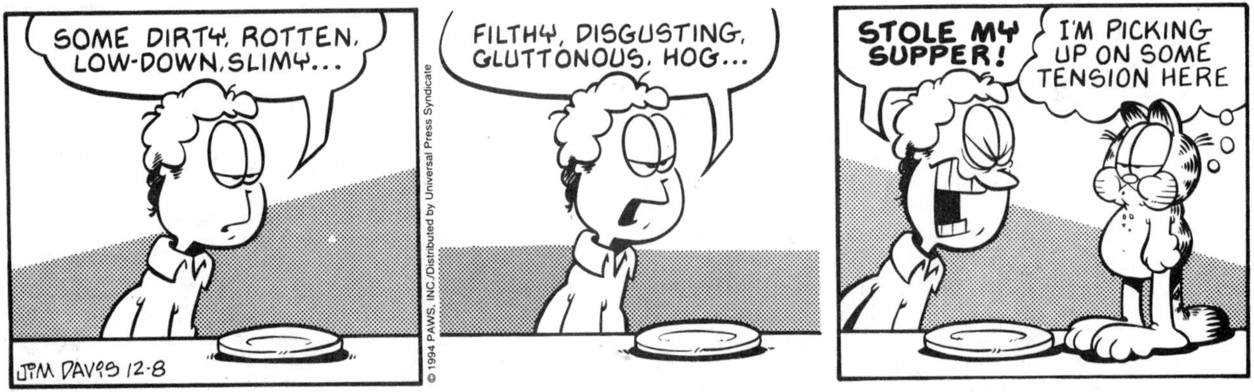
SOME DIRTY, ROTTEN, LOW-DOWN, SLIMY...
JIM DAVIS 12-8
FILTHY, DISGUSTING, GLUTTONOUS, HOG...
STOLE MY SUPPER!
I'M PICKING UP ON SOME TENSION HERE

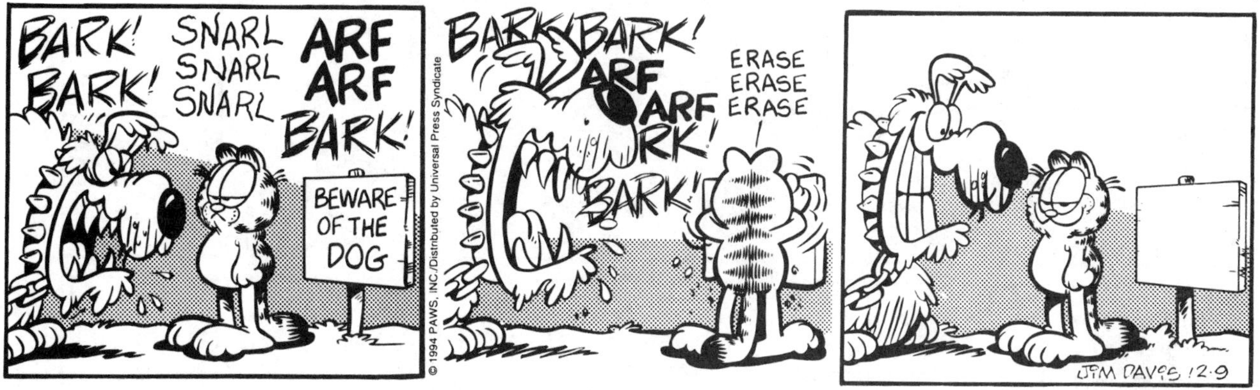
BARK! BARK!
SNARL SNARL SNARL
ARF ARF
BARK!
BEWARE OF THE DOG
BARK BARK!
ARF ARF
RK!
BARK!
ERASE ERASE ERASE
JIM DAVIS 12·9

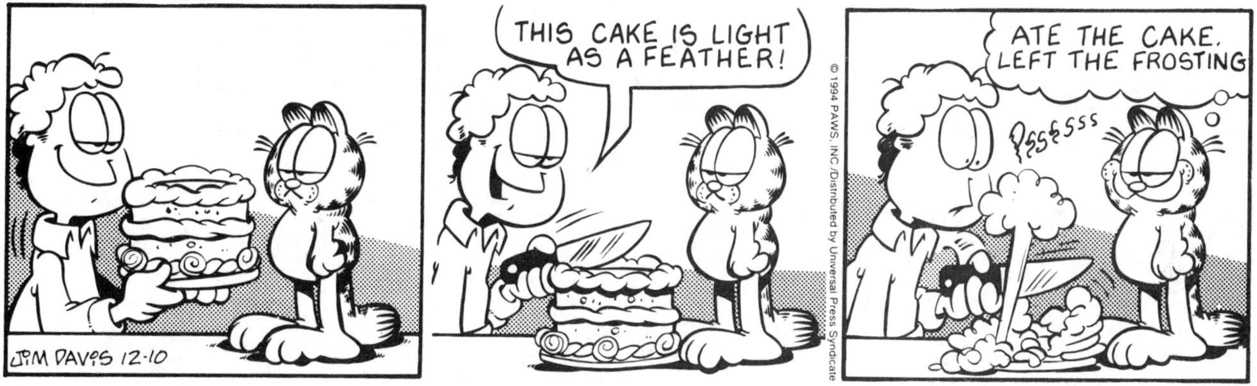
JIM DAVIS 12·10
THIS CAKE IS LIGHT AS A FEATHER!
ATE THE CAKE. LEFT THE FROSTING
PSSSSSS

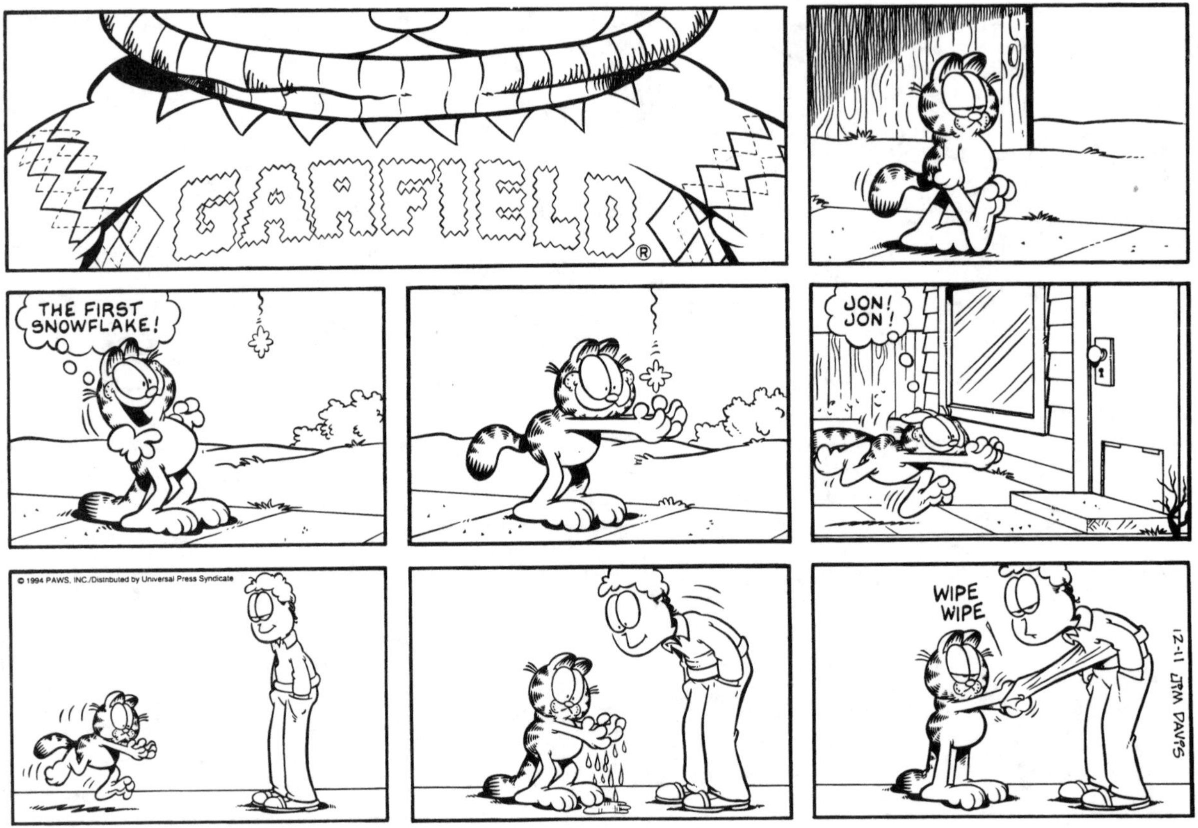
GARFIELD®
THE FIRST SNOWFLAKE!
JON! JON!
© 1994 PAWS, INC./Distributed by Universal Press Syndicate
WIPE WIPE
12-11 JPM DAVIS

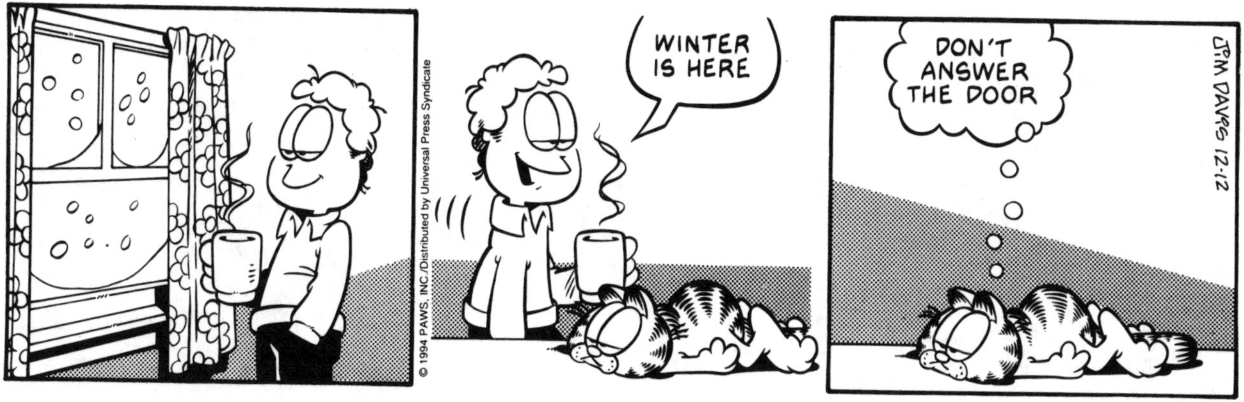
© 1994 PAWS, INC./Distributed by Universal Press Syndicate
WINTER IS HERE
DON'T ANSWER THE DOOR
JIM DAVIS 12-12

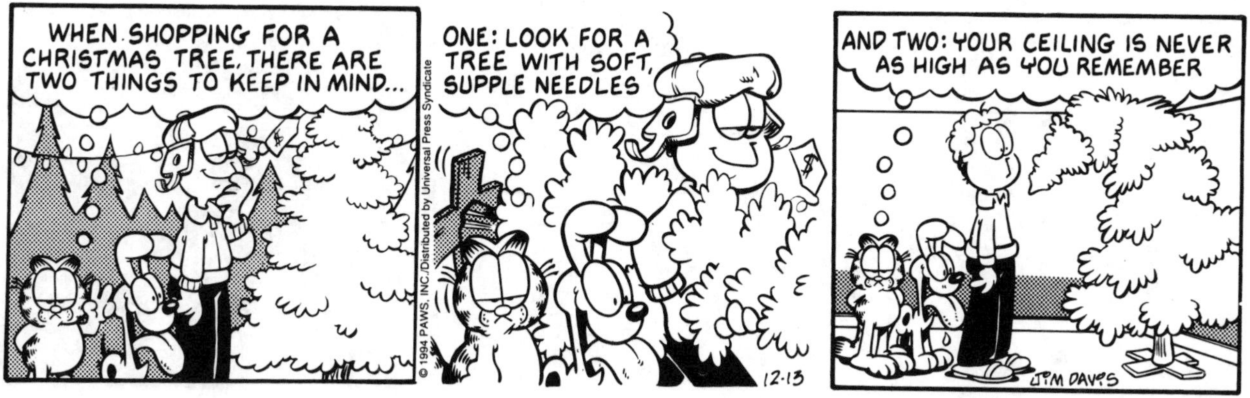
WHEN SHOPPING FOR A CHRISTMAS TREE, THERE ARE TWO THINGS TO KEEP IN MIND...
© 1994 PAWS, INC./Distributed by Universal Press Syndicate
ONE: LOOK FOR A TREE WITH SOFT, SUPPLE NEEDLES
12-13
AND TWO: YOUR CEILING IS NEVER AS HIGH AS YOU REMEMBER
JIM DAVIS

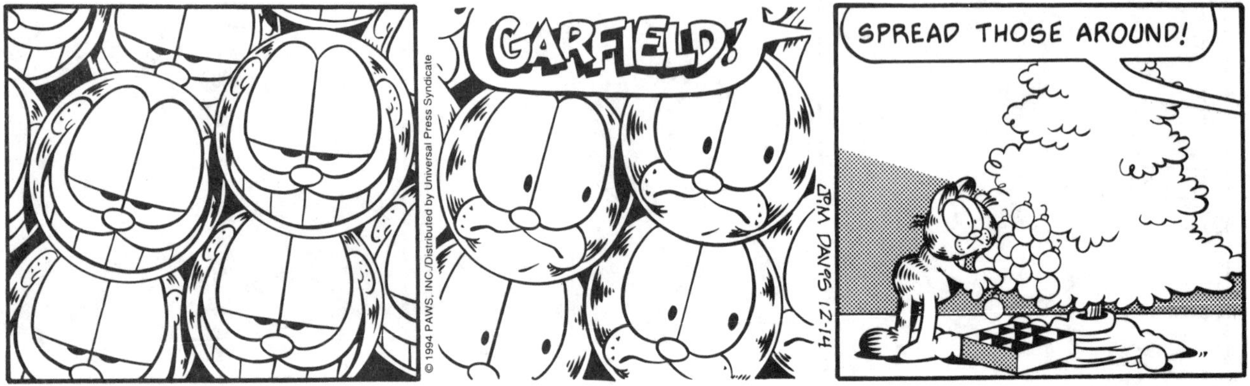
GARFIELD!
SPREAD THOSE AROUND!
© 1994 PAWS, INC./Distributed by Universal Press Syndicate
JIM DAVIS 12-14

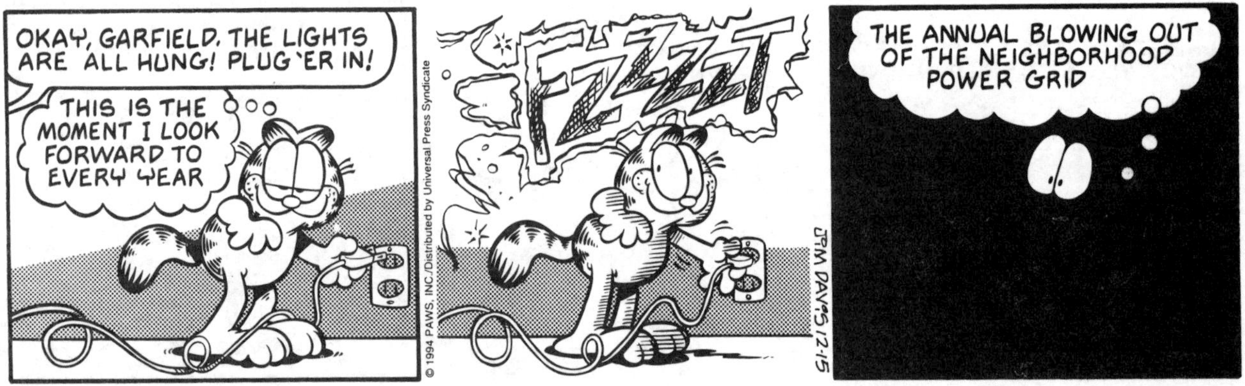
OKAY, GARFIELD. THE LIGHTS ARE ALL HUNG! PLUG 'ER IN!
THIS IS THE MOMENT I LOOK FORWARD TO EVERY YEAR
FZZZZT
THE ANNUAL BLOWING OUT OF THE NEIGHBORHOOD POWER GRID
© 1994 PAWS, INC./Distributed by Universal Press Syndicate
JIM DAVIS 12-15

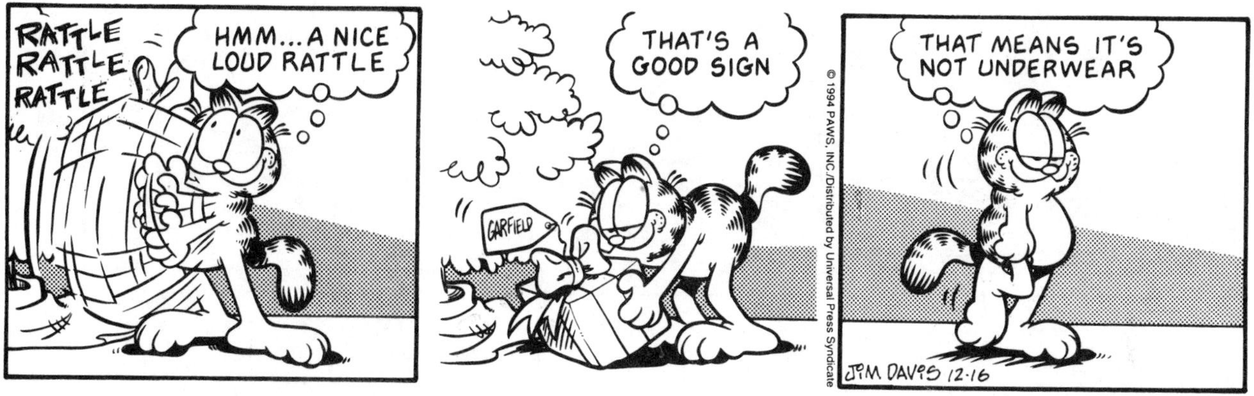
RATTLE RATTLE RATTLE
HMM... A NICE LOUD RATTLE
GARFIELD
THAT'S A GOOD SIGN
THAT MEANS IT'S NOT UNDERWEAR
JIM DAVIS 12-16
© 1994 PAWS, INC./Distributed by Universal Press Syndicate

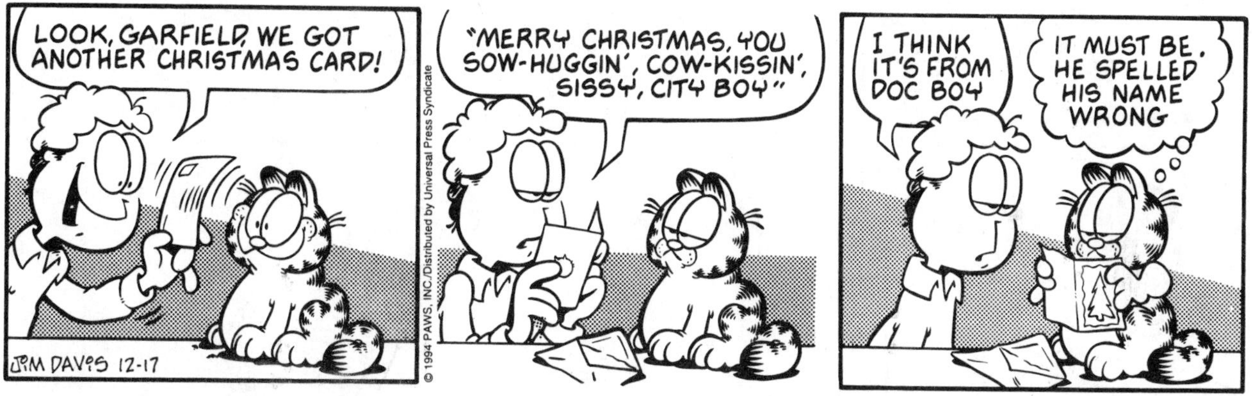
LOOK, GARFIELD, WE GOT ANOTHER CHRISTMAS CARD!
JIM DAVIS 12-17
© 1994 PAWS, INC./Distributed by Universal Press Syndicate
"MERRY CHRISTMAS, YOU SOW-HUGGIN', COW-KISSIN', SISSY, CITY BOY"
I THINK IT'S FROM DOC BOY
IT MUST BE. HE SPELLED HIS NAME WRONG

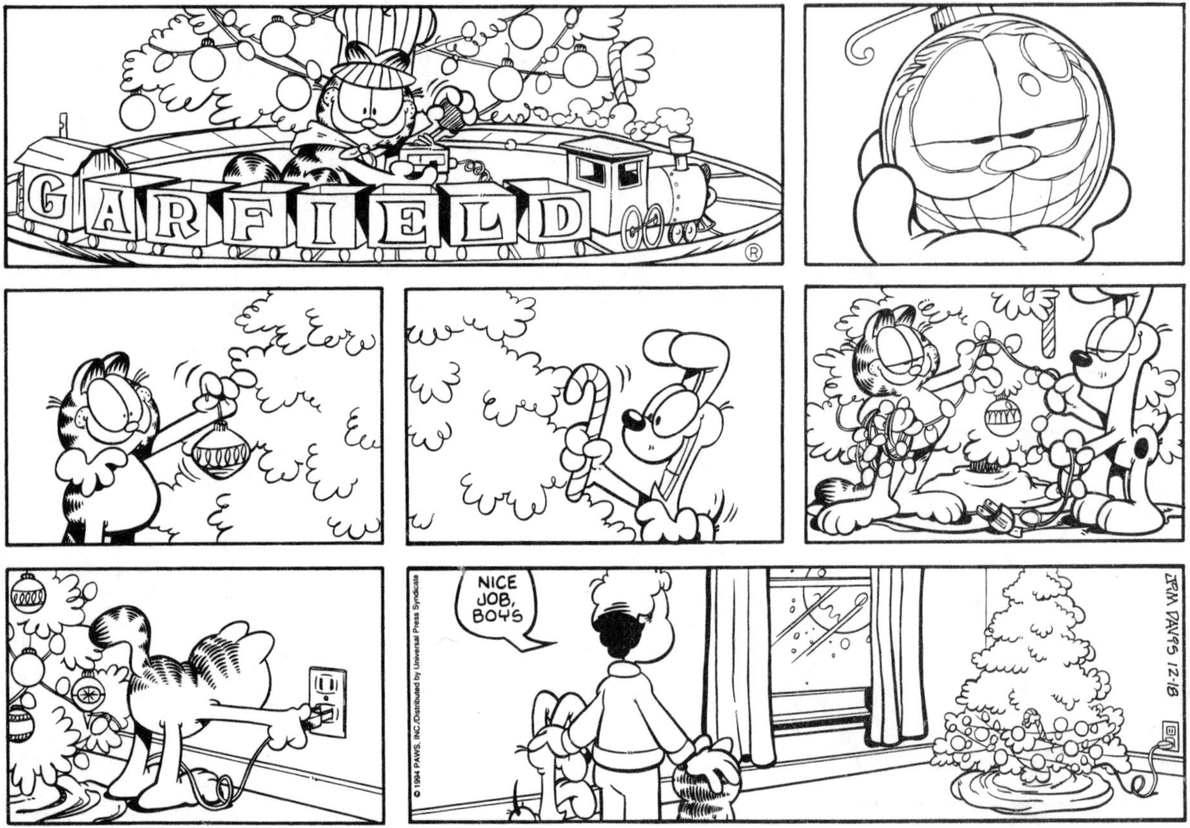
GARFIELD
NICE JOB, BOYS
© 1994 PAWS, INC./Distributed by Universal Press Syndicate

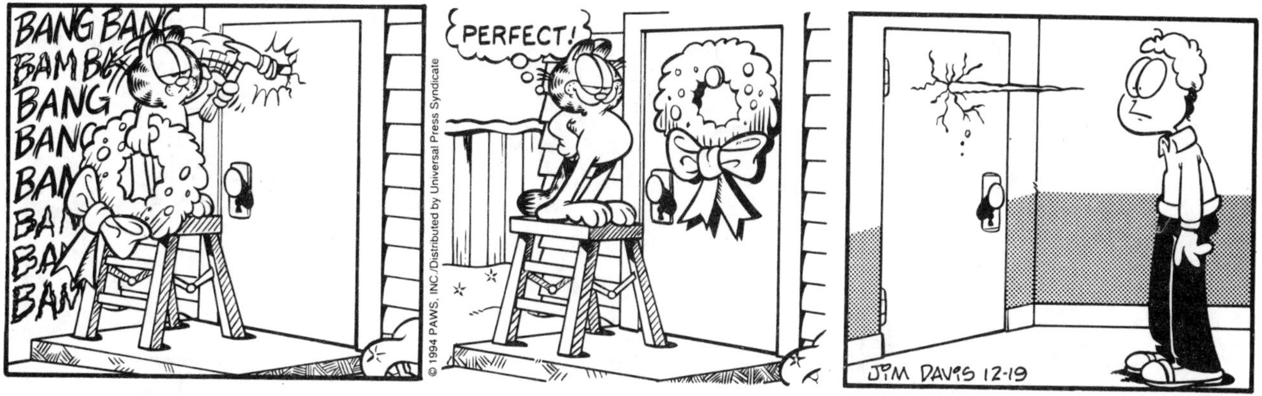
BANG BANG
BAM BANG
BANG
BANG
BANG
BANG
BANG
BANG
PERFECT!
© 1994 PAWS, INC./Distributed by Universal Press Syndicate
JIM DAVIS 12-19

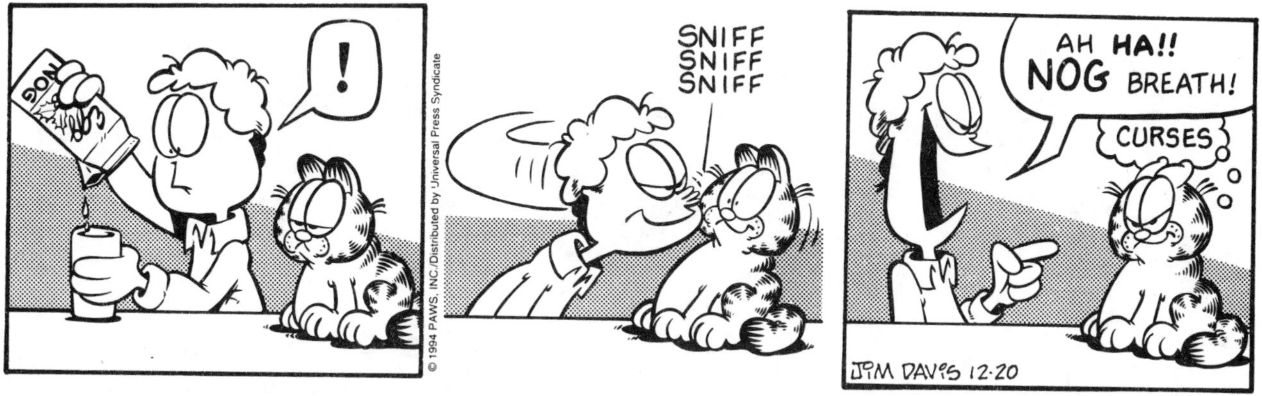
NOG
!
© 1994 PAWS, INC./Distributed by Universal Press Syndicate
SNIFF
SNIFF
SNIFF
AH HA!! NOG BREATH!
CURSES
JIM DAVIS 12-20

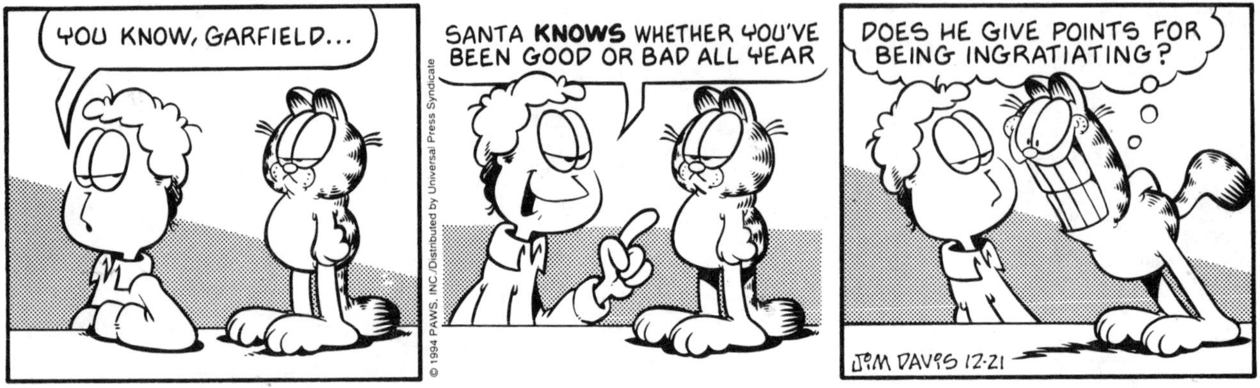
YOU KNOW, GARFIELD...
SANTA KNOWS WHETHER YOU'VE BEEN GOOD OR BAD ALL YEAR
DOES HE GIVE POINTS FOR BEING INGRATIATING?
JIM DAVIS 12-21
© 1994 PAWS, INC./Distributed by Universal Press Syndicate

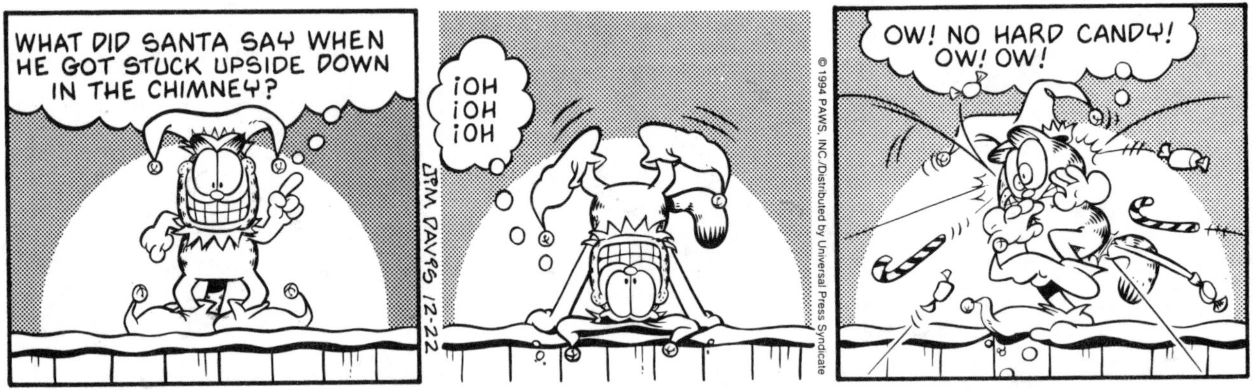
WHAT DID SANTA SAY WHEN HE GOT STUCK UPSIDE DOWN IN THE CHIMNEY?
JIM DAVIS 12-22
iOH iOH iOH
OW! NO HARD CANDY! OW! OW!
© 1994 PAWS, INC./Distributed by Universal Press Syndicate

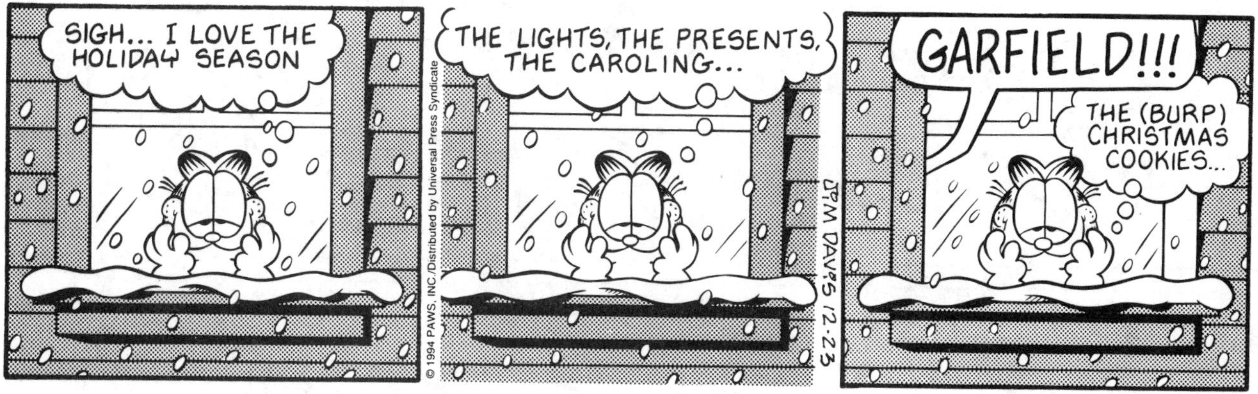
SIGH... I LOVE THE HOLIDAY SEASON
THE LIGHTS, THE PRESENTS, THE CAROLING...
GARFIELD!!!
THE (BURP) CHRISTMAS COOKIES...
© 1994 PAWS, INC./Distributed by Universal Press Syndicate
JIM DAVIS 12-23

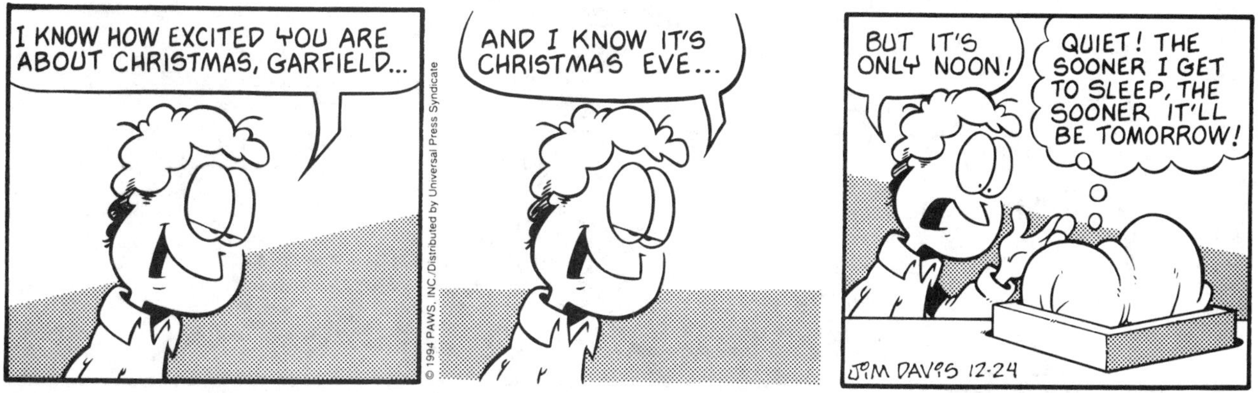
I KNOW HOW EXCITED YOU ARE ABOUT CHRISTMAS, GARFIELD...
AND I KNOW IT'S CHRISTMAS EVE...
BUT IT'S ONLY NOON!
QUIET! THE SOONER I GET TO SLEEP, THE SOONER IT'LL BE TOMORROW!
© 1994 PAWS, INC./Distributed by Universal Press Syndicate
JIM DAVIS 12-24

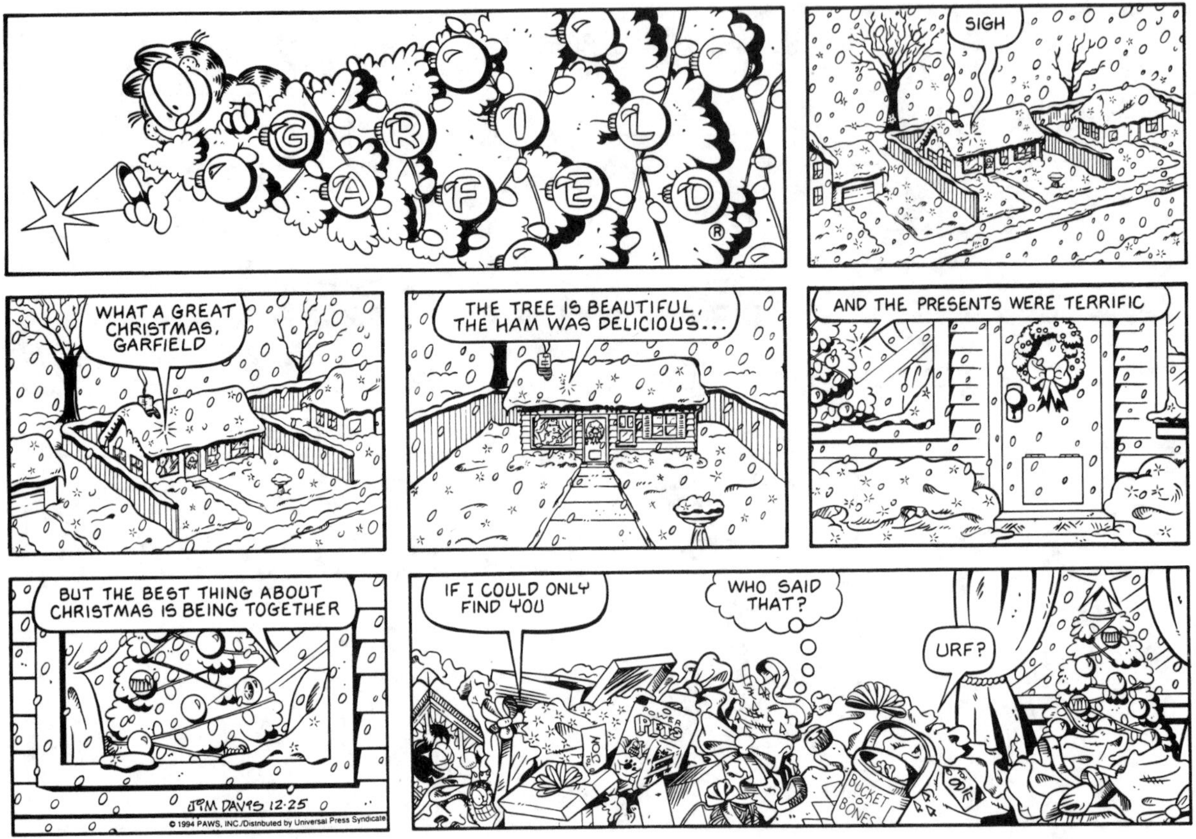
GARFIELD®
SIGH
WHAT A GREAT CHRISTMAS, GARFIELD
THE TREE IS BEAUTIFUL, THE HAM WAS DELICIOUS...
AND THE PRESENTS WERE TERRIFIC
BUT THE BEST THING ABOUT CHRISTMAS IS BEING TOGETHER
JIM DAVIS 12-25
© 1994 PAWS, INC./Distributed by Universal Press Syndicate
IF I COULD ONLY FIND YOU
WHO SAID THAT?
URF?
POWER PETS
TO: JON
BUCKET O BONES

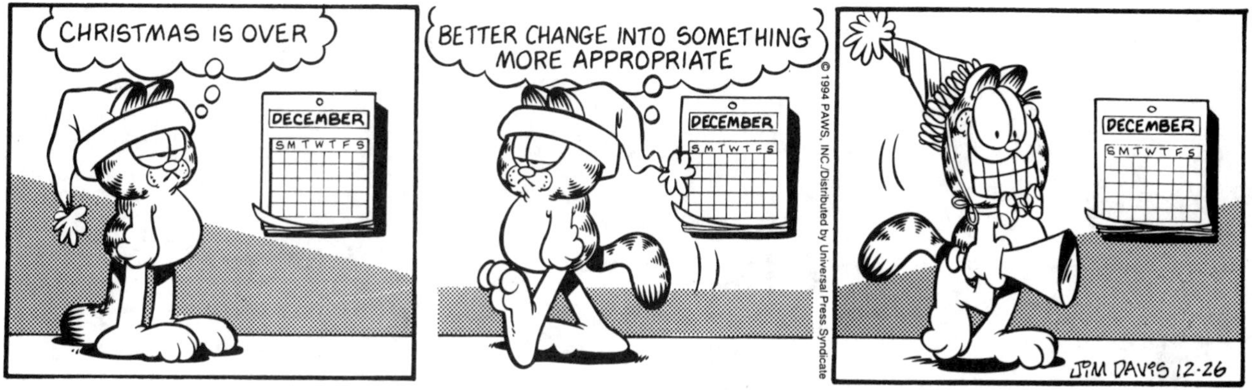
CHRISTMAS IS OVER
DECEMBER
S M T W T F S
BETTER CHANGE INTO SOMETHING MORE APPROPRIATE
DECEMBER
S M T W T F S
© 1994 PAWS, INC./Distributed by Universal Press Syndicate
DECEMBER
S M T W T F S
JIM DAVIS 12-26

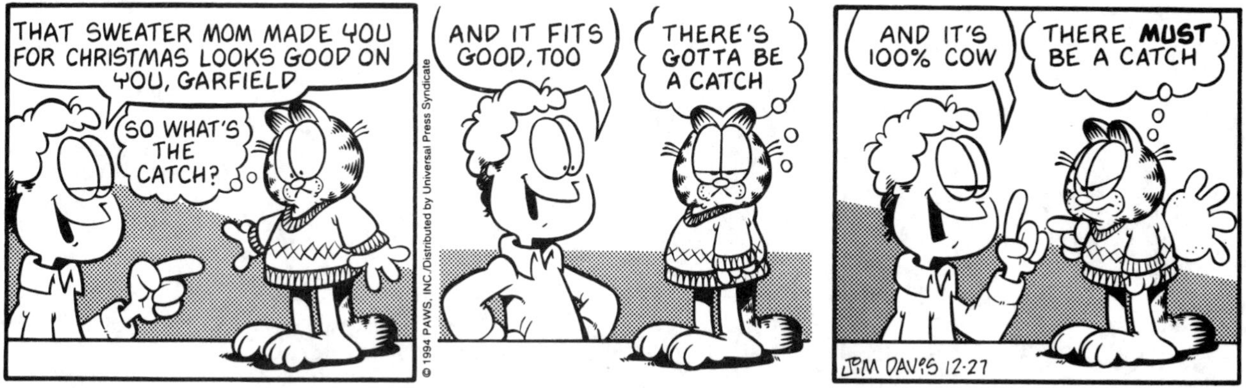
THAT SWEATER MOM MADE YOU FOR CHRISTMAS LOOKS GOOD ON YOU, GARFIELD
SO WHAT'S THE CATCH?
© 1994 PAWS, INC./Distributed by Universal Press Syndicate
AND IT FITS GOOD, TOO
THERE'S GOTTA BE A CATCH
AND IT'S 100% COW
THERE **MUST** BE A CATCH
JIM DAVIS 12-27

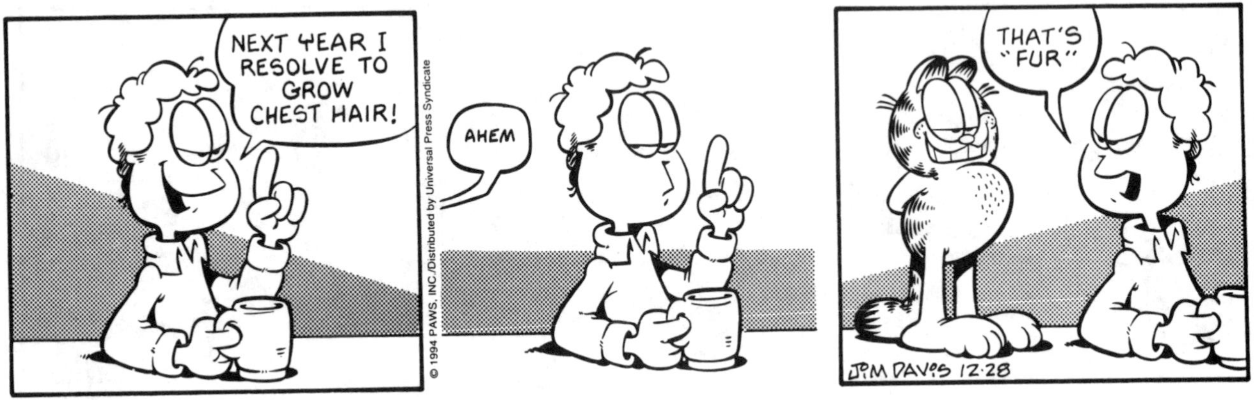
NEXT YEAR I RESOLVE TO GROW CHEST HAIR!
AHEM
THAT'S "FUR"
JIM DAVIS 12-28
© 1994 PAWS, INC./Distributed by Universal Press Syndicate

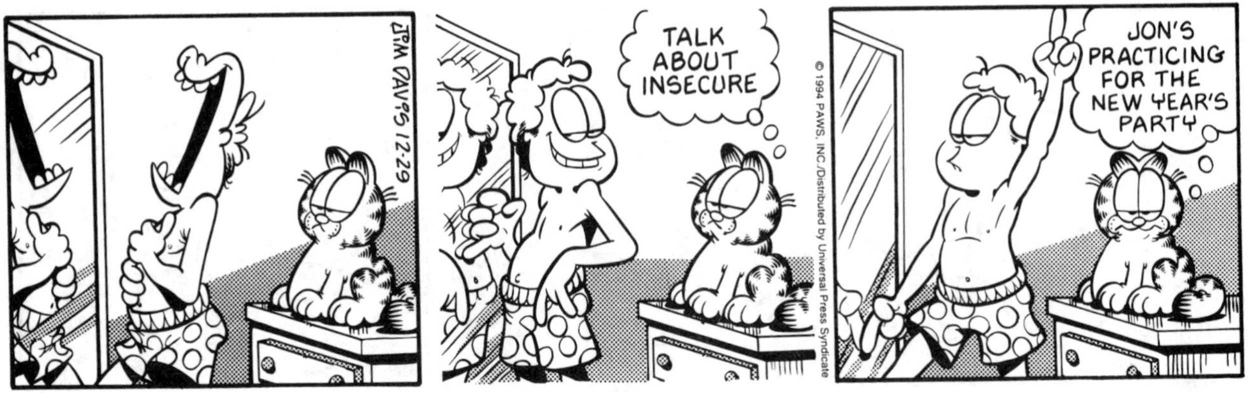
JIM DAVIS 12-29
TALK ABOUT INSECURE
JON'S PRACTICING FOR THE NEW YEAR'S PARTY
© 1994 PAWS, INC./Distributed by Universal Press Syndicate

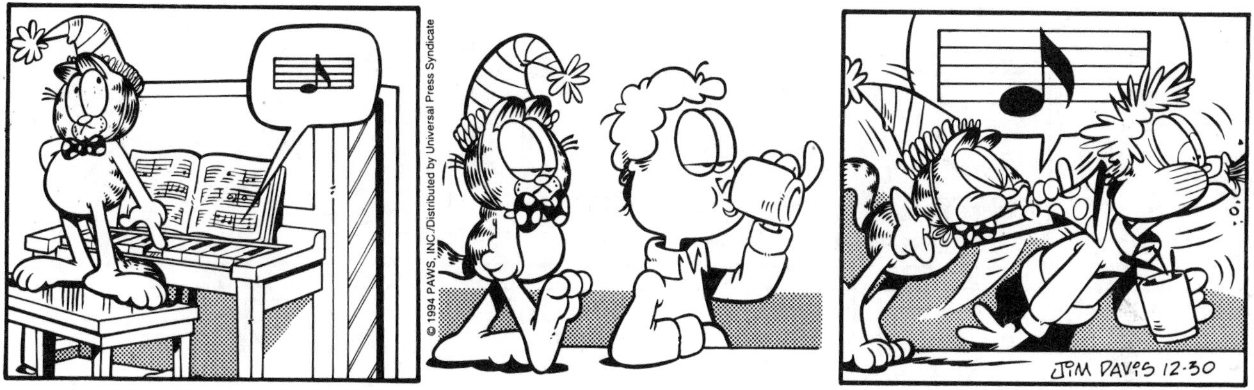
JIM DAVIS 12-30

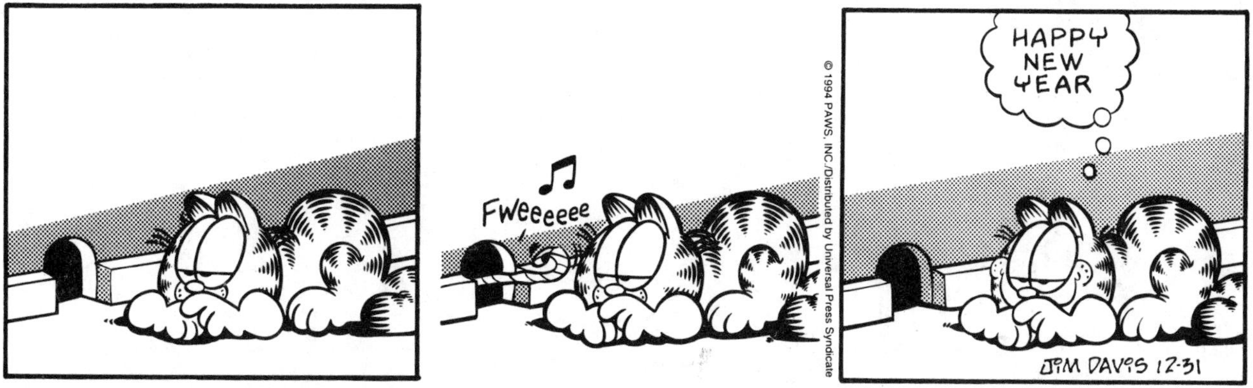
Fweeeeee
HAPPY NEW YEAR
JIM DAVIS 12-31

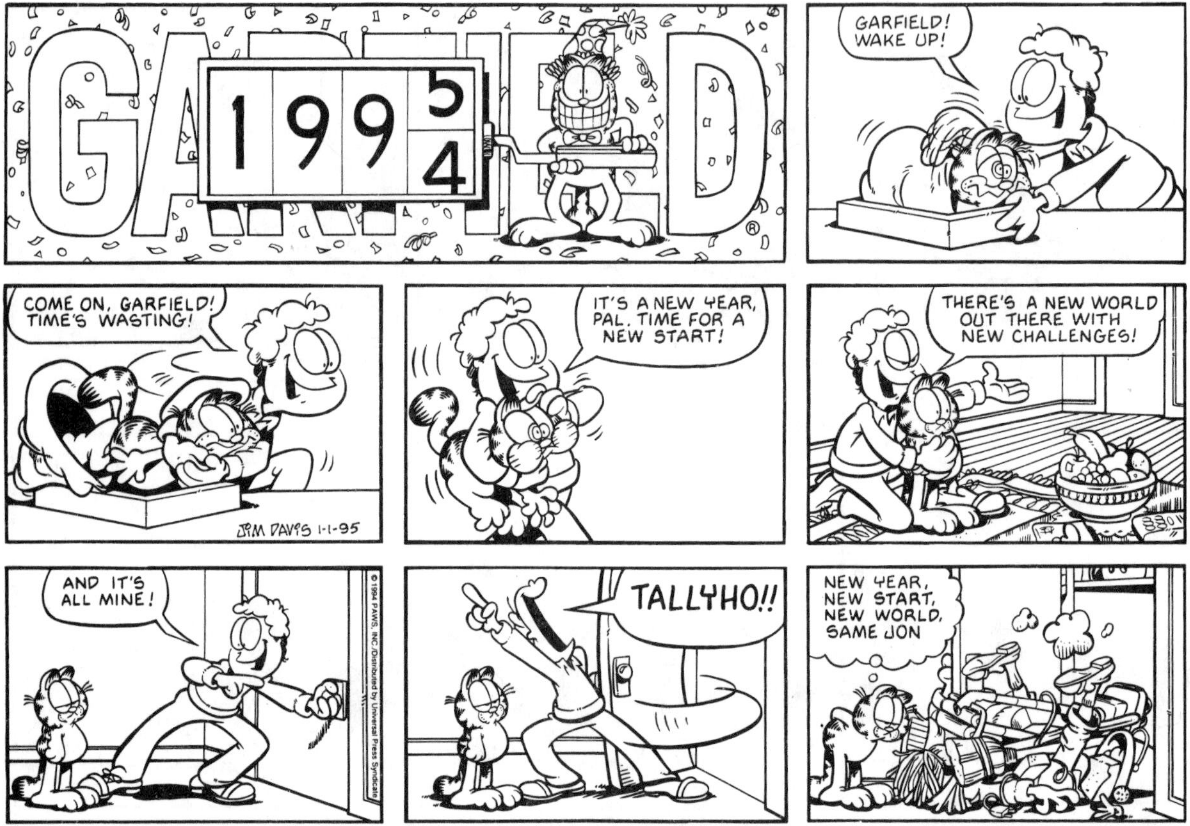
GARFIELD
1995
1994
GARFIELD! WAKE UP!
COME ON, GARFIELD! TIME'S WASTING!
JIM DAVIS 1-1-95
IT'S A NEW YEAR, PAL. TIME FOR A NEW START!
THERE'S A NEW WORLD OUT THERE WITH NEW CHALLENGES!
AND IT'S ALL MINE!
© 1994 PAWS, INC./Distributed by Universal Press Syndicate
TALLYHO!!
NEW YEAR, NEW START, NEW WORLD, SAME JON

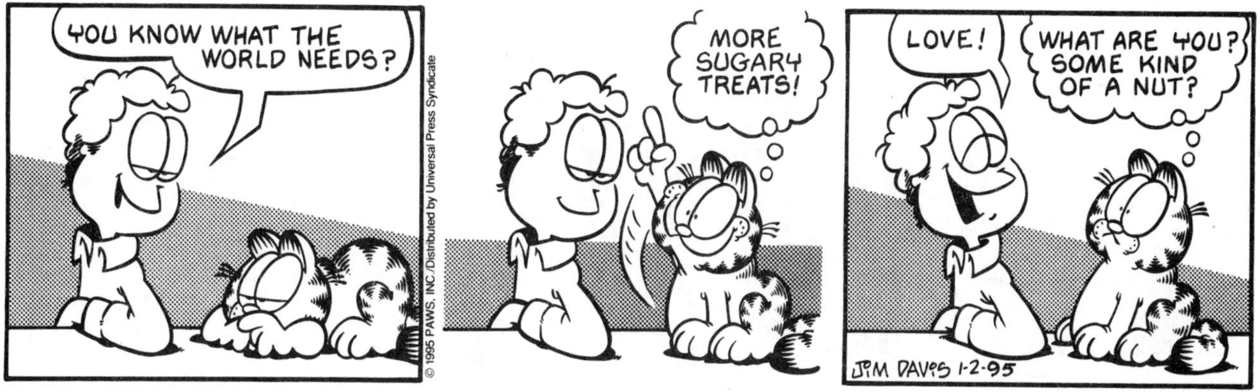
YOU KNOW WHAT THE WORLD NEEDS?
© 1995 PAWS, INC./Distributed by Universal Press Syndicate
MORE SUGARY TREATS!
LOVE!
WHAT ARE YOU? SOME KIND OF A NUT?
JIM DAVIS 1-2-95

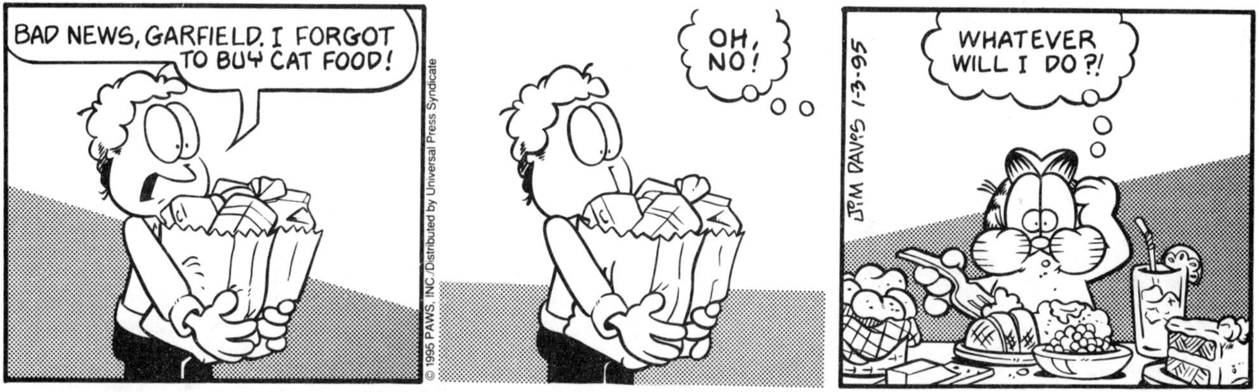
BAD NEWS, GARFIELD. I FORGOT TO BUY CAT FOOD!
© 1995 PAWS, INC./Distributed by Universal Press Syndicate
OH, NO!
JIM DAVIS 1-3-95
WHATEVER WILL I DO?!

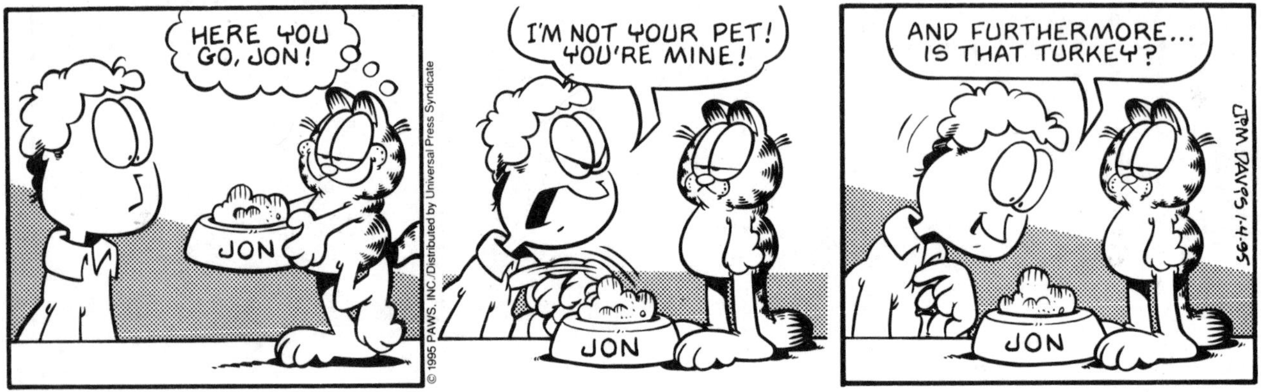
HERE YOU GO, JON!
I'M NOT YOUR PET! YOU'RE MINE!
AND FURTHERMORE... IS THAT TURKEY?
JON
JON
JON
JIM DAVIS 1-4-95

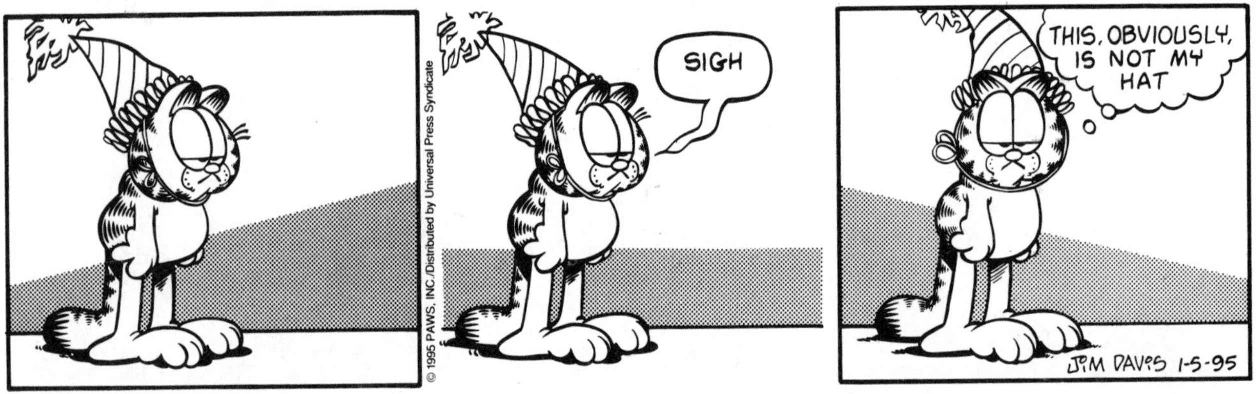
SIGH
THIS, OBVIOUSLY, IS NOT MY HAT
JIM DAVIS 1-5-95

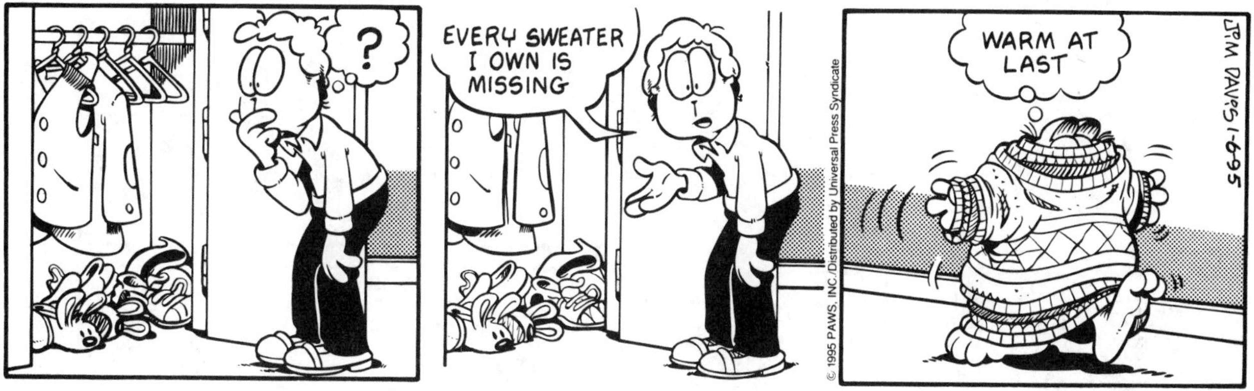
?
EVERY SWEATER I OWN IS MISSING
WARM AT LAST
JIM DAVIS 1-6-95

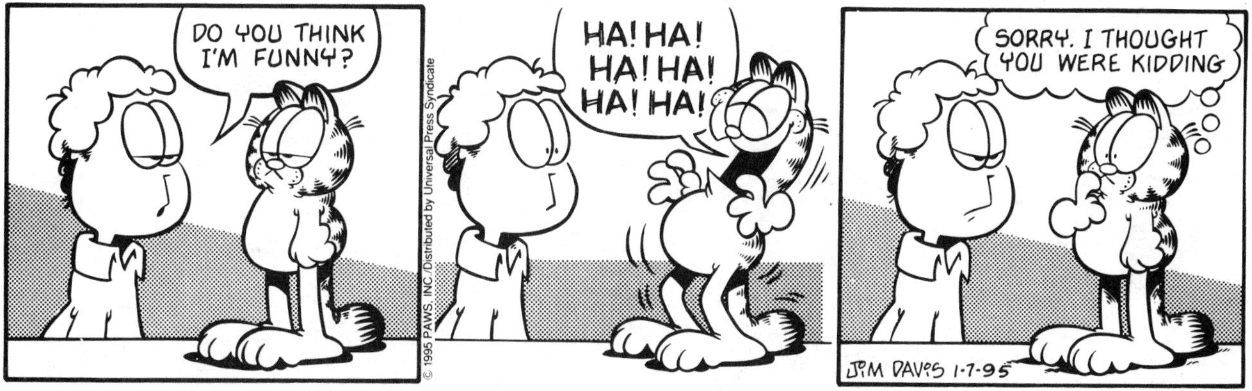
DO YOU THINK I'M FUNNY?
HA! HA! HA! HA! HA! HA!
SORRY. I THOUGHT YOU WERE KIDDING
JIM DAVIS 1-7-95

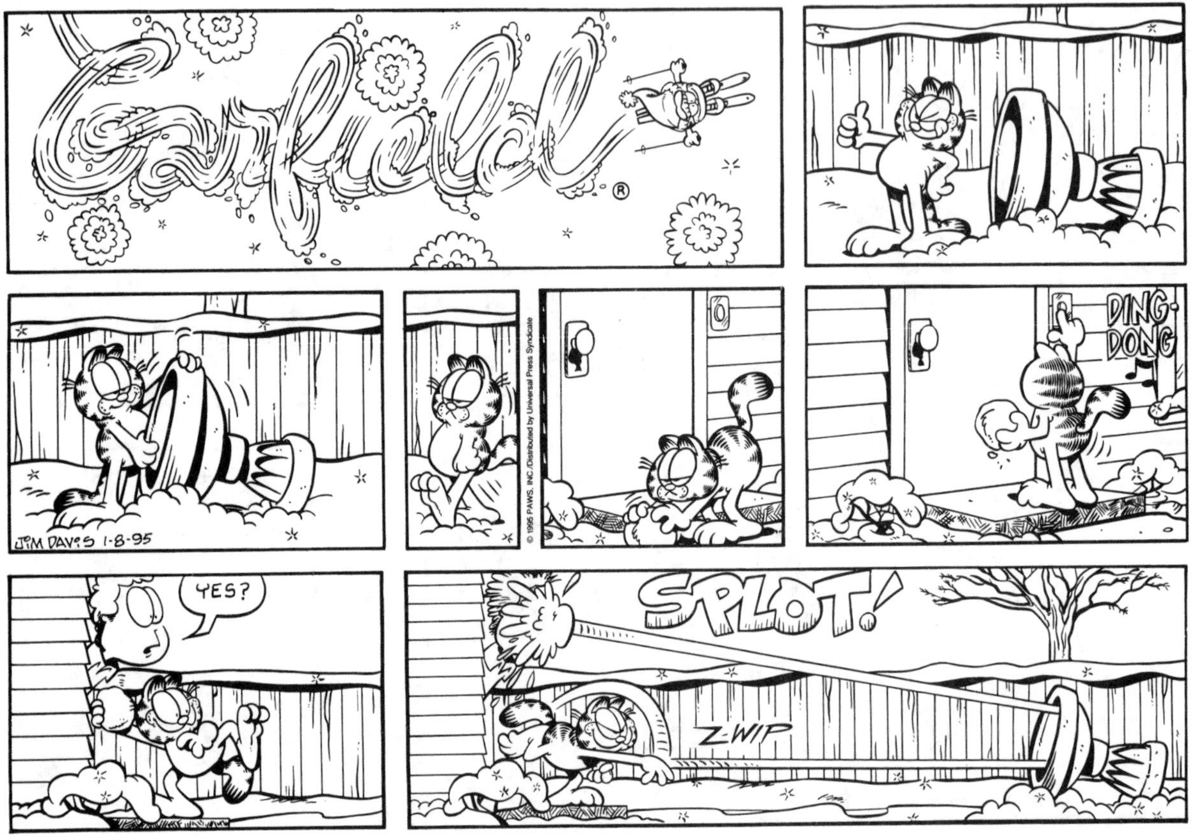
Garfield®
JIM DAVIS 1-8-95
© 1995 PAWS, INC./Distributed by Universal Press Syndicate
DING-DONG
YES?
SPLOT!
Z-WIP

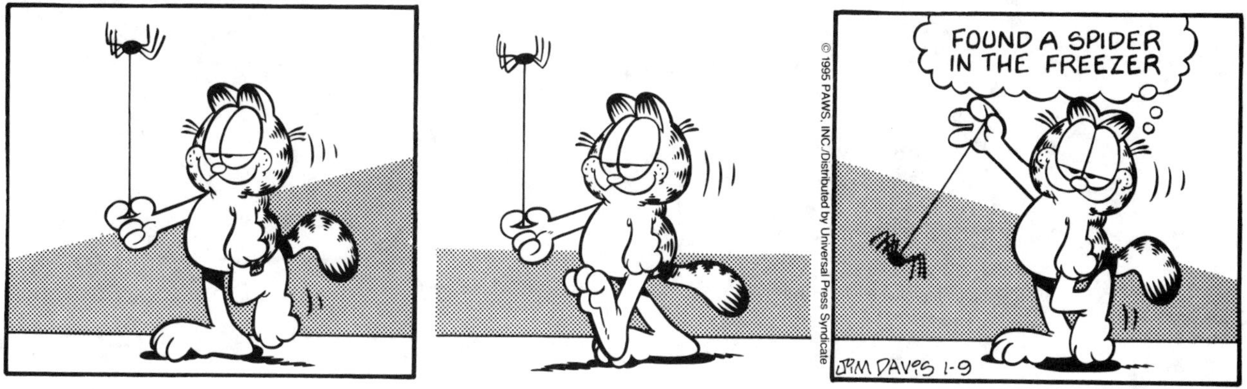
FOUND A SPIDER IN THE FREEZER
© 1995 PAWS, INC./Distributed by Universal Press Syndicate
JIM DAVIS 1-9

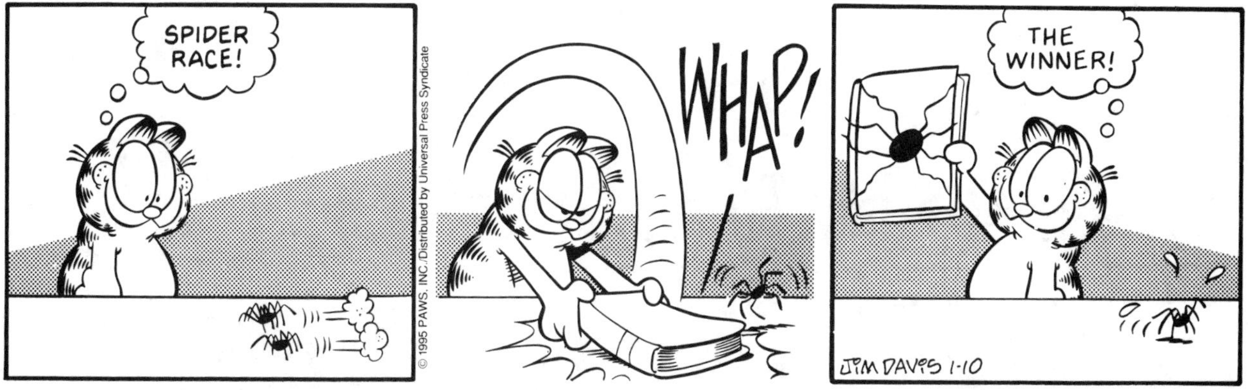
SPIDER RACE!
© 1995 PAWS, INC./Distributed by Universal Press Syndicate
WHAP!
THE WINNER!
JIM DAVIS 1-10

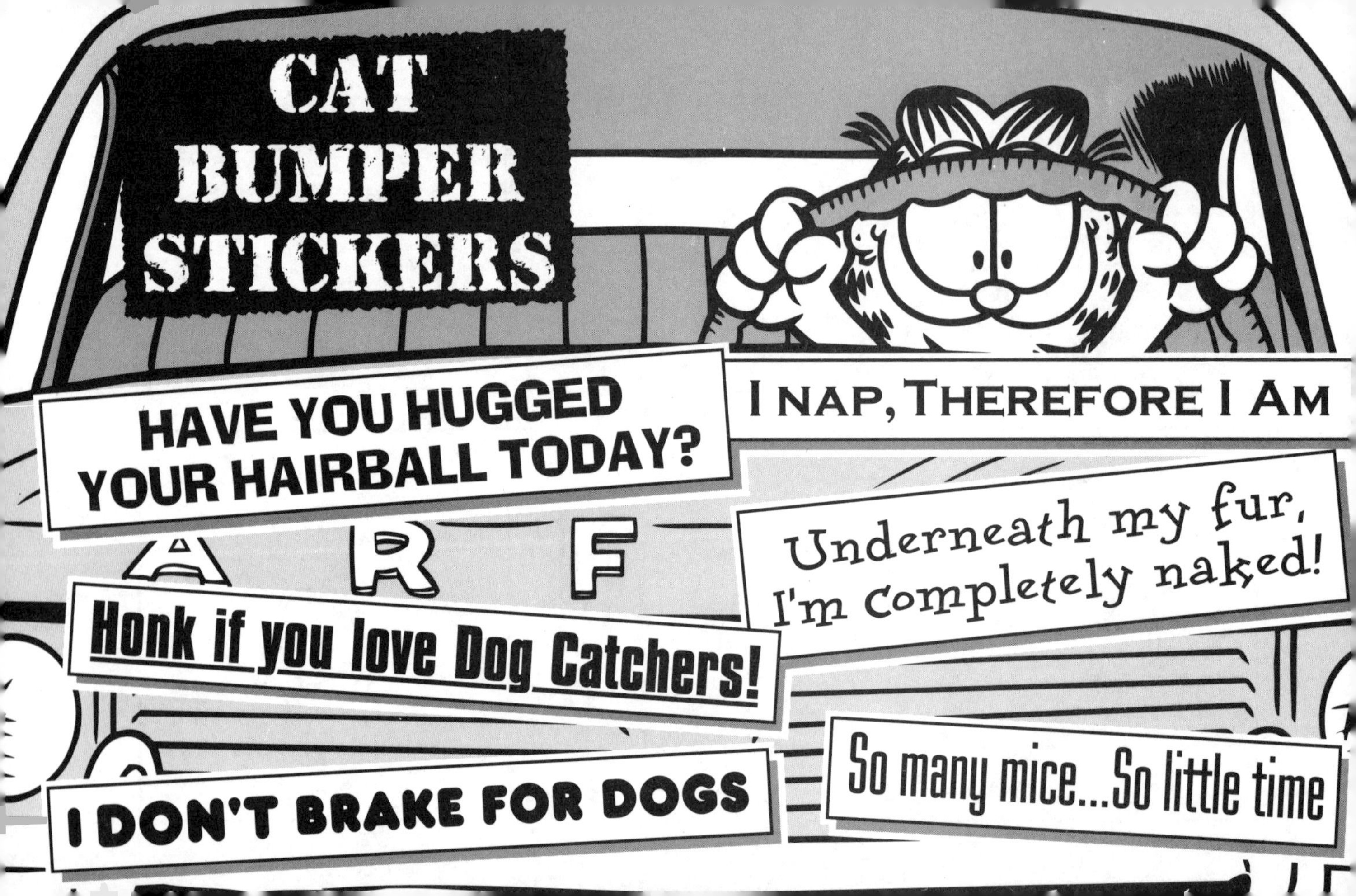
CAT BUMPER STICKERS
HAVE YOU HUGGED YOUR HAIRBALL TODAY?
I NAP, THEREFORE I AM
A R F
Underneath my fur, I'm completely naked!
Honk if you love Dog Catchers!
I DON'T BRAKE FOR DOGS
So many mice...So little time

STRIPS, SPECIALS, OR BESTSELLING BOOKS . . .
GARFIELD'S ON EVERYONE'S MENU
Don't miss even one episode in the Tubby Tabby's hilarious series!

__GARFIELD AT LARGE (#1)   32013/$6.95
__GARFIELD GAINS WEIGHT (#2)   32008/$6.95
__GARFIELD BIGGER THAN LIFE (#3)   32007/$6.95
__GARFIELD WEIGHS IN (#4)   32010/$6.95
__GARFIELD TAKES THE CAKE (#5)   32009/$6.95
__GARFIELD EATS HIS HEART OUT (#6)   32018/$6.95
__GARFIELD SITS AROUND THE HOUSE (#7)   32011/$6.95
__GARFIELD TIPS THE SCALES (#8)   33580/$6.95
__GARFIELD LOSES HIS FEET (#9)   31805/$6.95
__GARFIELD MAKES IT BIG (#10)   31928/$6.95
__GARFIELD ROLLS ON (#11)   32634/$6.95
__GARFIELD OUT TO LUNCH (#12)   33118/$6.95
__GARFIELD FOOD FOR THOUGHT (#13)   34129/$6.95
__GARFIELD SWALLOWS HIS PRIDE (#14)   34725/$6.95
__GARFIELD WORLDWIDE (#15)   35158/$6.95
__GARFIELD ROUNDS OUT (#16)   35388/$6.95

__GARFIELD CHEWS THE FAT (#17)   35956/$6.95
__GARFIELD GOES TO WAIST (#18)   36430/$6.95
__GARFIELD HANGS OUT (#19)   36835/$6.95
__GARFIELD TAKES UP SPACE (#20)   37029/$6.95
__GARFIELD SAYS A MOUTHFUL (#21)   37368/$6.95
__GARFIELD BY THE POUND (#22)   37579/$6.95
__GARFIELD KEEPS HIS CHINS UP (#23)   37959/$6.95
__GARFIELD TAKES HIS LICKS (#24)   38170/$6.95
__GARFIELD HITS THE BIG TIME (#25)   38332/$6.95
__GARFIELD PULLS HIS WEIGHT (#26)   38666/$6.95
__GARFIELD DISHES IT OUT (#27)   39287/$6.95
__GARFIELD LIFE IN THE FAT LANE (#28)   39776/$6.95

GARFIELD AT HIS SUNDAY BEST!
__GARFIELD TREASURY   32106/$11.95
__THE SECOND GARFIELD TREASURY   33276/$10.95
__THE THIRD GARFIELD TREASURY   32635/$11.00
__THE FOURTH GARFIELD TREASURY   34726/$10.95
__THE FIFTH GARFIELD TREASURY   36268/$12.00
__THE SIXTH GARFIELD TREASURY   37367/$10.95
__THE SEVENTH GARFIELD TREASURY   38427/$10.95
__THE EIGHTH GARFIELD TREASURY   39778/$12.00

Please send me the BALLANTINE BOOKS I have checked above. I am enclosing $_____. (Please add $2.00 for the first book and $.50 for each additional book for postage and handling and include the appropriate state sales tax.) Send check or money order (no cash or C.O.D.'s) to Ballantine Mail Sales Dept. TA, 400 Hahn Road, Westminster, MD 21157.

To order by phone, call 1-800-733-3000 and use your major credit card.

Prices and numbers are subject to change without notice. Valid in the U.S. only. All orders are subject to availability.

Name_____

Address_____

City_____ State_____ Zip_____

Allow at least 4 weeks for delivery   7/93

BIRTHDAYS, HOLIDAYS, OR ANY DAY . . .

Keep GARFIELD on your calendar all year 'round!

GARFIELD TV SPECIALS
__BABES & BULLETS   36339/$5.95
__GARFIELD GOES HOLLYWOOD   34580/$6.95
__GARFIELD'S HALLOWEEN ADVENTURE   33045/$6.95
  (formerly GARFIELD IN DISGUISE)
__GARFIELD'S FELINE FANTASY   36902/$6.95
__GARFIELD IN PARADISE   33796/$6.95
__GARFIELD IN THE ROUGH   32242/$6.95
__GARFIELD ON THE TOWN   31542/$6.95
__GARFIELD'S THANKSGIVING   35650/$6.95
__HERE COMES GARFIELD   32021/$6.95
__GARFIELD GETS A LIFE   37375/$6.95
__A GARFIELD CHRISTMAS   35368/$5.95

Please send me the BALLANTINE BOOKS I have checked above. I am enclosing $_____. (Please add $2.00 for the first book and $.50 for each additional book for postage and handling and include the appropriate state sales tax.) Send check or money order (no cash or C.O.D.'s) to Ballantine Mail Sales Dept. TA, 400 Hahn Road, Westminster, MD 21157.

To order by phone, call 1-800-733-3000 and use your major credit card.

Prices and numbers are subject to change without notice. Valid in the U.S. only. All orders are subject to availability.

GREETINGS FROM GARFIELD!
GARFIELD POSTCARD BOOKS FOR ALL OCCASIONS.
__GARFIELD THINKING OF YOU   36516/$6.95
__GARFIELD WORDS TO LIVE BY   36679/$6.95
__GARFIELD BIRTHDAY GREETINGS   36771/$7.95
__GARFIELD BE MY VALENTINE   37121/$7.95
__GARFIELD SEASON'S GREETINGS   37435/$8.95
__GARFIELD VACATION GREETINGS   37774/$10.00
__GARFIELD'S THANK YOU POSTCARD BOOK   37893/$10.00
ALSO FROM GARFIELD:
__GARFIELD: HIS NINE LIVES   32061/$9.95
__THE GARFIELD BOOK OF CAT NAMES   35082/$5.95
__THE GARFIELD TRIVIA BOOK   33771/$6.95
__THE UNABRIDGED UNCENSORED
  UNBELIEVABLE GARFIELD   33772/$5.95
__GARFIELD: THE ME BOOK   36545/$7.95
__GARFIELD'S JUDGMENT DAY   36755/$6.95
__THE TRUTH ABOUT CATS   37226/$6.95

Name_____

Address_____

City_____ State_____ Zip_____
30   Allow at least 4 weeks for delivery   7/93 TA-267